# The Music of Alban Berg

# The Music of
# ALBAN BERG

Douglas Jarman

University of California Press
Berkeley & Los Angeles

University of California Press
Berkeley and Los Angeles, California

Library of Congress Catalog Card Number: 77-76687
ISBN 0-520-03485-6

Printed in Great Britain

FOR MY MOTHER

# Contents

# Preface

Although the sources of relevant material from other writers are indicated throughout the following book I should here acknowledge my debt to the work of two authors who have had a particularly deep influence on my ideas. The origins of this book lie in an article written in 1969 in which I argued that the musical design of Berg's *Lulu* imposed upon the opera a subject other than that of the two Wedekind plays which form the libretto. A short article by Misha Donat, written independently of my own *Lulu* article and published some four months before it, showed that the design of *Wozzeck* had a similar significance and first suggested that the structures of the two operas provided an insight into Berg's use of similar formal plans in his instrumental music. The implications of this idea are discussed in the final chapter and I must acknowledge the stimulus which Mr. Donat's article provided. I must also, like anyone working on the music of the Second Viennese School in general and Berg in particular, acknowledge a particular debt to the work of George Perle. Professor Perle's *Serial Composition and Atonality* is not only an essential book for anyone wishing to understand the technical procedures employed in the music of Schoenberg, Berg and Webern but is also the source of the most precise definitions of the analytical terms applicable to this music and now in common usage and, as such, is frequently cited in the following text. Professor Perle's authoritative studies of *Lulu* and his more recent work on *Wozzeck* must inevitably influence the thought of anyone writing on Berg's music; readers familiar with Professor Perle's articles on the two operas will recognize the extent to which I am indebted to his analyses.

Throughout the book I have employed the terms 'set' and 'collection' to indicate a group of notes the identity of which depends on factors other than note order. The term 'set' I have applied to groups consisting of all twelve notes of the chromatic scale as well as to those containing fewer; the term 'collection' I have applied to groups consisting of fewer than twelve notes and usually, although not exclusively, to those groups that are associated with a fixed pitch level. The terms 'series' and 'row' I have regarded as synonymous and have reserved for twelve-note groupings that are specifically characterized by note order and interval sequence. Other terms are defined on their first appearance in the text. The different forms of a series are indicated by the initials 'P' (for the prime or original form), 'I' (for the inversion), 'R' (retrograde) and 'RI' (retrograde inversion). The most important pitch level associated with a series or a collection is indiated by the figure 'O'; other figures denote transpositions, the number indicating the number of semitone steps above this 'O' level at which the relevant transposition is to be found. The order of the notes in a series is here indicated by the numbers 1 to 12. Thus P–3 1–3 indicates the first, second and third notes of the prime form of a series at the transposition which begins on the note three semitones above that which I have regarded as its most important level.

The following book is not a biography. I have said in Chapter I below that the main features of Berg's life are already available in previous books on the composer. Recent research suggests that this statement is far from the truth and that an accurate biography remains, as yet, unwritten.

*September 1978*                                                            D.J.

# Acknowledgements

Frau Helene Berg, to whom, more than anyone, my thanks are due, died as I was completing the manuscript of this book. I should, however, like to acknowledge here her great kindness to me when I was in Vienna and to express my gratitude to her for allowing me access to many of the manuscripts in her possession.

My thanks are due to Frau Elena Hift and the Directors of Universal Edition, Vienna; Hofrat Dr. Franz Grasberger and the staff of the Musiksammlung of the Österreichische Nationalbibliothek; Dr. Ernst Hilmar, Stadtbibliothek, Vienna; Wayne D. Shirley, Manuscript Librarian of the Music Division, Library of Congress; the President of the Rychenburg Stiftung, Winterthur; and Mr. A. Hodges and the staff of the library of the Royal Northern College of Music, Manchester.

For answering various enquiries and helping me with a variety of problems I should like to express my gratitude to the late H. E. Apostel, Dr. Erich Alban Berg, Frau Kadidja Wedekind Biel, Mrs. Charlotte Bloch-Zavrel, Mr. Nicholas Chadwick, Frau Růžena Herlinger, Professor Rudolf Kolisch, Miss Elisabeth Lutyens, C.B.E., M. Jacques-Louis Monod, Professor George Perle, Professor Basil Smallman, Frau F. Schlesinger-Chapka, Professor Richard Swift, Mrs. Jeremy Thorpe, Miss Fanny Waterman, the late Dr. Egon Wellesz and Dr. Walter Jarry.

The British Academy and the Austrian Institute of London, on behalf of the Austrian Government, were kind enough to award the scholarships which enabled me to make two visits to Vienna in the course of my research; a fellowship from the Leverhulme Research Trust enabled me to devote some time to working on the material. I gratefully acknowledge the help of all three bodies.

For permission to reproduce copyrighted material my thanks are due to Universal Edition, Vienna for the use of extracts from all Berg's music except Op. 1 and Op. 2, permission for which was granted by Robert Lienau, Berlin; to the directors of the Alban Berg Stiftung, Vienna and to the editors of the *Musical Quarterly*, New York, the *Music Review*, Cambridge, *Perspectives of New Music*, Princeton, and *Soundings*.

I am deeply grateful to Dr. Donald Mitchell for his kindness and for the encouragement he gave me when I first began work on this book. I am also grateful to Dr. Mitchell, Mr. David Matthews, Miss Judith Osborne and the staff of Faber and Faber for their help when preparing the work for publication.

My thanks also go to the many friends who have helped me during the writing of this book and particularly to Mr. David Pinder, who read a number of the chapters in the early stages of preparation, to Mrs. Susan Davies who made the translation of Wedekind's 'Konfession' which appears in Appendix II, to Mrs. Susan Katzmann who has kept me in touch with Viennese events and publications, Miss Ann-Lynn Miller who provided me with a number of American publications and to Mrs. Susan Clarke and Mrs. Linda Taylor who together typed out the manuscript.

My especial thanks go to Mr. Michael Taylor who has been a constant and invaluable source of help, advice and information.

Finally, and despite her express wishes to the contrary, my thanks go to my wife Angela who not only read and corrected proofs but has helped, cheered, encouraged and tolerated me throughout.

# I

# Introduction

Of the three composers of the Second Viennese School, Berg has always been the most popular and the most widely performed. In the seven years from its première on 14 December 1925 to December 1932 *Wozzeck* alone received twenty-seven different productions[1] and, for most of the remaining years of his life following the initial production of *Wozzeck*, Berg, unlike either Schoenberg or Webern, was able to live on the royalties which he received from performances of his music.[2] The ban imposed by the Hitler Government at the end of January 1933, which effectively brought to an end all performances of Berg's music in Germany, coupled with the ever-increasing rate of inflation, seriously affected Berg's financial security. The fixed monthly allowance which Berg's publishers were giving him as an advance against the future performances of *Lulu* was insufficient without the income from royalties. Even so, if – with rare exceptions, such as Kleiber's courageous performance of the *Lulu* Suite in Berlin in 1934 – Berg's music

[1] Details of these productions are given in E. Hilmar, *Wozzeck von Alban Berg*, Vienna, 1975, pp. 88–92.

[2] A list (albeit incorrect and incomplete) in the files of Universal Edition, Berg's publishers, tables thirteen performances of Berg's music in the first six months of 1928. The following performances and artists are listed:

| | | | |
|---|---|---|---|
| Piano Sonata Op. 1 | Steuermann | Frankfurt Radio | 6.2.28 |
| | Frl. Jory Rosaska | Budapest | 7.3.28 |
| | Josefa Rosomska | Budapest | 7.3.28 |
| | Josefa Rosomska | Prague | 10.3.28 |
| | Josefa Rosomska | Vienna | 14.4.28 |
| Four Songs Op. 2 | Fr. Else Schürhoff | Berlin | 1.3.28 |
| | Fr. Růžena Herlinger | Paris | 22.3.28 |
| | Fr. Emmy Hein | Prague | 13.4.28 |
| | Fr. Emmy Hein | Paris (Sorbonne) | 4.6.28 |
| String Quartet Op. 3 | Peters Quartet | Munich | before 9.1.28 |
| | Peters Quartet | Frankfurt | 11.1.28 |
| Clarinet Pieces Op. 5 | Alfred Ruste and Ellen Epstein | Berlin | c.23.4.28 |
| *Lyric Suite* | Kolisch Quartet | Paris (Pleyel) | 22.5.28 |

The two Budapest performances are probably one and the same. The *Lyric Suite* performance should be dated 22.3.28. The list is by no means complete: the Chamber Concerto, conducted by Walter Straram, was also performed in Paris early in 1928 (see D. Jarman, 'Two Unpublished Letters from Berg', *Musical Times*, 113: 1550, April 1972).

was no longer performed in Austria and Germany, it was still widely performed abroad. As Berg ironically remarked in a letter to Růžena Herlinger
dated 17 November 1935:

> Mengelberg is doing the *Lulu* pieces on 8 Dec. . . . also on 11 Dec. . . .
> on the radio, on 17 Dec. Andreae in Zurich – Klemperer in U.S.A. at the
> same time. Subsequently Heuer (35/36) in Stockholm . . . Helsinki,
> Busch in Copenhagen, Stokowski (Philadelphia and poss. Cleveland). It
> will mean that there will be Austrian music everywhere but in Austria
> itself. Amusing, isn't it?!

In the forty years since his death many works by Berg, in particular
*Wozzeck* and the Violin Concerto, have established themselves as part of the
standard operatic and concert repertoire. Yet, in comparison with that of
Schoenberg and Webern, Berg's music has, until recently, received little
critical or analytical attention; as well as being the most generally popular of
the three composers of the Second Viennese School, Berg is also the one
whose aims and achievements are least understood.

To a large extent the relative popularity of Berg's music and the lack of
detailed analytical attention which it has received derive from the same
source. More than that of either of his colleagues, Berg's music belongs
emotionally to the world of late nineteenth-century romanticism and its
melodic and harmonic language is more reminiscent of that of earlier tonal
music than is the music of Schoenberg and Webern. It was these traditional
aspects of Berg's music which originally led to his being admired as 'the poet
of the atonal'[1] and for being 'more artist than doctrinaire';[2] it was these
same traditional elements that also led to his being ignored by many of the
composers who, in the late 1940s and early 1950s, rejected what they regarded
as the traditional aspects of Schoenberg's music and turned to the music of
Webern as offering a solution to the various problems with which they were
confronted. Before the late 1940s and early 1950s Schoenberg, as originator
of the twelve-note method, and as the senior, dominant and also the only
living member of the Second Viennese School, was the centre of heated
controversy. During and after the late 1940s the attention of young composers
was centred on the music of Webern, until then almost unknown.[3] Berg's
music was regarded as an unacceptable compromise between the old and
new orders and was virtually ignored by both composers and analysts.[4]

---

[1] See, for example, J. D. Bohm, 'Berg, Poet of the Atonal, tells of his new opera *Lulu*'
(*Musical America*, 51: 18, 28 Nov. 1931, p. 10).
[2] G. Abraham, *A Hundred Years of Music*, 3rd edn., London, 1964, p. 289.
[3] According to Donald Mitchell, (*The Language of Modern Music*, London, 1963, p. 27),
there was only one performance of the Op. 24 Concerto of Webern between the years
1935 and 1946.
[4] Boulez's 1948 article 'Incidences actuelles de Berg' (reprinted in *Relevés d'Apprenti*,
Paris, 1964) typifies the avant-garde composer's view of Berg at this time.

For many years, and particularly in the period since Hans Redlich published his valuable study of the composer,[1] any real assessment of Berg's music has been hindered by the fact that much of it has been unavailable to either scholars or the public. For over thirty of the forty years since Berg's death the orchestral scores of the *Altenberg Lieder, Der Wein,* the Seven Early Songs and *Lulu* remained unpublished, a fact which has inevitably discouraged performance of these works.[2] For a composer with such a small body of works as Alban Berg these four scores, including, as they do, two of his last three works, represent an important and substantial part of his output. Happily the full scores of the *Altenberg Lieder,* the Seven Early Songs, *Der Wein* and Acts I and II of *Lulu* are now published.

Excluding arrangements of his own works for media other than the original, Berg's published compositions now amount, at the most generous estimate, to a mere eighteen pieces. Even so small a number can only be arrived at by counting the two settings of 'Schliesse mir die Augen beide' as two separate works, by including the early Piano Variations (published only in Redlich's book on the composer),[3] the song 'An Leukon' and the four-part canon 'Alban Berg an das Frankfurter Operhaus' (published only in two of Reich's books),[4] and by regarding *Lulu* as a complete opera in the form in which it is at present published.

Of the works that are known to exist there remain as yet 72 early songs dating from the years 1900–8 and the Third Act of *Lulu* unpublished. The unknown early songs seem unlikely to affect the overall picture of Berg's output. The unpublished Third Act of *Lulu* I shall discuss later. The complete list of Berg's works[5] given in Appendix I includes two works – a choral piece and a Fugue for String Quintet and Piano, both dating from 1907 – which are unknown and the manuscripts of which are assumed to be lost. These and the other unknown works, such as the sketches for the symphony on Balzac's *Seraphita,* on which Berg was working in 1913, or for the projected opera on *Und Pippa tanzt,* may appear when all Berg's surviving manuscripts and sketches become available.

[1] H. F. Redlich, *Alban Berg: Versuch einer Würdigung,* Vienna, 1957. A shortened English version of this book (*Alban Berg: The Man and his Music*) was also published in 1957.
[2] The first complete performance of the *Altenberg Lieder* did not take place until 1953 when Jascha Horenstein conducted performances of the cycle in Paris and in Rome, eighteen years after Berg's death.
[3] Redlich, *Versuch einer Würdigung,* Vienna, 1957, p. 393f.
[4] W. Reich, *Alban Berg,* Vienna, 1937, Appendix, p. 16; *Alban Berg,* London, 1963, p. 116.
[5] Appendix I does not include the unpublished early songs, a list and a description of which can be found in N. Chadwick, 'Berg's unpublished songs in the ÖNB', *Music and Letters,* 52: 2, April 1971. Chadwick's suggested dates for Nos. 15–26 and No. 64 should be compared with those in Berg's own list published in Erich Alban Berg, *Alban Berg,* Frankfurt, 1976, p. 90. The opening pages of two of the songs (Chadwick Nos. 1 and 12) are given in E. A. Berg, pp. 77 and 78.

Now that the music of Schoenberg, Berg and Webern is part of music history, that the partisanship of the 1950s has disappeared and that it is no longer necessary to argue the validity of the twelve-note method before discussing the music to which it gave rise, it is possible at least to begin to appreciate Berg's true stature.

The role which tonality and other traditional elements play in Berg's music will be a recurring topic in the following chapters. The traditional aspects of Berg's music have been the subject of many writings on the composer, yet Berg's relation to the procedures and designs of earlier music is far more ambivalent than is generally realized. Alongside its more obviously traditional aspects, Berg's music shows a fascination with certain technical procedures of a kind that are quite foreign to the music of either Schoenberg or Webern and which are peculiarly relevant to musical developments since his death. That the traditional elements in his music have tended to obscure an appreciation of its more revolutionary features is itself an indication of Berg's great skill as a composer. During the course of his development, from the early songs to *Lulu*, Berg moved from romanticism to structuralism without ever abandoning the emotional intensity and apparent spontaneity which are the most striking features of his music. It is this apparently paradoxical fusion of technical calculation and emotional spontaneity that gives Berg's music its peculiar fascination and forms one of the main subjects of the following chapters.

Chapters II to V are each devoted to a consideration of one particular aspect of Berg's technique. The methods of pitch organization in the twelve-note and the pre-twelve-note music are discussed separately but I have not otherwise observed any strict chronological divisions. This method of approach has inevitable disadvantages in that it necessitates the consideration of different features of a single work at different points in the book. Given the limited size of Berg's output, I have hoped that the possibility, which such an approach affords, of studying the development and the consistency of Berg's preoccupation with certain highly individual organizational procedures over the course of his creative career, outweighs these disadvantages.

I have not attempted to give a biographical account of Berg's career. The main features of his life are already available in previous books on the composer. Since, however, the works are not dealt with in any strict chronological order, it will be useful to give a brief résumé of Berg's output and to attempt, in those cases where it is possible, to give more precise dates of composition than have hitherto been available. The list of Berg's compositions in Appendix I gives details of the whereabouts of the existing manuscripts as far as I have been able to discover them.

Berg began his studies with Schoenberg in October 1904.[1] The earliest of

[1] See E. Hilmar, *Wozzeck von Alban Berg*, Vienna, 1975, p. 8.

his published works – the first setting of the song 'Schliesse mir die Augen beide' of 1907 and the Seven Early Songs of 1905/8 – date from this period of study. The manuscripts of two of the early songs are dated[1] but it is impossible to date the five remaining songs, the Piano Sonata op. 1 of 1908 and the Four Songs op. 2 of 1909 (the first works to which Berg gave opus numbers) more precisely. The whereabouts of the manuscript score of the Piano Sonata op. 1 is unknown. The manuscript of the op. 3 Quartet of 1910, the last work written while Berg was studying under Schoenberg, is in the Austrian National Library.[2] The first movement of the work was completed by 30 May, on which date Berg wrote to Webern that he was busy rehearsing it and correcting the proofs of op. 1 and op. 2. The second movement was completed in July of that year. Op. 1 and op. 2 were published, at Berg's own expense, by Robert Lienau of Berlin later in 1910.

The five songs which make up the *Altenberg Lieder* op. 4 present two main historical problems. The first problem is the identity of the two songs which were included in the famous concert given by Schoenberg on 31 March 1913, a concert which, as a result of Berg's songs, ended in uproar and had to be abandoned. The second problem is a chronological one about the order in which the five songs were composed. The identity of the two songs included in the Schoenberg concert is no longer problematic for, although Reich, Redlich and Leibowitz all say that the songs performed were songs II and IV of the cycle, a report, published in the Boston Evening Transcript of 17 April 1913[3] and the discovery of Berg's own handwritten copies of the first violin parts used at the performance[4] confirm that the songs performed were songs II and III of the cycle as it now stands.

In his study of the *Altenberg Lieder*[5] Mark DeVoto makes the conjecture, on the musical evidence of the songs themselves, that the order of composition was: IV, III, V, II, I. The evidence of the unpublished correspondence between Berg and Webern suggests that this conjecture is correct. Berg began work on the cycle at the end of March 1912 and had finished the first song by 10 April when Webern wrote: 'How are you? Have you written any more orchestral songs? Send them soon to Schoenberg. He will be very pleased. The single song is marvellous.' By the end of August Webern knew that Berg had completed three songs. Webern had not at that time seen the

---

[1] The Wiener Stadtbibliothek manuscripts of 'Im Zimmer' and 'Liebesode' are dated Summer 1905 and 19.9.1906 respectively. The Österreichische Nationalbibliothek (ÖNB) manuscript of 'Liebesode' has the date 1905 crossed out.
[2] Redlich incorrectly describes the manuscript of the Op. 3 Quartet as lost (*Alban Berg*, London, 1957, p. 296). Berg's study with Schoenberg ended, officially, in May 1911.
[3] The report is published in Slonimsky, *Lexicon of Musical Invective*, New York, 1953, p. 53. I am grateful to Mr. Nicholas Chadwick for bringing this report to my attention.
[4] Published in Erich Alban Berg, *Alban Berg*, Frankfurt, 1976, p. 144.
[5] DeVoto, 'Alban Berg's Picture Postcard Songs', unpublished Princeton Univ. thesis 1967, p. 91.

third song, however, and, on 30 August 1912 wrote to Berg: 'Dear Friend, Your last letter refreshed me deeply. First, the news that you had completed the third of your orchestral songs. I am already very eager to see it. Is it a long one? You're really writing a cycle of orchestral songs.' In reply Berg wrote: 'My third song is a bigger one, about 2 or 3 times as long as the other two which you know. The fourth, which I shall finish soon, is shorter than all three. There will be five songs in all.'[1] In a fragment of a later letter, undated but probably written between 10–12 September 1912, Berg tells Webern that 'the song on which I am now working begins ". . . nach Schneestürmen"'.

Since this last fragment refers to the text of what is now the first song in the cycle, the 'bigger song', of which Berg speaks in his letter written at the beginning of September, is clearly the fifth song, the other large-scale song in the cycle. The 'fourth song' which 'is shorter than all three' is, presumably, the second and shortest song of the set.

It is thus possible to fix the order and approximate dates of composition of the last three songs to be written. It is impossible to be sure whether the 'single song' to which Webern refers in his letter of 10 April is the present third or fourth song. If DeVoto's conjecture, that the fourth song was the first of the cycle to be completed, is assumed to be correct, then the order and approximate dates of composition of each is:

Song IV: finished end of March/beginning of April 1912
Song III: composed sometime during summer (April/July) 1912
Song V: completed end of August 1912
Song II: completed beginning of September 1912
Song I: probably completed September 1912.

The length of time between the completion of Song IV, at the end of March or the beginning of April 1912, and the completion of Song V, at the end of August, with only the short third song written during the summer of 1912, is explained by the fact that Berg was engaged in making a voice and piano version of the third and fourth movements of Schoenberg's op. 10 Quartet at this time. He was also, as so often, ill for much of the summer, writing to Webern in early April: 'My health, in which I had only just begun to take pleasure after my recovery from jaundice, is already poor again. This time the asthma condition, which usually comes in July, has set in early.' Berg's jaundice returned in July;[2] he suffered from asthma throughout his life.

The precise dates of the composition of the op. 5 pieces for clarinet and

---

[1] Berg's letter is undated. Redlich, who quotes the letter (*Versuch einer Würdigung*, Vienna, 1957, p. 78) gives its date as 5 August 1912; the letter is, however, clearly a reply to Webern's letter of 30 August.
[2] See the letter of 22 July 1912 in Redlich, *Alban Berg*, London, 1957, p. 220.

piano are, again, difficult to ascertain. The published score has the date 'Spring 1913' at the end of the set yet both Redlich and, in the original edition of this book, Reich give the date of composition as 'Summer 1913'.[1] According to the chronology printed in the English edition of Berg's *Letters to his Wife*, the pieces were written in June 1913.[2] At the beginning of June of that year, however, Berg visited Schoenberg in Berlin, and on the final afternoon of the visit, the two had a lengthy argument. All commentators have maintained that this argument was caused by Schoenberg's hostile attitude to the op. 5 pieces. Berg had certainly returned from Berlin by 4 July,[3] so, unless the op. 5 pieces were completed immediately before Berg's visit to Schoenberg, it seems likely that the date in the published score, and in Reich's later book,[4] is correct. At any event, Berg began work on the 'Präludium' of the Three Orchestral Pieces op. 6 in the month following his visit to Schoenberg and by July of the following year (1914) was far enough advanced to tell Webern of his hopes of completing the score for Schoenberg's birthday on 13 September. The scores of the 'Marsch' and the 'Präludium' were finished in time for fair copies to be sent off to Schoenberg on 8 September.[5] The score of 'Reigen', the middle piece of the Three Orchestral Pieces, was not finished until the early summer of 1915. The precise date when 'Reigen' was completed is not known but the work was certainly finished in short score by 13 July 1915 when Berg wrote to Webern: 'I must finally finish the third of the Three Orchestral Pieces – that is to say, write out the score and bring it, nicely copied out, back to Vienna for Schoenberg'. A copy of 'Reigen' had been sent to Schoenberg by 5 August 1915.

While working on the Orchestral Pieces Berg was also actively engaged on the composition of *Wozzeck*, the earliest sketches for which are interspersed with sketches for the 'Marsch' of op. 6.[6] Berg had attended the first production in Vienna of Büchner's *Woyzeck*[7] at the Rezidensbühne on 5 May 1914 and had immediately decided to turn the work into an opera. The first sketches for the work date from May or June 1914 and are for the street scene of Act II, sc. 2, the first scene to be completed. Throughout Berg's work on *Wozzeck* the composition of the music and the arrangement of the libretto progressed simultaneously. Berg's work on the opera was continually interrupted: initially halted by Berg's military service during the first war,

[1] Reich, *Alban Berg*, Vienna, 1937, p. 11; Redlich, op. cit., p. 291.
[2] Berg, *Letters to his Wife*, London, 1971, p. 127.
[3] Reich, *Alban Berg*, London, 1965, p. 41.
[4] Ibid., p. 41 (cf. however, ibid., p. 113).
[5] Ibid., p. 42.
[6] The following details of the chronology of *Wozzeck* are drawn from E. Hilmar, *Wozzeck von Alban Berg*, Vienna, 1975.
[7] Although now usually called *Woyzeck*, the play was called *Wozzeck* at the Vienna performance which Berg attended. (See the reproduction of the programme in E. A. Berg, *Alban Berg*, Frankfurt, 1976, p. 149 and Perle, 'Woyzeck and Wozzeck', *Musical Quarterly* 53: 2, April 1967, p. 214.)

work on the composition was later disturbed by his involvement in Schoenberg's 'Society for Private Performances',[1] his dealing with the Berg family estate, the preparation of op. 3 and op. 5 for publication and his increasing literary activities as well as his ever-precarious health.

After the preliminary sketches of 1914, which, besides Act II, sc. 2, include fragments of Marie's Lullaby of Act I, sc. 3, and Andre's song in Act I, sc. 2, Berg did not resume work on *Wozzeck* until 1918. On 19 August 1918 Berg wrote to Webern: 'Up to now I have finished composing one scene and hope to get a second big one finished here.' The completed scene was the street scene of Act II, sc. 2; the 'second big one' the scene with the Doctor of Act I, sc. 4. Berg had finished Act I, sc. 1 by the early summer of 1919 and by 22 July had completed the whole of the first Act. On 29 July 1919, Berg wrote to tell Webern of the progress of the work:

> I was deep in work and also, I must admit, lazy. I'm not as far forward with *Wozzeck* as I hoped to be. Act I is quite finished (five scenes) and one big scene of Act II. Scarcely any is scored yet. But it's a big thing. Up to now about 900 bars are composed.

The following July (1920) Berg was at Trahütten working on the rest of Act II and, according to one letter to Webern, following a fairly strict routine: 'Daily from 7 to 1 on *Wozzeck*. After eating I have a little rest, then correspondence or tea and, towards evening, a walk.' By the end of July 1920 the overall plan of Acts II and III was fixed and, by the end of August, Act II, scenes 1, 3 and 5 completed. With Act II, sc. 2 already finished, the only scene of Act II still to be written was the big inn scene of sc. 4.

On 17 August of the following year (1921) Berg wrote to Webern: 'I have been so deep in work on *Wozzeck* that I couldn't get round to writing letters. . . . Things are going well for the first time here. The Second Act is finished. Only a quarter of the Third. I'll take it up again tomorrow.' On 28 September 1921 Berg wrote to Webern that he was about to start work on the final scene of the opera the following day. By mid-October the whole opera was complete in short score. The instrumentation was completed by April 1922.

The first details of the plan of the Chamber Concerto appear in a letter to Schoenberg written on 12 July 1923. The work was, at that point, intended as a piece for piano and violin accompanied by ten wind instruments.[2] By 1 September the first part of what Berg regarded as a 'single movement concerto' was finished – 'a variation movement of scherzo character'. The second movement was to be 'an Adagio; the third, a combination of the two preceding ones, a sonata movement'. The short score of the work was

---

[1] The Society was founded in 1918. Berg was one of the 'directors of performances'.
[2] See Redlich, *Alban Berg*, London, 1957, p. 115; the ten wind instruments eventually became thirteen.

finished by 9 February 1925, when Berg wrote the 'Open Letter' dedicating the work to Schoenberg, the sketch of the orchestral layout on 19 February, the complete full score on 23 July 1925.

Less than two months later, on 18 September 1925, Berg began work on the *Lyric Suite*. The first description of the nature of the piece on which he was working comes in a letter to Webern written on 12 October 1925:

> I too sent a love song, the words of which have no connection with the jubilee; or, rather, I sent two songs on the same poem, a very old song and a brand new one. The latter I composed up here – my first attempt at a strict twelve-note composition. However, in that art I am, unfortunately, not as far advanced as you so I can't tell you much about my present work on the String Quartet for the time being. It's not going easily at the moment. But perhaps I'm also tired, my health is not of the best and I was also wrong to spend so much time on the revision of the piano reduction of the concerto which is now going to the engravers. Such work really takes days and puts one in the wrong frame of mind. It should, however, become a suite for string quartet. Six movements, more lyrical than symphonic in character.[1]

Berg's remarks on the slowness with which the work progressed and on his difficulties in handling the unfamiliar twelve-note method is borne out by the manuscript score of the work. The manuscripts of the three twelve-note movements (movements I, III and VI) and the twelve-note tenebroso section of the fifth movement are covered in lines, letters and figures of different colours indicating the different row forms employed. On the reverse of each sheet of the manuscripts of the twelve-note movements, and interleaved between the movements themselves, are various sketches, jottings and comments. Bars 394–400 of the fifth movement, for example, are provided with an alternative first violin part ('in case the violinist cannot get so high') and bars 411–18 an 'ossia' for the cello. A further sketch on the reverse of one sheet of the fifth movement shows the method of row splitting employed in the final Largo.[2] Sketches for the final movement appear as early as the last page of the first movement, where there is a sketch for bar 31 et seq. of the finale. Interleaved between the first and second movements is a chart, headed 'Für das Largo', of the two sets employed in the finale, showing the relationship between the two sets as it appears at bar 30 of movement VI, and a sketch of the connection between the material of the finale and that of the first movement. In view of the unusual formal design of the *Lyric Suite*[3]

---

[1] The first paragraph of this letter is given in Redlich, *Alban Berg*, London, 1957, p. 131. The letter was sent from Trahütten, where most of the *Lyric Suite* was written. The two songs were the two settings of 'Schliesse mir die Augen beide' which Berg sent as his contribution to the celebrations of the silver jubilee of Universal Edition.

[2] See pp. 127–8 below.

[3] See pp. 180–1 below.

it seems likely that Berg had a clear and detailed plan of the whole work in mind when he began work on this manuscript.

Only the first two and the last movement of the Vienna manuscript of the *Lyric Suite* are dated. The first movement is dated 'Trahütten 23.10.25' and has the timing 2–2½ minutes indicated. The second movement is dated '12.6.26 Trahütten' and has an approximate time of 3½ minutes indicated. Particularly interesting is the manuscript of the sixth and final movement in which, in the Vienna manuscript, a text follows the main line throughout; I shall discuss this text in Chapter IV.[1] The finale is precisely dated 'Sept. 30, 1926, 1 o'clock in the morning'.

A feature of the manuscript of the third movement is the extent to which the instrumental effects employed in the movement differ from those in the published score. Berg was neither a string player nor, unlike Schoenberg and Webern, a performing musician. Although a competent pianist he made few public appearances as either pianist or conductor.[2] The third movement of the *Lyric Suite*, which in its final form makes highly original use of instrumental effects, is, in manuscript, covered with tentative suggestions and queries about the instrumentation. According to Rudolf Kolisch, Berg was unsure how best to achieve the effects he desired and the final details of the instrumentation were worked out between composer and performers in the rehearsals preceding the first performance.[3]

From early in 1926 Berg had been considering various plays as the basis of a new opera,[4] eventually being undecided about whether to use Hauptmann's *Und Pippa tanzt* or Wedekind's two *Lulu* plays, which he had seen in Karl Kraus's production at the Trianontheater on 29 May 1905. Berg's indecision lasted a long time. On 30 November 1927 he wrote asking Adorno's opinion. Adorno strongly advised him to set the Wedekind.[5] By 16 January 1928, however, Berg seemed to have finally decided, and told Webern that he was going to set the Hauptmann. On 17 January Webern wrote:

My dear Alban,
Only today have I realized what a fundamental event took place yesterday

[1] See p. 228 and footnote 1, p. 228 below.
[2] It is known that Berg played the piano part at the performance of his Fugue for String Quintet and Piano on 7 November 1907, the harmonium in the performance of arrangements of Strauss Waltzes on 27 May 1921, and that he accompanied Růžena Herlinger in the Paris performance of his op. 2 Songs and the *Wozzeck* Lullaby in 1928, but there are few other records of him having played the piano in public. His sole attempt at conducting (apparently a successful one, according to a letter from Webern written on 7 January 1913) appears to have been to take a rehearsal for the men's chorus of *Gurrelieder* on 30 December 1912.
[3] Personal communication from Prof. Rudolf Kolisch.
[4] Details of the plays which Berg considered are given in Carner, *Alban Berg*, London, 1975.
[5] See Adorno, *Alban Berg, Der Meister des Kleinsten übergangs*, Vienna, 1968, p. 41.

evening . . . namely your news that you are going to compose *Und Pippa tanzt*. Thank you for taking me into your confidence.

On 9 March 1928 Berg wrote to Kleiber that he had come to an agreement with Hauptmann, whom he had met in Rapallo, and that he hoped to start composing *Pippa* early that summer.[1] In April negotiations with Hauptmann's publishers broke down and Berg abandoned the project,[2] although even as late as 27 June Webern, at least, was still unsure about which subject Berg had chosen. Berg had certainly started work on the Hauptmann before the project was finally abandoned. He had already begun arranging the libretto and thinking about the music,[3] and also bought an ocarina which he intended to employ in the opera.

In October 1928 Berg and his publishers started negotiations with Frau Wedekind, the final details of which were not settled until July 1929, although Berg had already started work on the opera by that time and announcements to that effect had already appeared in the newspapers in June 1929. Berg's work on *Lulu* was interrupted twice: first by the composition of the concert aria *Der Wein* for Růžena Herlinger,[4] and secondly for the composition of the Violin Concerto for the American violinist Louis Krasner. *Der Wein* was begun towards the end of May 1929 and completed on 23 July of that year, the date on which Berg also wrote to Universal Edition (U.E.) to announce that he had reached a final agreement with Frau Wedekind on the *Lulu* negotiations. The Violin Concerto was started at the end of April 1935, following the death on 22 April of Manon Gropius, the 18-year-old daughter of Alma Mahler, to whom the work is dedicated. The short score of the concerto was finished on 15 July[5] and the full score on 12 August.[6] Despite these interruptions Berg worked on *Lulu* from 1929 onwards. On 22 June 1931 Berg was still engaged on Act I and wrote to Webern:

> The work is going steadily but slowly forward . . . I am still somewhat pestered by the weeks of pressure from U.E. to think of *Lulu* as a 'rush-job' for Philadelphia . . . but now I've freed myself from this coercion and work as always — that is, slowly! If I can wait so can U.E. and so can the U.S.A.

By 23 July 1931 Berg was writing the finale to Act I, arranging the libretto

[1] See Russell, *Erich Kleiber*, London, 1957, p. 125.
[2] See Carner, *Alban Berg*, London, 1975, p. 64.
[3] See the entry from the guest book of Alfred Kalmus reproduced in Carner, op. cit., p. 60.
[4] See Jarman, *Musical Times*, 113: 1550, April 1972.
[5] Redlich (*Alban Berg*, London, 1957, p. 295) has 12 July as the date of the completion of the full score. The above data is based on that given in a letter from Berg to Dr. Herlinger (published in Jarman, *Musical Times*, 113: 1550, April, 1972). See, however, footnote 2, p. 13 below.
[6] Ibid. has 11 August as the date of the completion of the full score. The above date is based on that given in a letter from Berg to Dr. Herlinger (published in Jarman, *Musical Times*, 113: 1550, April, 1972). See, however, footnote 2, p. 13 below.

at the same time as he wrote the music. Act II was finished by September of 1933: on 15 September Berg wrote to Webern: 'Things haven't been going well for some days. But they're now going quite well and I've finally, finally finished Act II. Now comes the most difficult – Act III, "splendour and decline".' In January 1934 Berg expected the work to be completed by the spring and the instrumentation by the autumn of that year; he wrote to Kleiber that the work, if it could be performed at all given the existing political situation, could be produced in the coming 1934/1935 season.[1] By the following month, February 1934, Berg was at work on the final scene of the opera.[2]

Berg now began to make plans for arranging a concert suite from the opera, as he had done with *Wozzeck* earlier, and on 23 May 1934 wrote to U.E. outlining his ideas for two concert works, a *Lulu* Suite and a *Lulu* Symphony.[3] According to Berg's letter the movements and their approximate durations were to be:

| | | |
|---|---|---|
| I | Rondo | 10 min. |
| II | Ostinato (Film music) | $3\frac{1}{2}$ min. |
| III | Variations | 4 min. |
| IV | Adagio | $4\frac{1}{2}$ min. |
| V | Lied der Lulu | $2\frac{1}{2}$ min. |

The Symphony was to include:

| | | |
|---|---|---|
| I | Allegro (Sonata movement) | $12\frac{1}{2}$ min. |
| II | Scherzo (with Trio) | $2\frac{1}{2}$ min. |
| III | Ostinato (Film music) | $3\frac{1}{2}$ min. |
| IV | Rondo | 10 min. |
| V | Quodlibet | c. $3\frac{1}{2}$ min. |
| VI | Lied der Lulu | $2\frac{1}{2}$ min. |
| VII | Variations | 4 min. |
| VIII | Adagio | $4\frac{1}{2}$ min. |

The idea of a *Lulu* Symphony was eventually abandoned. The Sonata Allegro, which formed the first movement of the projected Symphony, was to be a version of Dr. Schön's Sonata movement, the various sections of which are spread over Act I of the opera;[4] Berg intended, as in the Rondo movement of the *Lulu* Suite as it now stands, to excise the intervening episodes and bring the different sections together to form a single movement. The Scherzo and Trio of the Symphony would have been the orchestral interlude between Act I, scenes 1 and 2, of the opera. The 'Quodlibet' of the

---

[1] See Russell, *Erich Kleiber*, London, 1957, p. 142.
[2] Ibid., p. 143.
[3] See Volker Scherliess, 'Briefe Alban Bergs aus der Entstehungszeit der Lulu', *Melos*, No. 2, März–April 1976.
[4] See p. 201 f. below.

Symphony is more difficult to identify. Berg's letter of 23 May to U.E. says, with regard to the Rondo of the Suite: 'Only with movements I and V (Allegro and Quodlibet) of the Symphony will there be similar large adjustments and a number of pages to introduce.'[1] A jotting amongst Berg's sketches has 'Quodlibet III/i' but there is nothing in Act III, sc. 1 which fits Berg's description in his letter to U.E. It may be that the 'Quodlibet' was to be a version of the Ensemble scene in Act II, sc. 1.

Berg was working on the final scene of *Lulu* in February 1934 and had certainly finished the work by the end of April 1934. He had originally suggested to U.E. the idea of making a suite from the music of *Lulu* – a suite that would include music from the very end of Act III – sometime at the beginning of May 1934, for his letter of 23 May, quoted above, was written in reply to one from U.E. on 17 May asking specific questions about the Suite. The short score of the opera was, therefore, finished at least twenty months before Berg's death on 24 December 1935. With the exception of a period of about four months spent working on the Violin Concerto,[2] Berg spent these last twenty months working on the instrumentation of the opera. At his death he had scored Acts I and II, those sections of Act III which appear in the *Lulu* Suite and 268 bars of Act III, sc. 1.[3]

In view of the continuing non-publication of Act III of the opera and the preparatory note at the beginning of the present published score, the precise chronology of Berg's work on *Lulu* is of some interest and considerable importance. The posthumous history of *Lulu* is now generally known.[4] It will be sufficient to describe the state of the score as it stands at present, the existing material and the nature of the work necessary to complete the opera.[5]

With the exception of one short section in Act III, sc. 2 the Third Act of *Lulu* is complete in every detail other than instrumentation. The exceptional section is a passage of about twenty bars which at present consists of a recapitulation of the orchestral and the voice part of the 'Hymne' of Act II, sc. 2, and to which Berg intended to add vocal parts for Lulu, Schigolch and Countess Geschwitz. George Perle has suggested that Berg 'finding that he

---

[1] This section of Berg's letter is not published in Scherliess, *Melos,* No. 2, März–April 1976. Berg is here referring to the extent to which pages engraved for the full score of the opera can be bodily transferred to the *Suite* and observes: 'I hope you'll be pleased that I'm being so helpful and economical.'

[2] In a taped interview with Dr. Erich Schenk of the Phonotek in Vienna, Helene Berg said that the Violin Concerto (presumably the short score) was composed in six weeks.

[3] That is, almost to the end of the second Ensemble (see p. 206 below).

[4] For a résumé of the whole affair see Offergeld: 'Some Questions about *Lulu*', *Hi-Fi Stereo Review,* October 1964, pp. 58–76.

[5] The following description of the state of the score is based on my own study of the Particell and Berg's sketches, and on Perle's 'A note of Act III of *Lulu*' (*Perspectives of New Music,* 2, 1964) and '*Lulu* : The Formal Design' (*Journal of the American Musicological Society,* 17, Spring/Summer, 1964). I have been unable to examine Berg's scored section of III/1, the piano-vocal score of Act III prepared by Erwin Stein, and Berg's own copy of the Wedekind.

had not left sufficient space for filling in the missing details . . . probably completed them on a separate sheet'.[1] The only remaining work to be done, other than the addition of the vocal parts for this missing twenty-bar fragment, is the completion of the instrumentation 'in a manner consistent with Berg's style'.[2] The unusual formal design of the opera, in which extensive sections of material from Acts I and II reappear in Act III,[3] is such that Berg's intentions in this respect are peculiarly easy to ascertain. It would be possible to score 310 of the 670 bars of Act III, sc. 1 and 240 of the 590 bars of Act III, sc. 2 (that is, nearly half of the total Act) precisely in accordance with Berg's intentions. For the instrumentation of the remaining bars there are not only the occasional indications of the intended instrumentation which appear in the Particell itself but the various suggestions which appear in Berg's existing sketches.[4] Both Particell and sketches include specific and general notes on the instrumentation. The duet between Lulu and Schigolch in Act III, sc. 1, for example, includes, at various points in the Particell, indications of parts for horn, bass clarinet, clarinet, trumpet and strings. Throughout Acts I and II the figure of Schigolch is always associated with a chamber music-like texture and it is known that Berg intended to maintain this association in Act III;[5] a note amongst Berg's sketches suggests that, in Act III, Schigolch was to be associated with an instrumental combination similar to that employed in Schoenberg's First Chamber Symphony.[6] It was Berg's habitual practice, when working on a piece, to make occasional remarks about the most important features of the intended instrumentation in the margin of the manuscript – such remarks as, for example, 'new colour', 'very light' or 'wind' – and these too appear on both the sketches and the Particell of *Lulu*. There is reason to hope that Act III of *Lulu* will be completed and published in the near future. As I shall show in the following chapters, all Berg's mature works are characterized by a highly individual sense of formal balance and symmetry. In the two operas the symmetry of the formal design has particularly important dramatic significance. Although the fact that *Lulu*, even in the fragmentary form in which it has hereto been performed, has managed to establish itself as part of the international operatic repertoire, is a remarkable tribute to Berg's genius, the makeshift version of Act III both destroys the carefully calculated balance on which Berg's musical design is based and, by destroying the dramatic significance of this design, falsifies our understanding of the opera as a whole.

[1] Perle, *Perspectives of New Music*, 17, Spring/Summer, 1964, p. 9.
[2] Reich, *Alban Berg*, Vienna, 1937, p. 124. This sentence does not appear in Reich's later book.
[3] See pp. 210–11 below.
[4] The sketches for *Lulu* in the Ö.N.B. (see Appendix I) run to over 700 pages and include not only music, but remarks on instrumentation, on the effects to be achieved at certain points and, on occasions, diagrams plotting specific entries, exits and other stage action.
[5] See Reich, *Alban Berg*, London, 1965, p. 165.          [6] See p. 216 below.

# II

# Pitch Organization in the Early and 'Free' Atonal Works

The seventeen years which separate the composition of 'Im Zimmer' of 1905 (the earliest of the songs published as Seven Early Songs) from the completion of *Wozzeck* in 1922,[1] saw the development of Berg's musical language from one firmly rooted in tonality to one in which tonality was one of many available compositional resources. The third act of *Wozzeck*, each scene of which demonstrates how a musical element, other than tonality, can be exploited as a means of organizing a large musical structure, gives some indication of the other compositional resources upon which Berg was able to draw at the time of writing the opera. Tonal elements never completely disappear from Berg's work, however, and, although these elements do not have many of the functions that they have in a traditional tonal piece, it would be wrong to minimize the important role which they play in his music. It will be useful to attempt to define this role before considering other aspects of Berg's musical language.

Any discussion of the role played by tonal elements in what is usually termed 'atonal' music is beset by a number of problems. The general lack of agreement amongst theorists as to the extent to which a sense of key operates, or is intended to operate, in atonal music need not concern us here; there has been unanimous agreement amongst all commentators, from Schoenberg onwards,[2] that tonal references of some kind are felt when listening to Berg's music and that these tonal references were intended by the composer. I shall assume that the reader agrees with these commentators.

A more difficult problem is presented by the lack of any convenient terminology to define the different roles which tonal elements may play in 'atonal' music. The function of the tonal references, their range and the extent to which they operate in Berg's music differs from work to work and

---

[1] See Ch. I, p. 8 above. Reich (*Alban Berg*, Vienna, 1937, p. 12), and Redlich (*Alban Berg*, London, 1957, p. 292), both give, incorrectly, April 1921 as the date of the completion of *Wozzeck*.
[2] See Schoenberg, *Style and Idea*, London, 1975, pp. 244–5.

from passage to passage within a single work. Traditional music theory has no terms which can distinguish between these different functions.

In the *Harmonielehre* Schoenberg characterizes the two basic functions of tonality as being to unify and to articulate. The tonal allusions in Berg's music, at least in the works from the op. 3 String Quartet until the late twelve-note works, may be said to have an articulative and expressive, rather than a unifying, function.

The peculiar expressive power of Berg's music springs primarily from the fact that, for long sections, it encourages tonal interpretation while, at the same time, refuses to confirm this interpretation.[1] While the melodic patterns and the individual harmonic formations are frequently reminiscent of those of earlier music, the harmonic formations themselves are rarely arranged in a succession organized according to traditional, functional harmonic procedures. Since many other aspects of Berg's music – the phrase structures, the metrically organized rhythmic patterns,[2] the methods of thematic development and continuity – are clearly related to those of earlier music, the appearance of vertical structures reminiscent of those of tonal music inevitably calls forth traditional associations and suggests the operation of traditional, diatonic criteria.

It may not be possible for the listener to say, with any sense of certainty, how the individual chords in Berg's music should be resolved since, within its context, each chord may be so tonally ambiguous that a number of different resolutions will seem equally possible and equally satisfactory; nonetheless, the chords are similar enough to those of traditional music for the listener to feel them as dissonances which require some kind of resolution. The characteristic emotional intensity of Berg's music derives from the fact that, for extensive passages, the individual chord structures imply a resolution which does not take place.[3]

George Perle has rightly criticized those writers who, by an 'unwarranted projection of these (tonal) criteria . . . attribute tonic functionality to "atonal" motives',[4] yet all Berg's music works against a background of tonality and deliberately exploits the listener's previous experience of tonal music.

The balance between tonal confirmation and tonal denial in Berg's music affords a very flexible method of articulating the musical structure. The

---

[1] See Edward Cone's remarks in 'Music: A View from Delft' in *Perspectives on Contemporary Music Theory*, New York, 1972, p. 68.

[2] Some of the rhythmic procedures employed in Berg's music are, however, based upon non-metric methods of organization. These procedures are discussed in Ch. IV below.

[3] See Rosen, *Schoenberg*, Glasgow, 1967, Ch. II, for a consideration of the same phenomenon in Schoenberg's music.

[4] Perle: 'The Musical Language of *Wozzeck*', *Music Forum*, I, New York, 1967, p. 207. An extended, and unconvincing, attempt to analyse *Wozzeck* in traditional tonal terms can be found in Werner König's *Tonalitätsstrukturen in Alban Bergs Oper 'Wozzeck'*, Tutzing, 1974.

resolution of the dissonance implied by the structure of a chord may be used as a means of obtaining a point of momentary relaxation; the extent to which a resolution is anticipated by the chord sequence which precedes it, the extent to which it is defined by the sense of movement towards a 'tonic' which the preceding passage generates, and the extent to which the resolution itself is asserted as a stable element all provide means of manipulating the degree of relaxation which the resolution produces. On a larger scale, the extent to which a passage or a section of music invites or discourages tonal interpretation can characterize or articulate large sections of a piece. To this extent the precariously maintained tonal ambiguity of Berg's music can be regarded as an extension of the musical language of the late nineteenth century.

However, although the handling of tonal implications and the manipulation of degrees of tension and relaxation in Berg's music articulate the musical design in a way comparable to that of the tensions and relaxations in traditional diatonic music, the tonal areas on to which the music occasionally resolves do not have the unifying function of tonic keys in eighteenth- and nineteenth-century music. These tonal areas do not usually give rise to an ordered hierarchy of functional relationships or subsidiary areas as does a traditional 'tonic' nor, as a consequence, do they exert any long-term sense of 'pull' towards themselves. The tonal areas on to which the music resolves are, usually, of only local significance and any sense of 'pull', or of movement, towards a tonal area operates over only a short length of time. The D minor area which marks many of the cadences of the Three Orchestral Pieces op. 6,[1] for example, serves to emphasize important structural points and to separate the different sections from one another but has no long-term, architectural function of the kind one associates with a tonic in traditional music.

The final orchestral interlude of *Wozzeck* is exceptional in that, as Perle has shown,[2] the move to the D minor tonic of the interlude is carefully prepared throughout the preceding scenes. Ex. 1 demonstrates how the D minor of the interlude is the focal point towards which the harmonic structure of the hundred bars of the opera which precede its appearance is moving. A chromatic inflection of the chord which ends Act III, sc. 3 (Ex. 1a) produces the hexachord which governs the harmonies of Act III, sc. 4. Ex. 1b shows this hexachord at its original and primary pitch level, to which level it returns at the end of the scene. A further chromatic inflection of this chord (Ex. 1c) produces the opening chord of the D minor interlude.[3] By its placing within the dramatic structure of the work, the interlude acts as the

---

[1] 'At least once in each of the three pieces there is a strong resolution to the note D or to a chord whose most prominent tones form a D minor triad.' (Archibald, 'The Harmony of Berg's "Reigen" ', *Perspectives of New Music*, 6, Spring/Summer, 1968, p. 73.)
[2] See Perle, *Music Forum*, I, New York, 1967, pp. 245–7.
[3] See Perle, ibid., p. 247, Ex. 64.

resolution of the tensions built up during the course of Act III and, indeed, as the resolution of the tensions built up during the course of the whole opera. The dramatic significance of the interlude is underlined by its musical significance as the resolution of a harmonic progression which has stretched over the two preceding scenes.

Ex. 1

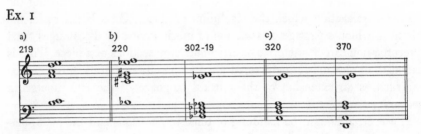

The long-term 'pull' towards a tonic exerted by the D minor[1] of the final interlude of *Wozzeck* is unusual in that, unlike the momentary tonal allusions and the tonally orientated passages that appear elsewhere in the opera, it has more than local significance. Even so, its significance is not comparable to that of a traditional tonic; the key of D minor has no large-scale, architectural function over the opera as a whole, nor – even within the two preceding scenes – does it act, as does a tonic key in diatonic music, as a referential element to which every harmonic and melodic formation can be related. It is a curious and typically paradoxical feature of Berg's stylistic development that, with the exception of the D minor interlude of *Wozzeck*, the most overtly 'tonal' passages in Berg's works after the Four Songs op. 2 are to be found in the late twelve-note works, that is, in the music based upon a method originally intended to provide an alternative to tonality as a means of organizing music.

While tonal references are usually of only local significance in Berg's pre-twelve-note music, what George Perle has called 'tone centres'[2] – by which is meant either single notes or a collection of notes at a specific pitch

---

[1] Berg seems to have had a peculiar fondness for the key of D minor, which appears as the tonic key of op. 2 No. 1, the key of the central section of op. 2 No. 2, at many of the main cadences of the op. 6 Orchestral Pieces and as the main 'home area' of the later *Der Wein*, as well as being the tonic of the final orchestral interlude of *Wozzeck*. It was for long generally thought that the projected 'Seraphita' Symphony, upon which Berg was working in 1912 and which was in D minor, provided some of the material of both the op. 6 pieces and the *Wozzeck* interlude; recent research suggests that the *Wozzeck* material may have come from a *Klavierstuck* which Berg wrote for Helene Berg and which, presumably, was also in D minor. A sentence in a letter which Berg wrote to Helene on 16 July 1909 – in which he says: 'How wrong you were to call this enchanting humour silly nonsense. On the contrary, it's the most superb sense, in which the most glorious D minor chords of your soul sound forth in their full magnificence.' (Berg: *Letters to his Wife*, London, 1971, p. 62) – suggests that the key may have had some deeply personal, psychological significance to him.

[2] Perle, *Serial Composition and Atonality*, 2nd edn., London, 1968, p. 34.

level which, while implying no kind of functional or hierarchical relationship amongst the remaining notes, are asserted in such a way that they acquire a certain priority and, thus, function as referential elements – are often of great importance as a means of organizing the music. Although such note-collections may operate independently of thematic elements a particularly important aspect of Berg's handling of such referential 'tone centres' is his habit, in both his pre-twelve-note and twelve-note music, of associating specific themes with specific pitch levels. Examples of such 'tone centres' and fixed pitch levels operating in Berg's music will be discussed later in this chapter.

In the earliest of Berg's published works (the Seven Early Songs, the Piano Sonata op. 1 and the Four Songs op. 2) a weakening of the sense of tonal direction is achieved mainly through the use of harmonic and melodic formations based on superimposed fourths or the whole-tone scale. The feeling of tonal ambiguity which such formations produce results from the fact that they are built of only one interval type. There are, for example, only two whole-tone scales: that beginning on C natural and that beginning on C sharp. Transpositions of either of these two scales produce not new scales but rearrangements of the notes of one of these two six-note hexachords, a process which, as Arnold Whittall has pointed out, is one of 'permutation rather than of transposition'.[1] Since each whole-tone scale consists of a sequence of equal interval steps there is no way of differentiating between the six whole-tone scales that can be derived from the notes of one hexachord; a feeling of priority amongst the notes of the hexachord can only be achieved through stressing one note by registral, dynamic or other compositional means. Whereas the lack of intervallic balance in chords built of, for example, a perfect fourth and a superimposed augmented fourth seems to generate a sense of forward movement, whole-tone formations and those built entirely of superimposed perfect fourths have an intervallic equality which produces a feeling of harmonic stasis or suspended tonal movement.[2]

Already in the opening bars of 'Nacht', the first of the Seven Early Songs, the whole-tone scale is employed as a means of creating a tonally ambiguous harmonic and melodic area. As Ex. 2 shows, the sentences of the text of 'Nacht' are differentiated from one another, and a slight sense of forward movement is achieved in the opening section, by the shift from one whole-tone hexachord to the other. Here, as elsewhere in the Seven Early Songs, the whole-tone harmony is eventually integrated into a diatonic context and the tonal ambiguity of the opening bars resolved by the move into a clear A major at bar 9 of the song. The resolution to A major has been

[1] Whittall, 'Tonality and the Whole-Tone Scale in the Music of Debussy', *Music Review*, 36: 4, 1976, p. 262.
[2] For a discussion of Berg's use of quartal formations see Archibald, 'Harmony in the Early Works of Alban Berg', unpublished Harvard Univ. thesis, 1965 (in particular p. 34).

prepared by the constant emphasis laid on the note E as the bass note in the first eight bars of the song, the whole-tone scale on E being treated as a chromatically altered dominant chord to the tonic A.

Ex. 2

Whole-tone formations, whether integrated into a predominantly diatonic context, as in the Seven Early Songs, or into a more complex chromatic style, are an important feature of Berg's musical language up to and beyond the period of *Wozzeck*. The two examples below, from the second movement of the *Lyric Suite,* illustrate the extent to which whole-tone elements permeate even the last of Berg's non-twelve-note movements. Ex. 3a shows the shift from one whole-tone hexachord to the other employed, as in 'Nacht', as a means of providing a sense of harmonic movement. In Ex. 3b the feeling of harmonic movement is produced by the shift from a six-note chord, built of four of the notes of one whole-tone hexachord plus two 'wrong' notes, to a similar chord based on the other whole-tone hexachord. One of the two main referential harmonic formations in *Wozzeck* consists of a similar 'whole tone plus wrong note' formation.[1] Although whole-tone formations do not play a large role in Berg's twelve-note works, a feeling of harmonic progression, similar to that generated in the earlier works by the shift from one whole-tone hexachord to another, is obtained by a similar shift from a 'white-note'

[1] See p. 49f., below.

to a predominant 'black-note' harmonic area. The contrast of 'white-' and 'black-note' areas plays an important role in the first movement of the *Lyric Suite* and in much of *Lulu* and will be considered in Chapter III.[1]

Ex. 3

Many of Berg's pre-twelve-note works have certain other procedures which promote a feeling of directed movement and of harmonic continuity in common. Although I shall discuss the specific melodic and harmonic features of each of the pre-twelve-note works in some detail below it will be useful to give a brief survey of these common procedures first.

One of the primary devices for obtaining a sense of directed movement in Berg's early music is his use of melodic and harmonic wedge patterns.[2] The harmonic skeleton of the last scenes of Act III of *Wozzeck* in Ex. 1 above shows this wedge pattern operating over a large scale. Ex. 4a, the main theme of the opening of the first of the *Altenberg Lieder*, shows this wedge principle embodied in a single melodic line, the opening two notes of which progress outwards chromatically; Ex. 4b, from the op. 3 String Quartet, shows a chord sequence above a repeated bass figuration. The systematic progression of the individual voices, each of which moves chromatically outwards from the opening chord, has a sense of directed movement which makes the vertical formations seem logical and justified.[3]

It is a characteristic of all non-tonal music that the sense of directed movement generated by any perceptibly consistent progression gives a feeling of logic and continuity. Berg frequently exploits this characteristic, not only in his use of wedge patterns, but also in passages the harmonic structure of which is based on chords moving in parallel motion and, in passages such as those shown in Exx. 5a and 5b, where each of the individual voices moves in consistent intervallic steps. Thematic and harmonic material derived from pitch cycles consisting of a specific interval class is a frequent and consistent feature of Berg's music. The opening movement of the Chamber Concerto,

[1] See pp. 82–3 and p. 87f., below.

[2] See Archibald, 'Harmony in the Early Works of Alban Berg' (unpublished Harvard Univ. thesis, 1965) and DeVoto, 'Alban Berg's Picture Postcard Songs' (unpublished Princeton Univ. thesis, 1967), for extended discussions of such wedge formations.

[3] See Perle, *Serial Composition and Atonality*, 2nd edn., London, 1968, p. 24.

Ex. 4                                                      (Op. 4, I)

(Op. 3, Movt. II)

which is especially notable for its use of such interval cycles and from which Ex. 5b below is taken, is discussed in greater detail below. The extent to which this method of generating material permeates Berg's later twelve-note works is illustrated by the basic series of the song 'Schliesse mir die Augen beide' and the first movement of the *Lyric Suite* which consists of two inter-locking cycles of fifths.[1]

One of the problems facing the analyst of 'free' atonal music is the immense variety of the procedures employed and the difficulty in classifying these procedures according to neat, self-contained categories. The techniques employed in 'free' atonal music cannot be referred to any generally accepted or understood criteria applicable to a considerable body of works, as can those of tonal music, nor can they be referred to a set of theoretical propositions of the kind upon which twelve-note music is based. Each work creates afresh the compositional context within which it operates, a context which becomes clear only as the piece itself progresses. Any aspect of the music – from a traditionally-shaped melodic pattern to a tiny intervallic cell, a rhythmic figure or harmonic formation, a timbre or a single pitch – may act

[1] See pp. 129–30 below. Since the above was written George Perle has published an article discussing the wider implications of such interval cycles and relating them to coupling of the prime and inverted forms of a twelve-note set of the kind discussed on p. 95f., below. (See Perle, 'Berg's Master Array of the Interval Cycles', *Musical Quarterly*, Vol. 63, No. 1, January, 1977, pp. 1–30.)

Ex. 5                                      (Op. 3, Movt. II)

(Chamber Concerto, Movt. I)

as a cohesive element if the composer chooses to assert it in a way that enables it to operate as such.

The analytical problem is less acute when considering the 'free' atonal music of Berg than when considering that of Schoenberg and Webern, since Berg's music, for the most part, works within a more obviously traditional thematic context. Only in the shorter forms of the op. 5 Clarinet Pieces of 1913 and, to a lesser extent, the central songs of the *Altenberg Lieder* of 1912, does Berg's music show that concentration on the manipulation of tiny cellules within an athematic context that is so characteristic of the music that both Schoenberg and Webern were writing at that time.

The source of almost all the material in the op. 5 pieces is the figuration on the solo clarinet which opens the first piece. This figuration is shown in Ex. 6; the two phrases which make up the figuration are marked *x* and *y* in the example. Phrase *y* has one note in common with *x*.

Ex. 6

Both *x* and the composite collection *xy* act as referential elements and each
of the remaining pieces opens with a statement of one of these collections.
The second piece opens with an expanded statement of *xy* at T–O;[1] the
repeated piano dyad consists of those notes of *y* which do not appear in *x*,
above which the clarinet gradually unfolds the remaining notes of *xy* at T–O
with the addition of one extra note, D flat (Ex. 7a). The fourth piece begins

Ex. 7

with a statement of *x* at T–O. The piano chords which open the piece consist
of five of the six notes of *x*; the missing A natural is the goal of the chromatically descending three-note figure on the clarinet in bar 2 (Ex. 7b). The third

---

[1] The terms employed to designate pitch levels and set forms are explained in the
Preface (p. ix above).

piece opens with a statement of the complete collection $xy$ at T–4.[1] The collection is partitioned into two separate units, as it was at the beginning of the first piece, the piano presenting the notes of $x$, and the following clarinet phrase beginning with the two notes of $y$ which do not appear in $x$ (Ex. 7c).

The clarinet statement of $xy$ which opens the first piece also acts as the source of a number of three- and four-note intervallic cells which form the motivic material of the four pieces. Ex. 8a shows the five cells which dominate the first piece of the set and demonstrates their derivation from the collection $xy$; Ex. 8b shows how these cells, superimposed and combined in various ways, provide the material of the first five bars of the first piece. The five cells shown in Ex. 8a run through all four pieces, although additional cells, similarly derived from the original $xy$ collection, appear during the course of the work. The reordering of $x$ when it appears in the piano part at the beginning of the third piece, for example, produces an augmented triad, while the continuation of the clarinet phrase, at bar 1 of the same piece, outlines a diminished seventh chord. Both formations, which have already appeared at the end of the second piece, spring from the fact that the total content of $xy$ can be ordered in such a way as to form a chain of ascending or descending thirds, a feature which determines many of the harmonic formations in the work.

The melodic and harmonic structure of the second of the *Altenberg Lieder* is based almost entirely on two intervallic cells. These two cells are marked $i$ and $ii$ in Ex. 9a, which shows the opening vocal line of the song. The vocal line consists of two statements of $i$ – one in its prime and one its inverted form – which frame a central statement of $ii$, an ABA structure that mirrors that of the song itself. Cell $i$ is the main motivic element in the song. Ex. 9b shows the opening bars of the orchestral accompaniment and illustrates the way in which the melodic and harmonic formations in this accompaniment are completely derived from overlapping versions of $i$ in its retrograde form; the retrograde inversion of $i$ is treated in a similar manner in the second half of the song.

The *Altenberg Lieder*, as a whole, are more obviously thematic in character than the op. 5 Clarinet Pieces and the most important feature of the cycle is the reappearance of themes from one song to the next.[2] The significance of cells $i$ and $ii$ springs primarily from the fact that both appear elsewhere in the cycle as components of more extensive and more important themes. Cell $ii$ plays only a limited role within the confines of the second song, appearing in the form shown in Ex. 9a only in the opening and closing vocal phrases. During the course of the song, however, it gives rise to the variant

[1] See A. Forte, *The Structure of Atonal Music*, Yale University Press, New Haven and London, 1973, pp. 32–3.
[2] The form of the cycle as a whole is discussed in Ch. V below (see p. 182).

Ex. 8

shown in Ex. 10, a figuration, derived from the inversion of *ii*, which has already appeared in the first song of the cycle and which develops into one of the main motives of the final song. Cell *i* is a component of two of the most

important recurrent themes in the cycle. Its role in the work as a whole is discussed in greater detail below.[1]

Ex. 10

The op. 5 Clarinet Pieces are something of an oddity amongst Berg's output. His most significant achievements are in his handling of large-scale structures and both the scale and the style of op. 5 set the pieces outside this central line of development. Nonetheless, the technical procedures employed in op. 5 are of considerable importance in relation to Berg's subsequent works. The use, as in op. 5, of a referential pitch collection which acts as the source of the most important melodic and harmonic formations in the work, reappears as one of the chief organizational techniques in *Wozzeck*.

Apart from those in the athematic op. 5, referential note collections and intervallic cells which act as integrative elements are usually absorbed into or work alongside more clearly defined thematic elements. Thus the different movements of the *Lyric Suite* are unified not only by the reappearance of clearly recognizable material from one movement to the next,[2] but by

[1] See pp. 36–7.
[2] These quotations from movement to movement will be discussed in Ch. V below (see pp. 180–1).

certain less obvious thematic relationships and by the recurring four-note collection *z*, shown in Ex. 11, which, while not associated with any single thematic contour, is gradually established as a referential element.

Ex. 11

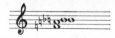

The four-note collection *z* appears at a variety of transpositions during the course of the *Lyric Suite*. The pitch level shown in Ex. 11 is that at which it is first established, at which it appears at many of the most important points of the work and at which it therefore acts as a referential tone centre. I shall call this level T–O. The significance of the collection is first established in the outer 'Allegro misterioso' sections of the third movement. The extent to which the choice of set forms and transpositional levels employed in this movement is determined by the desire to enhance this collection as a tone-centre will be discussed in the following chapter; it is significant that when the twelve-note set of the third movement appears briefly during the second movement (bars 24–5 on viola; bars 30–1 on second violin) it is at a level at which it includes the four notes of collection *z* as adjacencies.

Collection *z* at T–O opens the 'Trio estatico', the central section of the third movement; the opening melodic phrase of the Trio consists of horizontal statements of *z* at various transpositional levels (Ex. 12). Collection *z*,

Ex. 12

at T–O, recurs prominently at bar 84 of the 'Trio estatico' and, transposed, forms the basis of the first violin figuration at bar 90; on its reappearance at bar 38 of the fourth movement this violin figuration is transposed so as to give a statement of *z* at its primary referential level, T–O. Bars 38–44 of the fourth movement present a number of versions of a new melodic figure derived from *z* at various transpositional levels, beginning and ending with a statement of *z* at T–O on the first violin. The statement on first violin at bar 44 introduces the first appearance of a quotation from Zemlinsky's *Lyric Symphony*. The climax of the fourth movement (bar 54–8) and the opening of the following 'molto adagio' section concentrate almost exclusively on *z* at T–O.

Of the two twelve-note sets employed in the final movement of the *Lyric Suite* one[1] contains a single statement of *z*, the other incorporates two

[1] See pp. 127–8 below.

statements. The four-note collection thus permeates the whole movement. The referential function of $z$ at T–O, and its significance in the overall structure of the work, is again emphasized by its appearance at three of the most important points of the final Largo: at bars 25–6 (where $z$ at T–O introduces a quotation from *Tristan und Isolde*), at bars 34–5 (where its appearance on the first violin introduces the final 'tempo primo' section) and at bar 39 when it is incorporated into a reminiscence of the first movement of the work.

In addition, the main themes of many of the twelve-note[1] and the non-twelve-note movements of the *Lyric Suite* are related through certain structural similarities. Ex. 13 illustrates the way in which the segments of the basic set of the twelve-note first movement (13a) are rearranged to produce the main theme of the non-dodecaphonic second movement (13b).

Ex. 13a  (Movt. I)

Ex. 13b  Main theme. T-0                                        (Movt. II)

Another repartitioning and rearrangement of the segments of the first movement set (Ex. 14a), at the same transpositional level as that shown in Ex. 13, produces the main theme of the non-twelve-note fifth movement (Ex. 14b).

Ex. 14a  (Movt. I)

Ex. 14b  Main theme. T-0                                        (Movt. V)

A further relationship can be seen between the main theme of the second movement (Ex. 15a) and bars 75–6 of the third movement's 'Trio estatico' (Ex. 15b). This relationship is confirmed at bar 30 of the fourth movement,

---

[1] The relationships between the sets of the twelve-note movements of the *Lyric Suite* is discussed in Ch. III below (see p. 126f.).

[2] The fifth movement theme has already appeared on the viola as an accompaniment figure at bars 45–6 of the fourth movement (see p. 181 below).

Ex. 15a  (Movt. II)

Ex. 15b (Movt. III)

when the opening theme of the second movement is juxtaposed with the material from the 'Trio estatico'.

The Four Songs op. 2 are bound together by a similar web of melodic, harmonic and rhythmic interrelationships. Ex. 16 shows the piano part at bars 20–21 of the fourth song of the set. The chain of ascending perfect fourths in the left-hand part is a repetition of that which formed the bass line in the opening bars of the second song whilst the chromatically descending chords in the right-hand part are derived from the two chords in the right-hand piano part at bars 7–8 of the first song.

Ex. 16

The main melodic motive of the third song presents the 'tritone plus a fourth' structure of the right-hand chords of Ex. 16 as a horizontal formation (Ex. 17). The third song is also related to the first song tonally, in that the

Ex. 17

D minor of the central section of the song is a return to the main tonality of the first song, and to the second song through the rhythmic pattern which appears in the final bars of each.[1]

The four-note collection of the *Lyric Suite*, discussed above, is unusual in that it has no primary thematic form. Melodic and harmonic cells of this kind, which link the different sections of a piece to one another, are more often integrated into clearly defined thematic patterns. The increasing com-

[1] Berg's handling of such rhythmic motives will be discussed in Ch. IV below.

plexity of the thematic structure, and the increasing skill with which Berg handles the motivic interrelationships, is one of the most noticeable characteristics of the works which precede *Wozzeck*. The manipulation of integrative motivic cells and the kind of thematic transformations that are a feature of Berg's music are, however, already apparent in the Piano Sonata op. 1 where the themes themselves are very closely linked motivically and the traditional formal structure of a sonata exposition – the division into first and second subject groups and codetta themes – is articulated by the different tempo associated with each theme.

The opening phrase (bars 1–4) of the first theme of the first subject group is marked 'Mässig bewegt' and is shown in Ex. 18a. I shall designate this theme *SI/i*. The two most important motives in this phrase are marked *x*

Ex. 18

and *y* in Ex. 18a. *x*, the three-note figure, consisting of a rising fourth and a tritone, which opens the work is the source of many of the melodic and harmonic formations in the piece. The opening dotted rhythm of *x* acts as a means of associating this first theme with other themes. Motive *y* consists of two falling major thirds. Together, the notes of the falling thirds constitute a segment of the whole-tone scale and, in the variant of this opening phrase which appears at bars 5–8 (Ex. 18b), the thirds of *y* develop into a complete whole-tone scale figuration (*z*). Ex. 18c shows the first theme of the second subject group (*SII/i*). The theme, which begins with the dotted rhythm of *SI/i* and which, like *SI/i*, includes motives *x* and *y*, is characterized by the tempo marking 'Langsamer'. A comparison of this example with Ex. 18d, which shows the main first subject theme (*SI/i* of Ex. 18a) transposed to T–11, will reveal the extent to which *SII/i* is based on *SI/ii*.

A similar relationship links the second themes of the first and second subject groups. Ex. 18e shows the second of the themes of the first subject group (*SI/ii;* marked 'Rascher') which consists of a figuration and its free inversion (the two indicated by 'P' and 'I' in the example) and which contains, in a permuted form, the major third pattern of motive *y*. The second theme of the second subject group (Ex. 18f; *SII/ii*) combines the contour and opening note collection of *SI/ii* with the whole-tone figure *z* of the first subject at bar 7. *SII/ii* is marked 'Rasch' and is, thus, also related to *SI/ii* in tempo.

The closing codetta theme of the exposition (Ex. 18g; marked 'Viel Langsamer') is a slow, rhythmically altered version of *SII/ii* and *SI/ii;* all three have the opening pitch collection E–F–F sharp–A–C in common.

Such motivic and thematic interconnections between the different themes of the sonata exposition have an important effect on the overall formal design of the movement for, since the individuality of the different themes depends primarily on the characteristic tempo associated with each, the whole sonata form becomes very fluid and ambiguous. The formal structures of Berg's music will be considered in Chapter V.

A technique of thematic integration similar to that found in the Piano Sonata is employed in the String Quartet op. 3 where the relationships between the different themes within each movement, and between the two movements themselves, depend on the constant transformation and rearrangement of tiny intervallic cells. Ex. 19 shows the main themes of the first movement and some of the variants to which they give rise in the course of the movement. The main integrative elements are the five cells marked *i*, *ii*, *iii*, *iv*, *v* in Ex. 19a which shows the main theme of the movement. Exx. 19b and 19c show two melodic patterns – the first subject's cadential figure (19b) and the second theme of the second subject group (19c) – derived from the whole tone segment embodied in *i* of Ex. 19a.

Exx. 19d, 19e and 19f show three figurations based on cell *ii* of Ex. 19a. Ex. 19d, the second theme of the first subject group, consists of repeated statements of the inverted form of cell *ii*. Ex. 19e links cell *ii* to cell *v*. Ex. 19f presents a variant of Ex. 19d as an accompaniment to a further variant of the whole-tone segment of cell *i*. Ex. 19g shows a rhythmic variant of cell *i* accompanied by statements of cell *ii*.

Ex. 19

Example 20 illustrates the relationship between the material of the first and second movements of the Quartet. Ex. 20a shows the main theme of the second movement, which includes cell *iii*, at the pitch at which it appeared at the beginning (Ex. 19a) and the end of the first movement, cell *ii* and cell *v*. Ex. 20b shows the second theme of the first subject group of the second movement; the opening of this figuration is an inversion of, and has the same rhythm as, that shown in Ex. 19b; the tail consists of cell *v*.

Ex. 20c is a variant of the first movement theme shown in Ex. 19d; Ex. 20d a second movement variant of cell *iv*, at the pitch at which it originally appears in the first movement (Ex. 19a), coupled to the rhythm of cell *i* at bar 1 of the first movement; Ex. 20e shows one of the second movement themes based upon the whole-tone cell *i*.

Ex. 20

In the *Altenberg Lieder* op. 4 the most obvious recurring elements are clearly defined figurations. These figurations are generally associated with a specific melodic contour and with a particular pitch level although they also, on occasions, appear as simultaneities and are subjected to various rhythmic transformations. The most important of the recurring figurations in the *Altenberg Lieder* are shown in Ex. 21.[1]

*A*, *B* and *D* in Ex. 21 form the main material of the Passacaglia of the fifth song. All three appear in the first song of the cycle. *A* gradually evolves in the celesta part during the course of the orchestral introduction to the first song, acquiring its 'definitive' form at bar 9. The figuration makes a single appearance in this definitive form at the centre of the second song. *B* first appears as a simultaneity at the climax of the orchestral introduction to the

---

[1] For a more detailed study of the *Altenberg Lieder* see DeVoto's 'Some notes on the unknown *Altenberg Lieder*', *Perspectives of New Music*, 5, Fall/Winter, 1966, pp. 37–74, and 'Alban Berg's Picture Postcard Songs', unpublished Princeton Univ. thesis, 1967, two important studies from which much of the material which follows is drawn.

Ex. 21

first song (bar 14) and later appears as a horizontal formation in the voice part at bar 29 of the song. The celesta figure which closes the first song (bar 36) also incorporates a statement of *B*. The figuration reappears in a clearly recognizable form at bar 14 of the fourth song and makes a less obvious, almost 'hidden', appearance in the second (this is discussed below). *D* is the main thematic element in the orchestral introduction to the first song, gradually unfolding on the violas from bar 9 onwards. *D*, as such, makes no further appearance in the cycle until it returns as one of the main themes of the fifth song.

*A, B* and *D* – the three most important themes in the *Altenberg Lieder* – are, throughout the cycle, associated with the pitch levels shown in Ex. 21. *A* and *D* always appear at the pitch levels illustrated. On its appearance in the second and fifth songs *B* is associated with the pitch level shown in Ex. 21. As a component of the web of figurations which makes up the introduction to the first song, however, *B* is subjected to the series of progressively ascending transpositional shifts which affects the whole complex of figurations. It is significant that when it first acquires its 'definitive' shape at bar 9 of the introduction *B* appears at the pitch level shown in Ex. 22, at which level the two groups of rising fourths (*x* and *y* in Ex. 22) appear at the same pitch as in Ex. 20.

Ex. 22

*C* in Ex. 21, which has four of its five notes in common with *B*, appears in the first and fifth of the *Altenberg Lieder*. The transformation of a vertical statement of theme *B* into one of *C* at bars 14–15 marks the climax of the introduction to the first song; the final bars of the fifth song are devoted to the transformation of a horizontal statement of *C* into one of *B*.[1]

[1] See DeVoto, *Perspectives of New Music*, 5, Fall/Winter, 1966, p. 72.

Motivic cells derived from *A* and *D* appear throughout the work and give rise to a number of subsidiary melodic figurations. The cells of *D* which are marked *i, ii* and *iii* in Ex. 21 are particularly important integrative elements. *E*, which appears in the form shown in Ex. 21 in the third and fifth songs, is an offspring of *D* and incorporates two statements of cell *ii*. *E* is characterized by both its melodic and rhythmic features. The rhythmic pattern of *E*, which evolves gradually during the course of the cycle and often operates independently of the thematic characteristics of *E*, with which it is later associated, will be discussed in Chapter IV.[1]

Cell *ii* of *D* forms the main material of the second song of the cycle, which has been discussed above,[2] and appears prominently in the vocal part at bars 2–3 and bar 13 of the third and the opening phrase of the fourth song. It is also a component of the variant of *E* which appears on the cor anglais at bar 7 of the fourth song (Ex. 23). Although a component of neither *A* nor *B*,

Ex. 23

cell *ii* is momentarily related to both in the second song of the cycle. Cell *ii* is associated with *A* at bars 8–9 of the second song, when the celesta has an arrangement of the fourth-figures of *A*, the upper notes of which form a statement of cell *ii* (Ex. 24a), and with *B* when, at bars 4–5, overlapping statements of cell *ii* lead to a brief 'hidden' appearance of *B* on the violas. The viola statement is shown in Ex. 24b; although the order of the first two notes is exchanged, the relationship to *B* is confirmed by the fact that the viola statement is at the pitch level with which *B* is consistently associated throughout the work.

Ex. 24

Cell *i* of *D* at T–1 appears on the trumpets as the most prominent of the figurations which make up the orchestral introduction to the first song. Cell *i*, at T–0, and associated with the falling sixth of *E*, provides one of the most important new motives of the fifth song (Ex. 25). Cell *iii* of *D* at T–0 is a component of the two sets of fourths (marked *x* and *y* in Exx. 21 and 22) of *A*. *D* and *A* are momentarily associated at bars 45–50 of the final song of the

[1] See p 149f., below.
[2] See p. 25f., above.

Ex. 25

cycle, when the last notes of *A* on the tuba are extended to form a statement
of the closing notes and cell *i* of *D* (Ex. 26a). The relationship between *D* and
the fourths of *A* is also exploited in the second song where the opening vocal
phrase (which, as Ex. 26b shows, includes cell *iii* and is based on *D*) is followed
by a statement of *A*.

Ex. 26

The motivic complexity of Berg's music reaches its height in the Three
Orchestral Pieces op. 6, and particularly in the last piece, 'Marsch'. The
three pieces are related to one another by a number of integrative melodic
and harmonic cells and by certain recurring themes to which these cells give
rise. Three such integrative cells link the majority of the melodic, and many
of the most important harmonic, formations in the work. I shall deal with
each cell, and the most prominent of the recurring themes to which it gives
rise, separately.

The most important of the three cells is that shown in Ex. 27, which I
shall call *x*. At the pitch level shown in Ex. 27 (T-0) *x*, in its prime form,

Ex. 27

appears as the opening notes of the main theme of the first piece ('Präludium')
and, in its inverted form, as the opening notes of the main theme of the
second piece ('Reigen'); the bass figuration at the beginning of the third
piece ('Marsch') is derived from *x* in both its prime and inverted forms, at
T–3.

Cell *x* first appears at bar 8 of the introduction to the 'Präludium' when *x*–P and *x*–I are announced simultaneously by bassoon and trumpet (Ex. 28).

Ex. 28

These initial statements develop into the opening of the main theme of the 'Präludium' (Ex. 29).

Ex. 29

A variant of this main theme (bar 24 f.; Ex. 30a), based on *x*–I at T–O, becomes the starting point of the introductory theme of the second piece (Ex. 30b). The main waltz theme of the second piece combines both *x*–P and *x*–I at T–O (Ex. 30c). As in the 'Präludium', the initial statement of cell *x* in 'Reigen' is given to trumpet and bassoon.

Ex. 30

The march figure in the cellos at the beginning of the third piece is a modified version of the waltz theme of 'Reigen' at T–3 (Ex. 31).

Ex. 31

Two overlapping horizontal statements of *x* produce the theme shown in Ex. 32, which appears in the first and third pieces. This theme, which I shall call 'theme *I*', is first announced at the end of the introduction to the 'Präludium' (bars 11–13), reappears at the end of the 'Präludium' (bars 38–40) and, accompanied by the original harmony from bars 11–13 of the 'Präludium', at the climax of the final 'Marsch' (bars 160–1). All three appearances of this theme are at the pitch shown in Ex. 32.

Ex. 32

(Movt. I)

A variant of theme *I*, in which the contour is modified through octave displacement, is also employed in the third piece. The variant (Ex. 33) appears at bars 5, 23 and 125 and, in a slightly altered form, at bars 29, 35 and 89 of the final 'Marsch':

Ex. 33

Theme *II* (Ex. 34) appears for the first time in the coda of the 'Präludium' and, thereafter, plays an important role in both 'Reigen' and the 'Marsch'. Like theme *I*, theme *II* contains two overlapping statements of cell *x* and, indeed, the end of theme *II* can be regarded as a contracted statement of theme *I*. The lower stave of Ex. 34 shows the chords with which theme *II* is harmonized on its first, and on a number of subsequent, appearances.

Ex. 34

(Movt. I)

Theme *II*, at T–1, appears in the opening bars of 'Reigen' as an accompaniment to the theme shown in Ex. 30b. Theme *II* appears in both its prime and inverted form during the course of the second and third pieces. The inversion of theme *II* first appears at bars 49–51 of 'Reigen', where it is gradually unfolded by the horns (Ex. 35).

When theme *II* appears in its inverted form, the 'tail' of the theme is

Ex 35

usually modified, appearing either as shown in Ex. 35 or, as most often occurs in the final 'Marsch', in the form shown in Ex. 36. Statements of theme *II*

Ex. 36                                                    (Movt. III)

in this inverted form can be seen at bars 126, 129 and 162 of the 'Marsch'. For much of the 'Marsch', however, the 'tail' of theme *II* leads an independent existence. Both the theme itself (in its P and I forms) and the 'tail' give rise to a number of variants.

Although cell *x* has little direct effect upon the harmonic structure of the work it permeates the thematic and motivic structure of all three pieces.

Cell *y* is shown in Ex. 37a. Its most characteristic form is that shown in Ex. 37b, where it forms the 'tail' of a theme which I shall call theme *III*.

Ex. 37                                                    (Movt. I)

Theme *III* incorporates both cell *y* (in its prime and inverted forms) and cell *x*. The theme first appears at the climax of the 'Präludium' where its initial statement coincides with the restatement of theme *I*. The theme reappears at bar 6 of 'Reigen' and, rhythmically altered, forms the continuation of the main waltz theme of the central section of the piece (bar 19f.; see Ex. 38).

Ex. 38

Theme *III* gradually develops out of the bass figurations which open the final piece to become one of the main themes of the 'Marsch' (Ex. 39).

Ex. 39

Cell *y* plays an important role in determining the harmonic structure of many passages of the work. After the initial announcement of theme *III* in 'Reigen', the fanfare-like statement of cell *y* with which the theme ends is extended by the horns to provide an arpeggio-like accompaniment figuration which appears throughout the rest of the introductory section. At bar 20 this figuration evolves into the accompaniment to the main waltz theme.

Cell *z*, shown in Ex. 40, is the opening chord of the whole work. The most

Ex. 40

important feature of cell *z* is its characteristic superimposed fourths. Such superimposed fourths, emphasized by the spacing with which they are usually associated, are a feature of many of the harmonic formations of the work, appearing as either pure fourth chords (the most notable example of which is the twelve-note chord, built entirely of fourths, at bars 66–7 of 'Reigen') or as chords, such as those shown in Ex. 41, which are formed from

Ex. 41

cells *z* and *y* superimposed. The chord shown in Ex. 41a accompanies the first appearance of theme *I* at bar 9 of the 'Präludium'; both theme *I* and the accompanying chord return at the end of the 'Marsch'. Bars 161–4 of the final piece consist entirely of chromatically ascending statements of this chord. The climax of the 'Präludium' presents five different horizontal versions of cell *z* (Ex. 40) simultaneously, over a six-note chord built of superimposed fourths. The overall shape of the 'Präludium' is based on a sequence of chords – most of which are derived from cell *z* or from super-imposed versions of cells *z* and *y* – which is announced in the opening bars of the piece, repeated in both its complete and fragmentary form in the centre of the movement and finally restated in retrograde at the end of the piece.[1]

[1] See Archibald, 'Harmony in the early works of Alban Berg', unpublished Harvard Univ. thesis, 1965, pp. 90–7.

In both their textural density and their handling of thematic development the op. 6 Orchestral Pieces, and especially the final 'Marsch', are, perhaps, the most complex music in Berg's output. Berg himself said that the 'Marsch' should sound as if 'Schoenberg's [Five] Orchestral Pieces and Mahler's Ninth Symphony were played together'.[1] In the op. 5 Clarinet Pieces the basic intervallic cells are constantly rearranged to produce a variety of frag-mentary athematic figurations; in the op. 6 Orchestral Pieces the manipu-lation of the basic cells – their rearrangement, expansion and superimposi-tion – is employed, in what appears to be a relatively traditional thematic context, to produce not fragmentary figurations but a profusion of fully-formed melodic ideas. The 'Marsch' in particular presents so many variants of its basic material, and such an overwhelming number of apparently new themes, that the recurring themes discussed above act merely as recognizable signposts to which the ear clings amidst the unrelenting flow of thematic variation. Large sections of the 'Marsch' derive their sense of forward movement from the momentum generated by the constant presentation of 'new' material.

It is impossible to give any kind of comprehensive survey of the numerous transformations which the basic cells and the recurring themes undergo during the course of the 'Marsch'. A few examples, however, will serve to illustrate the kind of developmental techniques employed. Ex. 42a shows one of the most prominent themes of the 'Marsch', an apparently new theme which makes its first appearance only at bar 152 towards the end of the piece; Ex. 42b illustrates the derivation of this theme from cells *y* and *z*.

Ex. 42

Ex. 43 (a–d) illustrates a more slowly evolving process of transformation. Ex. 43a shows a figuration which appears at bar 34 of the 'Marsch'. Ex. 43b, a rhythmically and intervallically modified version of theme *III* which appears at bar 135, clarifies the relationship between theme *III* and the opening notes of the figuration illustrated in Ex. 43a. Ex. 43c and 43d show two of the many variants which spring from the figuration of Ex. 43a. In Ex. 43c a variant, recognizably related to Ex. 43a in its contour and rhythm

---

[1] Quoted in Adorno, *Alban Berg,* Vienna, 1968, p 29.

but modified in such a way that it also includes cell *z*, is followed by its inversion; in Ex. 43d a further variant of this figure is followed by a retrograde-like permutation.

Ex. 43

Ex. 44 illustrates the kind of rhythmic metamorphosis to which the themes of the 'Marsch' are subjected. Ex. 44a shows the trombone theme from bar 5 of the piece, a theme which grows out of the rhythm of the cor anglais motive and the *x*-figurations with which the cellos open the 'Marsch'; Ex. 44b shows a rhythmic transformation of the previous trombone theme. The theme of Ex. 44b has been transposed to the pitch of Ex. 44a in order to facilitate comparison.

Ex. 44

In the 'Marsch' any aspect of a musical idea – its contour, intervallic, rhythmic or harmonic characteristics – may be used as a link with or become the starting point for another idea. Thus, from a larger melody (Ex. 45a), one section may be extracted and modified in some way (in this case by having one segment inverted) so as to produce a new theme (Ex. 45b); the resulting figuration may then, in turn, give rise to yet more new variants (Exx. 45c and 45d).

Ex. 45

The textural density of many passages in op. 6 results from Berg's tendency to state a number of such motivic and thematic variants simultaneously. The first appearance of the main theme of the 'Präludium', for example, is surrounded by a web of $x$ and $y$ figurations, the significance of which becomes clear only later in the work (Ex. 46).

Ex. 46                                                         (Movt. I)

Many commentators[1] have remarked on the similarities between certain melodic and rhythmic patterns in Berg's op. 6 Orchestral Pieces and those of Mahler's Sixth and Ninth Symphonies, on the Mahlerian emotional atmosphere of op. 6 and on the fact that the hammer blow of the finale of Mahler's Sixth Symphony reappears in Berg's 'Marsch'. The most important Mahlerian feature of the Three Orchestral Pieces, and of much of Berg's music, lies in the handling of thematic and motivic development. Erwin Stein, himself significantly a pupil of Berg, said that Mahler 'shuffles motifs like a pack of cards, as it were, and makes them yield new melodies'.[2] Mahler's description of his own developmental techniques is a precise description of the techniques employed in the op. 6 Orchestral Pieces and in much of Berg's music: 'Often the thousand little fragments of the picture change so kaleidoscopically that it is impossible to recognise it again.'[3]

In the op. 6 Orchestral Pieces, as in all Berg's 'free' atonal music from the String Quartet op. 3 onwards, the harmonic structure is determined primarily by motivic considerations. In some cases chords are obtained by stating melodic figurations as vertical formations (as happens frequently in both the *Altenberg Lieder* and the op. 6 Pieces),[4] in others the individual notes of a melodic figuration may determine the pitch at which other melodic figurations are presented. In the final bars of 'Reigen', for example, each note of an augmented statement of theme *II* in its prime form gives rise to a statement of theme *II* in its inverted form (Ex. 47).

Ex. 47

At the end of the 'Marsch' three overlapping statements of theme *II* in its prime form are arranged in such a way that, together, the initial note of each spells out cell *y* (Ex. 48). A similar example occurs at the beginning of the first of the *Altenberg Lieder* where the successive transpositions of one of

[1] See, for example, Redlich *Alban Berg*, London, 1957, pp. 69–71.

[2] Stein, *Orpheus in New Guises*, quoted in Mitchell, *Gustav Mahler: the Wunderhorn Years*, London, 1976, p. 28.

[3] Natalie Bauer-Lechner, *Erinnerungen an Gustav Mahler*, quoted in Mitchell, op. cit., pp. 28–9.

[4] See, for example, the statement of *B* (Ex. 21) at bar 14 of the first song and in the final bar of the last song of the *Altenberg Lieder* and the statement of Theme *II* (Ex. 34) at bars 128–9 of the 'Marsch' of op. 6.

Ex. 48

the most prominent figurations (on piccolo, first clarinet, glockenspiel, xylophone and first violins) are arranged in such a way that the initial notes of each transposition together form a statement of theme *B*, one of the cycle's most important themes. Further examples of this procedure, in which each note of a statement of one thematic pattern gives rise to a subordinate statement, can be found elsewhere in Berg's music.[1]

Elsewhere in the op. 6 Orchestral Pieces and Berg's earlier music the vertical formations often result from the superimposition of different thematic figurations. The desire to produce a music balanced between tonality and atonality, to obtain vertical structures which are, at least to some extent, reminiscent of those of traditional diatonic music, seems to be the most important of the factors determing the way in which these different horizontal figurations are superimposed. Berg's harmonic language in the works from op. 3 to op. 6, although consistent within the context created by each piece, is not referable to any single criterion and can perhaps best be described as empirical, obtained, as DeVoto has remarked of the harmonic structure of the last of the *Altenberg Lieder*, by a process of 'trial and error'.[2]

One of the most remarkable features of Berg's output as a whole is the extent to which, while still maintaining that characteristically Bergian intensity of emotional expression, more and more aspects of the music are organized according to precompositional, apparently abstract, schemes and progressively fewer elements left to purely subjective choice. The two operas are the key works in this, as in other, respects: *Wozzeck* is the culmination of Berg's musical development from the time of the Seven Early Songs onwards, *Lulu* that of the period which begins with the Chamber Concerto. Many of the compositional procedures employed in *Wozzeck* can be found in Berg's earlier music. In *Wozzeck,* however, these procedures not only acquire dramatic significance but are more systematically applied and have a vastly extended structural function.

The following discussion of *Wozzeck* does not attempt to be a comprehensive survey of either the musical material or the compositional procedures employed in the opera; it is an attempt to show the way in which the most

[1] See, for example, the statements of Countess Geschwitz's trope at bar 427f. of *Lulu*, II/1.

[2] DeVoto, 'Alban Berg's Picture-Postcard Songs', unpublished Princeton Univ. thesis, 1967, p. 42.

important melodic and harmonic features of the work are related to one another and to indicate the similarities between the techniques employed in *Wozzeck* and those found in Berg's earlier music.

In his 1929 lecture on *Wozzeck* Berg draws attention to the fact that each act of the opera ends on 'the same quasi-cadential chord', observing that 'the point where in a tonally conceived composition the return and confirmation of the main key becomes distinctly evident even for the layman, should also be the place where in an atonal work the circle of harmony comes full close'.[1]

Each act of *Wozzeck* ends with a statement of the two chords shown in Ex. 49. Segments or modified versions of these chords, in both their vertical and horizontal forms, give rise to many of the most important harmonic and melodic formations which appear in the opera and also act as referential pitch areas over large sections of the work. The structural significance of these two chords, which bring the 'circle of harmony' to a 'full close', lies, not simply in the fact that they end each act of the opera but in that they represent the source of much of the musical material of the work.

Ex. 49 shows the two chords in their most characteristic form and at the pitch level at which they close all three acts of the opera. I shall call this pitch level T–O and shall refer to these two chords as cadential chord *A* and cadential chord *B* respectively. As referential pitch areas the note collection

Ex. 49

G–D–A, which is common to both chords but is especially notable in cadential chord *A* where it is emphasized as the three lowest notes by the characteristic spacing shown in Ex. 49, and the dyad B–F of cadential chord *B* are particularly important.

The collection G–D–A first appears prominently at bar 317 of Act I[2] and is held as a pedal throughout the passage from bar 317 to bar 332. This passage introduces the first appearance of the Drum Major and of the Military March with which he is associated.

The notes G–D of this collection reappear at the beginning of the orchestral interlude between Act I, sc. 4 and Act I, sc. 5 as a pedal (bars 656–9) against which is heard the first statement of the music which accompanies

[1] Reprinted in Redlich, *Alban Berg,* London, 1957, p. 262.
[2] Although a segment of cadential chord *A* appears at a number of points in I/1, the passage at bar 317f. marks the first appearance of an important version of the cadential chord; the passage is discussed in detail below (pp. 60–1).

the Drum Major's seduction of Marie. The 'seduction music' returns as part of the waltz played by the on-stage band in Act II, sc. 4 (bar 529f.). On its return at the end of Act I, sc. 5 as the bass of the cadence which ends the first act, the G–D dyad is preceded (bars 709–11) by a pedal on the notes G and A. All three notes of the collection are included in the cello figuration which opens Act II.

The association between the three-note collection G–D–A and the character of the Drum Major, established during the course of Act I, is further exploited in Act II, sc. 3, the central scene of the opera in which Wozzeck confronts Marie and charges her with infidelity. Wozzeck's references to the Drum Major are accompanied by fragments of the Drum Major's motives over a repeated figure in the bass on the notes G and A, two notes of this three-note collection. The repeated figure on these notes is arranged in such a way that it resembles one of the motives associated with Wozzeck himself (compare Ex. 50 and Ex. 54). Marie's replies (bars 388–9, bars 390–1, bars

Ex. 50

392–3) are accompanied by reminiscences of the 'seduction music' and the Trio of the March of Act I, sc. 3 over a pedal point on the note collection G–D–A.

Although the interval of a tritone plays a particularly important motivic role in the work, George Perle has observed that the tritone B–F which is a component of cadential chord *B* functions as 'a tone centre in the context of both the largest and smallest dimensions of the work'.[1] Perle has shown[2] how the desire to emphasize the B–F tritone not only determines the pitch at which many of the principal leading motives appear in the course of the work but is also frequently associated with the rise or fall of the curtain at the beginning or end of a scene. The significance of the emphasis placed on the notes B and F becomes clear in Act III. The note B acts as a pedal point throughout Act III, sc. 2, in which Wozzeck murders Marie, and eventually leads to the great double crescendo on B which is the basis of the orchestral interlude between Act III, scenes 2 and 3; the complementary note F is emphasized by both the vocal and the orchestral parts throughout the scene of Wozzeck's own death, Act III, sc. 4.[3] The appearances of this dyad in a

[1] Perle, *Music Forum*, I, New York, 1967, p. 210.
[2] Ibid., pp. 210–18.
[3] F is, for example, the highest note of the level of the hexachord upon which the scene is based: see III/4, bars 220–2, 246–51, 257–62, 302–20. In particular, see Wozzeck's cry of 'murder' at bars 233–4.

number of the most important leading motives in the opera will be pointed out as they occur in the following discussion of the musical material of the work.

I shall first discuss each cadential chord separately and shall then attempt to show the relationships between the material derived from each. The transpositional level allotted to each of the individual harmonic or melodic formations discussed below is chosen with reference to the primary level (T–O) of the two chords as they appear at the end of each act, as shown in Ex. 49.

## Cadential Chord B

As the final chord of each act, and of the opera as a whole, cadential chord *B* is the more important of the two chords.

Vertical statements of both cadential chord *B* and of a five-note segment of the chord play an important structural role in Act I, sc. 1. These will be discussed below.

Apart from the statements of cadential chord *B* which end each act of the opera, there are no vertical statements of the complete chord outside Act I, sc. 1.

Ignoring the spacing which characterizes appearances of this chord at the end of the three acts (that shown in Ex. 49) the total content of cadential chord *B* at T–O can be regarded as consisting of five ascending whole tones and an ascending semitone and may be represented in the form shown in Ex. 51.

Ex. 51

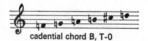

cadential chord B, T-0

### 1. *Horizontal Statements*

A number of figurations in the opera reproduce the content of cadential chord *B* in its entirety.

1(a) The figuration shown in Ex. 52a appears at the beginning of the orchestral interlude between Act I, scenes 4 and 5. It reappears when the opening bars of this interlude return as part of the final orchestral interlude in Act III (bar 352). A distorted version of this figure appears, amongst

Ex. 52

cadential chord B, T-2

other reminiscences of the material associated with the Drum Major, in Act III, sc. 3 (bars 394–5).

1(b) The phrase shown in Ex. 53a, the final vocal phrase of Marie's Lullaby in Act I, sc. 3, includes a complete statement of cadential chord *B* at T–9. The phrase returns in its entirety in the final scene of the opera (Act III, sc. 5, bars 377–8) when the children learn of the discovery of Marie's body. That part of the phrase which consists of the six notes of cadential chord *B* (indicated by a square bracket in Ex. 53a) returns at bars 244–6 of Act III, sc. 4. Although this phrase includes a complete statement of the notes of

Ex. 53

cadential chord B, T–9

cadential chord *B* at T–9, the separation by a crotchet rest of the last note from the first five notes of this statement is significant. The five-note group defined in this way acquires particular associations during the course of the opera and is discussed in section 2(b) below.

1(c) The figure shown in Ex. 54a is the subject that represents Wozzeck in the triple fugue of Act II, sc. 2. It is derived from the inversion of cadential chord *B* at T–O (Ex. 54b) at which level it contains, like the original, the tritone B–F. (As Perle has pointed out,[1] in the fugal exposition of Act II, sc. 2, the three fugue subjects appear at pitch levels at which all three include the tritone dyad B–F.) The figuration reappears at the climax of the final orchestral interlude (Act III, bar 365f.).

Ex. 54

cadential chord B, inversion T–0

1(d) The figuration shown in Ex. 55a appears in the opening bars of Act II, sc. 4, bars 445–7, where it acts as the final cadence of the 'Langsamer Ländler' which forms the orchestral interlude between Act II, scenes 3 and 4. The phrase recurs as the cadence of the mock-sermon at bar 633 of the same scene, and is recalled in the following scene (Act II, sc. 5) at the beginning and the end of the fight between Wozzeck and the Drum Major (bars 784–5; bars 802–4).

[1] See Perle, *Music Forum*, I, 1967, p. 211.

Ex. 55

2. *Five-note Segments*

2(a) The figuration shown in Ex. 56a is one of a number of leading motives
associated with Wozzeck. At the pitch shown in Ex. 56a, at which level the
leading motive usually appears, it contains five of the notes of cadential
chord *B* at T–1. This five-note segment is indicated by the beamed notes of

Ex. 56

Ex. 56b. The leading motive, which is usually associated with entrances or
exits, appears in this form at Act I, sc. 3, bar 427; Act II, sc. 3, bar 373 and
Act II, sc. 4, bar 395. A modified version of the leading motive, which
reverses the order of the last two notes, appears in Act I, sc. 4 (bars 524–5;
bars 528–32) and in Act III, sc. 1 (bar 44). Wozzeck's exits in Act I, sc. 3
and Act III, sc. 2 are marked by the figuration shown in Ex. 57 which, while
inverting the contour, maintains the pitch content of the original. The second

Ex. 57                                                           (Act III, sc. 2)

of the two chords which open the opera is a verticalization of this leading
motive;[1] its role in Act I, sc. 1 and in the opera as a whole is considered
below.[2]

2(b) The five-note segment indicated by the beamed notes of Ex. 58b
forms the first five notes of the final phrase of Marie's Lullaby; the five notes,
separated by a rest from the remaining part of the phrase, which were noted

Ex. 58                                                           (Act I, sc. 3)

[1] See Forte, *The Structure of Atonal Music,* Yale University Press, New Haven and
London, 1973, p. 25.
[2] See pp. 56–62 and 66–7 below.

in section 1(b) above. In its prime form (Ex. 58a) this segment links much of the music associated with Marie to a number of important motives and will be discussed in greater detail below.[1] In its inverted form it is the basis of the leading motive which symbolizes the ear-rings[2] (Ex. 60) and the leading motive which represents Marie's guilt.[3] In both its prime and inverted forms it is usually presented as a chain of thirds, as it is in its appearance in the Lullaby of Act I, sc. 3. The prime and inverted forms of this five-note motive are shown in Ex. 59.

Ex. 59

prime            inversion

At the pitch shown in Ex. 59 the inverted form of the motive is the basis of the main theme of the Sonata movement in Act II, sc. 1 (Ex. 60). Not only

Ex. 60

does it appear at a number of points throughout the Sonata movement in this its horizontal 'thematic' form, but important features of the harmonic structure of the movement are governed by this five-note segment. During the course of the movement many harmonic formations are derived from this five-note segment in both its P and I forms or from the composite five-note cell (shown in Ex. 60) derived from the P and I forms of the segment (shown in Ex. 59) when both are transposed so that the augmented triad in each appears at the same pitch level.[4]

Ex. 61

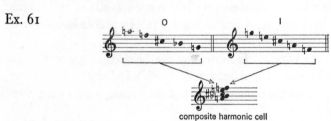

composite harmonic cell

[1] See pp. 56–7 below.
[2] See, for example, II/1, bar 6f., bars 59–63, 96–8 and 128–31.
[3] The descriptive titles used to identify leading motives are those suggested by Perle in his 'Representation and Symbol in the music of *Wozzeck*', *Music Review*, 32, No. 4, Nov. 1971.
[4] See the harmonic analysis of the Sonata movement of Act III, sc. 1 in Perle, *Music Forum*, I, New York, 1967. Of the three five-note cells shown in Ex. 60 the P version of the five-note segment corresponds to Perle's 'pentad xp', the inversion to Perle's 'pentad x' and the composite cell to Perle's 'basic pentad'.

A four-note segment of this composite harmonic cell (the four upper notes of the form shown in Ex. 61) is associated with the child. As a horizontal formation the four-note collection appears in inversion as the opening vocal phrases of the Lullaby in Act I, sc. 2. In its vertical form the collection acts as the basic harmonic cell of the second subject group of the Sonata movement in Act II, sc. 1, the section specifically associated with the child, reappears in those sections of Act III, sc. 1 in which Marie addresses the child, and forms the basis of the chords which open the final scene of the opera. Ex. 62 shows, in diagrammatic form, bars 29–34 of Act II, sc. 1 (Ex. 62a) bars 19–20 of Act III, sc. 1 (Ex. 62b and the opening of the final scene of the opera (Ex. 62c).

Ex. 62

The Sonata theme, transposed and rhythmically altered, reappears at the moment of Marie's death in Act III, sc. 2 (bar 104). The inverted form of the five-note segment, representing the ear-rings which the Drum Major gives to Marie, also becomes associated with Marie's guilt through its appearance in Act II, sc. 1, bar 105 at her words 'bin ich ein schlecht Mensch?' ('am I a wicked person?') and its appearance in a retrograde statement at bars 126–8 of the same scene, with the words 'ich bin doch ein schlecht Mensch!' ('I am after all a wicked person').

The relation between the six-note figure which appeared as a component of the final phrase of the Lullaby in Act I, sc. 3 – the figure illustrated in Ex. 53a and discussed in Section 1(b) above – and the inversion of the five-note segment which, as the first subject of the Sonata movement, accompanies Marie as she admires the ear-rings in Act II, sc. 1 is revealed in Act III, sc. 4 bars 244–5. Wozzeck's reference to the ear-rings in this scene ('Was that crimson necklace, like the ear-rings, earned by your sins?') is set to the horizontal statement of the six notes of cadential chord *B* at the pitch and in the

Ex. 63

form in which they appeared to the words 'Lauter kühle Wein muss es sein' in the Lullaby of Act I, sc. 3 (Ex. 63).[1]

### 3. *Four-note Segments*

3(a) Two important motives are derived from the four-note segment of cadential chord *B* indicated by the beamed notes of Ex. 64. The most

Ex. 64

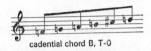

cadential chord B, T-0

important of these is that associated with the words 'Wir arme Leut' ('We poor folk'), a phrase which recurs constantly throughout the opera and which constitutes the most important verbal leading motive of the work. The figuration shown in Ex. 65, with which the sentence is associated, plays a correspondingly important role in the musical development of the opera. The

Ex. 65

Wir    ar - me    Leut!

relation between this four-note segment and cadential chord *B* is briefly revealed at bar 142 of Act I, sc. 1 when a statement of this motive at T-8 on the horn is accompanied by the remaining notes of the cadential chord.

The four-note segment which, stated horizontally, gives rise to the 'Wir arme Leut' motive also produces, when presented as a vertical formation, the chord shown in Ex. 66 below, a minor triad with an added major seventh.

Ex. 66

This chord, at the pitch shown in Ex. 66, gradually acquires the importance of a leading motive during the latter part of the opera. The first appearance of the chord as an independent formation occurs in Act II, sc. 4, bar 670 at the end of Wozzeck's conversation with the Idiot. The Idiot's prophetic sentence 'Ich reich Blut!' (bars 667–8) is a premonition of the final tragedy. At bar 668f. Wozzeck repeats the word 'Blut' to a melodic line which consists of three notes of the E flat minor chord with added major seventh shown in Ex. 66. At bar 670 the full orchestra enters fortissimo with a two-chord figure which is repeated throughout the following ten bars and which centres on the chord of Ex. 66. Wozzeck's next sentence – 'Mir wird rot vor den Augen', 'I see red before my eyes' – is set to the same three notes of the E flat

[1] See Perle, *Music Forum*, I, New York, 1967, p. 296.

minor⁷ chord as the word 'Blut' at bars 668–70 (see Ex. 67). The significance of this E flat minor⁷ chord in the rest of the opera depends on its association

Ex. 67

here, in Act II, sc. 4, with the first appearance of the word 'Blut'. I shall henceforth refer to vertical statements of the four-note segment shown in Ex. 64 at the pitch shown in Ex. 66 as the 'blood' chord.

Ex. 68

On its first appearance the chord gradually evolves from the melody of the 'Langsamer Ländler' which forms the orchestral interlude between Act II, scenes 3 and 4 and which reappears at a number of points during Act II, sc. 4 (Ex. 68). Three of the four notes around which the Ländler centres are included in the 'blood' chord. The opening four notes of the Ländler form an ostinato bass figure which appears below a repeated E flat minor chord at bar 589f. This passage returns in Act III, sc. 3, the scene following the murder scene, when the E flat minor chord appears in the orchestral part while the vocal line has a distorted version of the Ländler melody (Act III, sc. 3, bar 180f.).

The 'blood' chord not only has the same total content as, but also maintains the relative pitch levels of the notes of, the 'Wir arme Leut' motive, a feature which is significantly exploited towards the end of Act II, sc. 5 when, after a number of vocal and instrumental statements, the 'Wir arme Leut' motive is finally stated at the pitch level at which it forms an E flat minor chord with an added major seventh. The notes of this statement are sustained to form the 'blood' chord which, after being held as a pedal chord for five bars, eventually resolves on to the second of the chords of the orchestral figure shown in Ex. 67 (see Ex. 69). The relationship between the 'Wir arme Leut'

Ex. 69

motive and the 'blood' chord illustrates the subtlety of Berg's use of such musical symbols. The musical relationship between the two figurations underlines the dramatic relationship between the final tragic outcome of the opera, represented by the 'blood' chord, and Wozzeck's economic and social situation, represented by the 'Wir arme Leut' motive.

It is equally significant that the four-note segment of cadential chord *B* which generates both the 'blood' chord and the 'Wir arme Leut' motive is included in both the five-note segment discussed in section 2(a) above, which gives rise to Wozzeck's 'entrance motive' (Ex. 56a), and in the original form of the five-note segment associated with Marie (see Ex. 59). On most of its appearances in the opera[1] Wozzeck's entrance motive appears at the pitch shown in Ex. 56a, at which level it reproduces this four-note segment as an E flat minor chord with an added major seventh, the pitch associated with the 'blood' chord. The relation between Marie's five-note figure and the 'Wir arme Leut'/'blood' motive is exploited in the passages which begin and end Act II, sc. 3. The introduction to the scene is shown in Ex. 70a and consists of a gently oscillating four-note figure; together these notes form the four-note segment from which originate the 'Wir arme Leut' motive and the 'blood' chord. The same passage returns at the end of the scene (bars 405–7) but with an additional note in the bass. The additional note converts the vertical statement of the 'Wir arme Leut' motive into a statement of Marie's five-note segment (Ex. 70b).

3(b) The four-note segment indicated by the beamed notes of Ex. 71a is the basis of the leading motive associated with the Doctor. The motive first appears in Variation 13 of the Passacaglia of Act I, sc. 4 (bars 362–4) and acts as the Doctor's fugue subject in the triple fugue of Act II, sc. 2 (Ex. 71b).

[1] See I/3 (bar 427), I/4 (bars 524, 528, and 530), II/4 (bar 495) and III/2 (bar 107).

Ex. 70

The relationship between cadential chord *B* at T–O and both the Doctor's motive and Wozzeck's entrance motive (Ex. 56a) is shown at bars 345–7 of

Ex. 71

the final orchestral interlude of Act III when the two motives are juxtaposed. The one note of the cadential chord which does not appear in either the Doctor's motive or its accompanying harmony at bars 346 and 347 of the final interlude is the opening note of the statement of the motive associated with the Captain which follows (Ex. 72).

Ex. 72

As Ex. 51 above demonstrates, the total content of cadential chord *B* consists of a five-note fragment of the whole tone scale plus one superimposed conjunct semitone. The characteristic five whole tones 'plus one "odd" note'[1] structure of this collection is reflected in many of the most important melodic figurations in the opera. Thus, for example, the first melodic figuration to be heard in the opera (oboe, bars 1–3), which returns at various points during Act I, sc. 1 and the following orchestral interlude[2] is composed of two such collections. The figuration begins with the five-note segment G–A–B–C sharp–D sharp plus the one 'odd' note C (the collection marked *x* in Ex. 73). The addition of the note F sharp on the bassoon in bar 2 links this figuration

[1] Perle, *Serial Composition and Atonality*, London, 2nd edn., 1968, p. 38.
[2] See I/1, bars 29–30, 62–3, 153, 173f.

to the inverted form of the cadential chord *B* (the collection marked *y* in Ex. 73).

Ex. 73

Collection *y* relates this figuration to that which represents Wozzeck in the Fugue of Act II, sc. 2 (Ex. 54a above), which is also based on the inverted form of cadential chord *B*, and to one of the figurations which appears in Act I, sc. 5 and is associated with the Drum Major (Ex. 74).

Ex. 74

The collection *x* links the figuration to that which symbolizes the Doctor's dreams of immortality in Act I, sc. 4, one of a number of elements which suggests a relationship between the Captain's and the Doctor's own peculiar forms of mania (Ex. 75).[1]

Ex. 75

Although cadential chord *B* gives rise to one figuration associated with Marie (Ex. 58), it is primarily associated with Wozzeck himself through much of the opera. The opening bars of the opera are shown in Ex. 76. They present three figurations: the sequence of two chords marked *I* (*i* and *ii*), the predominantly whole-tone figuration (*II*) which was discussed above and the two-chord figure marked *III* (*i* and *ii*) in Ex. 76. The two opening chords will be discussed in detail later; as can be seen from Ex. 76, however, the second of these chord (*I/ii*) is a verticalization of that five-note segment of cadential chord *B* which generates Wozzeck's entrance motive (cf. Ex. 56a above).[2] The final chord of Ex. 76 (*III/ii*) presents a different five-note segment of cadential chord *B*.

[1] These, and other related 'whole-tone plus one "odd" note' figurations are discussed in Perle, *Music Forum*, I, New York, 1967, and Redlich, *Versuch eine Würdigung*, Vienna, 1957, pp. 126–7.
[2] See Forte, *The Structure of Atonal Music*, New Haven, 1973, p. 25.

Ex. 76

Formally, Act I, sc. 1 is designed as a Suite consisting of:

| | |
|---|---|
| Prelude | bars 1–29 |
| Pavane | 30–50 |
| Cadenza I | 51–64 |
| Gigue | 64–108 |
| Cadenza II | 108–14 |
| Gavotte | 115–35 |
| Air | 136–54 |
| Postlude | 154–71 |

The following diagram shows how the most important structural points of the scene – the beginning and the end of each of the movements which make up the Suite – are marked by a return of the chords of either *I* or *III* of Ex. 76. Since chords *I/ii* and *III/iii* both represent five-note segments of cadential chord *B*, I shall denote the pitch level at which they appear by reference to the primary level of the cadential chord. Thus in the following diagram the first two chords of Ex. 76, the opening chords of the opera at the pitch at which they originally appear in bar 1, will be denoted by the symbol *I/i–ii* T–6; the last two chords of Ex. 76 at the pitch shown in this example will be denoted by the symbol *III/i–ii* T–10. Particularly important are the appearance of *III/ii* at T–O, the level at which cadential chord *B* appears at the end of each act of the opera. Only in the final bars of Act I, sc. 1, does chord *III/ii* acquire the additional note which converts this five-note segment into a complete statement of cadential chord *B*.

*WOZZECK: ACT I, sc. 1*

**Prelude**

| bar 1 | bar 3 | bar 6 (first vocal entry) | | bar 24 | bar 26 |
|---|---|---|---|---|---|
| I/i–ii | III/i–ii | III/ii | | I/i–ii | III/i–ii |
| T–6 | T–10 | T–O | | T–6 | T–10 |

**Pavane**

| bar 30 | | | bars 47–50 |
|---|---|---|---|
| III/ii | | | III/ii |
| T–11 | | | T–O |

**Cadenza I**
bar 58                    bars 63–5
I/i–ii                    III/i
   T–6                       T–10


**Gigue**
bar 65
III/ii
   T–10


**Cadenza II**

**Gavotte**
bar 115
III/ii
   T–10


**Air**
bar 142f.
'Wir arme Leut' motive = four-note segment of cadential chord *B*.

**Postlude**
bar 153        bars 154–6                              bar 170
I/i–ii         III/i–ii                                III/ii+A
   T–6            T–10                                    = cadential chord *B*
                                                            T–O
**Orchestral Interlude**
bar 173
III/ii
   T–11


The chords *I/i–ii* and *III/i–ii* of Act I, sc. 1 are briefly recalled when the Captain reappears in Act II, sc. 2.[1]


## Cadential Chord A

Cadential chord *B* is usually associated with Wozzeck and plays an important role in Act I, sc. 1, the first scene in which he appears. Cadential chord *A*, on the other hand, is the main source of the material associated with Marie and statements of this chord frame Act I, sc. 3, the first scene in which she appears.

Whereas in Act I, sc. 1 cadential chord *B* is always presented as a five-note chord, only reaching its full six-note form in the final chord of the scene cadential chord *A* is usually presented in an extended form as the seven-note chord shown in Ex. 77. It is in this version, which I shall call cadential chord *A1*, that it first appears in the opera at bar 317 of the orchestral interlude

[1] See II/2, bar 174 (Chord *I/i* T–6), bar 179 (Chord *III/i* T–10) and bar 190 (Chords *III/i–ii* T–10). In the first two of these appearances the upper and lower parts of the chords are displaced.

between Act I, scenes 2 and 3, the moment at which the music of Act I, sc. 2 first begins to give way to the military music which introduces the March of

Ex. 77

the following scene. On its first appearance at bar 317, a horizontal statement of cadential chord $A_1$ at T–O appears above a vertical statement which is sustained as a pedal chord throughout bars 317–20 (Ex. 78).[1]

Ex. 78

The same horizontal figuration, at T–5, reappears at bar 481 of the orchestral interlude which follows Act I, sc. 3 (Ex. 79).

A comparison of the two examples above with Ex. 53 will show that the horizontal statement of cadential chord $B$ which forms the closing phrase of Marie's Lullaby at bar 400 of Act I, sc. 3 is at a level at which it intersects with the two statements of cadential chord $A_1$ which frame the scene.

The most important of the musical characteristics associated with Marie, other than the five-note figure discussed in section 2(b) above, are derived from cadential chord $A_1$. These characteristics are:

(i) The melodic cell $z$, consisting of a minor third and a semitone, shown in Ex. 80a. Cell $z$ is a component of both cadential chords. Extensive sections of Marie's vocal line are constructed on this cell; Ex. 80b illustrates one such section from Act II, sc. 1. The square brackets above the example indicate

[1] H. F. Redlich has commented on the resemblance between the melodic figure at bars 317–8 (the horizontal statement of cadential chord $A_1$) and the 'Abblasen' retreat signal of the Austrian Army (*Versuch einer Würdigung*, Vienna, 1957, p. 117).

appearances of the melodic cell; the single dotted bracket and beams below show how the original version of Marie's five-note figure, derived from cadential chord *B* (see section 2(b) above), is incorporated into this phrase.

Ex. 80

(ii) Harmonic formations built of superimposed fourths or fifths.

(iii) Harmonic progressions in which the notes progress chromatically in contrary motion.

All of these characteristics can be found at bar 363 of Act I, sc. 3 when the melodic cell *z* shown in Ex. 80a first appears in the opera.[1] As can be seen from Ex. 81a the first note of the melodic cell is here harmonized with a chord built of three superimposed fourths (*x*), the notes of which shift chromatically to form the chord on the third note of the melodic cell (chord *y*). Both *x* and *y* are components of cadential chord *A1* at T–5, *x* consisting

Ex. 81

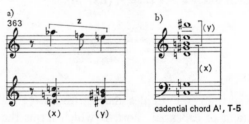

cadential chord A¹, T-5

of the four lower notes, *y* the four upper notes of the chord. Ex. 81b, which shows cadential chord *A1* at T-5, demonstrates the way in which the harmonic progression of Ex. 81a is derived from the cadential chord. A similar displacement of the upper and lower notes of cadential chord *A1* (at T–11) forms the harmonic basis of the opening phrase of Marie's Lullaby in the same scene (Ex. 82).

The melodic and harmonic structure of this Lullaby reappear in Marie's song to the child in Act II, sc. 1 (bar 43f.) and Wozzeck's song in the pub scene of Act III, sc. 3 (bar 145f.). The opening two vocal phrases of the Lul-

[1] In his list of leading motives in *Wozzeck* Perle has called this particular form of the melodic cell 'Marie as mother' (*Music Review*, 32: 4, 1971, p. 278).

laby are linear statements of the inverted form of the four-note collection (derived from the composite cell shown in Ex. 61) associated with the child and discussed above.[1] The harmonic and melodic structure of the final scene

Ex. 82

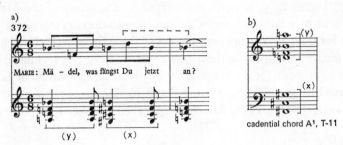

of the opera, in which the child hears of the discovery of Marie's body, is based on this four-note collection, which includes the melodic cell $z$, and upon chords $x$ and $y$ of Ex. 81. Chord $y$ in Exx. 80 and 81 is the harmonic basis of the leading motive shown in Ex. 83, a leading motive which, according to Berg, expresses Marie's 'aimless and indefinable attitude of waiting, an attitude that finds its final solution only in death'.[2] Ex. 83a shows the motive in its original form, in which it appears in Act I, sc. 3, bars 412–5; Ex. 83b shows the variant which appears at bar 425 of the same scene when the interval of a fourth (F–C) in the bass part of the original is converted to the interval of a tritone on the notes F and B, the 'fateful' tritone dyad, the significance of which has already been discussed.

Ex. 83

[1] See p. 53 above.
[2] See Berg's lecture on *Wozzeck* in Redlich, *Alban Berg*, London, 1957, p. 272.

The conversion of the fourth F–C at bar 412 to the basic tritone dyad of the opera at bar 425 is brought about by the introduction of reminscences of music from the Military March. During the passage from bar 412 to bar 425 an arpeggio figure, which presents the notes of Ex. 83a (that is to say, of chord *y*) horizontally, is twice interrupted by fragments of the March; at bars 419–20 by a reminiscence of the fanfare introduction from bars 328–31 and, at bar 423, by the opening phrase of the March itself. Both of these March fragments emphasize the tritone F–B; the fanfare by including the two notes as adjacencies (at the point marked by the square brackets in Ex. 84a), the March by its rhythm and contour (Ex. 84b). At bar 423 the last two chords of the opening phrase of the March are absorbed into the arpeggio figuration.

Ex. 84

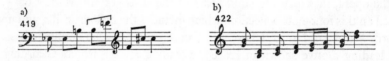

The introduction of the basic tritone dyad of the opera has a double significance at this point. On one level it announces the arrival of Wozzeck, who appears in the following bars; at a less immediate level it anticipates, by being introduced through the March material, the role which the Drum Major will play in bringing about the tragedy. Marie's exclamation 'Es ist Alles eins', the turning point of the drama (Act I, sc. 5, bar 709), is set to the notes of the inversion of the variant of her 'waiting' motive; Act II, sc. 3, in which Wozzeck charges Marie with infidelity, is introduced by a statement of Marie's 'waiting' variant as a long held pedal chord (bar 370f.). Marie's 'waiting' motive, in both its original and variant forms, usually appears at the pitch shown in Ex. 83. The appearance of the variant form at a different transpositional level at the beginning of Act II, sc. 3 (bars 372–4) is exceptional; elsewhere the original form is always associated with the notes A–E–F–C and the variant A–E–F–B. The relationship between the two forms of the leading motive and the other musical material associated with Marie can be seen in the fact that whereas the leading motive in its original form (Ex. 83a) is identical with chord *y* (Ex. 81 and 82), the variant form of the motive has three of its four notes in common with the four-note collection which gives rise to the opening phrases of Marie's Lullaby – a relationship which is exploited at the end of the opera when a statement of this form of the leading motive on the notes A–E–F–B (bar 379) is followed by a reminiscence of the Lullaby on the same notes (bar 386) (see Ex. 85).

The same phrase from the Lullaby is, as I have pointed out above, also related to the five-note collection, derived from cadential chord *B*, which is associated with Marie.[1] After its initial appearance in Act I, sc. 3, Marie's 'waiting' motive usually takes the variant form shown in Ex. 83b. Only in the final act of the opera, in the murder scene of Act III, sc. 2 and after, does the original form (Ex. 83) reappear and then in conjunction with the variant – the missing C from the original being added to the variant form to produce the five-note collection A–E–F–B–C, symbolizing the closing of the circle as Marie's 'aimless waiting' finds its final resolution in her death.

Ex. 85

This composite five-note collection appears briefly at the beginning of Act III, sc. 2 when Marie's words 'Aber ich muss fort' are set to a horizontal statement. More significant is the statement at the actual moment of Marie's death (bar 106): the orchestra plays the variant form of the leading motive and Wozzeck adds the missing C on the word 'Tod'.

In Act III, sc. 2 (bar 152) when Wozzeck, suddenly overcome by the memory of his crime, desperately calls for Margaret to dance with him, a horizontal statement of the composite five-note collection in the vocal part is accompanied by the orchestra playing the variant form of Marie's 'waiting' motive. On its reappearance in Act III, sc. 4 (bars 241–2), as Wozzeck sees Marie's body on his return to the scene of the murder, the waltz theme of Act II, sc. 4 (bar 480f.) is transposed to a level at which its opening notes are those of Marie's pitch collection. Both forms of Marie's 'waiting' motive are contained in cadential chord *A1* (see Ex. 86). Although it is only in Act III

Ex. 86

cadential chord A¹, T-2

that the significance of the two forms of the 'waiting' motive becomes clear, the note-collection formed by the superimposition of the two forms of the leading motive (the collection shown in Ex. 86b which appears at the moment

[1] See p. 53.

of Marie's death in Act III, sc. 2) is the opening chord of the opera. The first
chord of the opera thus presents the five-note segment of cadential chord *A1*
represented by Marie's 'waiting' motive and its variant; the second chord of
the opera is a verticalization of the five-note segment of cadential chord *B*
which generates one of the most important of Wozzeck's leading motives
(Ex. 87).

Ex. 87

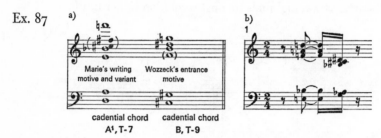

As the final chords of Acts I, II and III both cadential chords appear at
the level which I have designated T–O, at which level the two chords have
four notes (in particular, the open fifth G–D in the bass) in common. The
two five-note segments which form the opening chords of the opera do not
represent the two cadential chords at equivalent transpositional levels – the
first chord of the opera being contained in cadential chord *A1* at T–7, the
second in cadential chord *B* at T–6. When juxtaposed at these levels the two
five-note segments have no notes in common and the content of each is
distinct.

The pitch relationship between Marie's 'waiting' motive and Wozzeck's
entrance motive exposed in the opening chords of the opera appears at a
number of significant points in the course of the work. The statement of
Marie's 'waiting' motive and its variant at Act I, sc. 3 (bars 421–6) is followed,
at bar 427, by Wozzeck's appearance accompanied by his five-note entrance
motive (Ex. 56 above) derived from cadential chord *B* at T–1; the same five-
notes are presented as a harmonic formation in the following bars. The order
of and relationship between the two motives presented in this passage –
Marie's 'waiting' motive and its variant and Wozzeck's entrance motive –
are the same as those presented by the first two chords of the opera. Bars
412–28 of Act I, sc. 3 thus present an extended version of the two chords of
Act I, sc. 1, bar 1.

The same two figurations, and the same pitch relationship between them
as appears at Act I, sc. 3 bars 412–28, reappear as the curtain rises on Act II,
sc. 3 (bars 373–4) – the central scene of the opera – and at the end of the murder scene of Act III, sc. 2 (bars 105–8: cf. Exx. 88 and 87b).

George Perle has described Wozzeck's entrance motive as specifically
'representing the "distracted" Wozzeck entering or leaving Marie's pre-

sence'.[1] The intimate relationship, first unfolded in the opening bar of the opera, between Wozzeck's motive and Marie's 'waiting' motive – each

Ex. 88

representing a five-note segment of one of the two cadential chords – may, perhaps, indicate why Wozzeck's motive acquires this particular association, It is significant that when Wozzeck's entrance motive appears in Act I, sc. 4, the orchestral parts gradually settle on to the harmonic area associated with Marie's 'waiting' motive (bar 528) although Marie herself is neither present nor mentioned in the text at that point.

Much of the thematic and harmonic material in *Wozzeck* not directly derived from the two cadential chords has, nonetheless, many features in common with the material discussed above.

Thus the first phrase of the orchestral interlude between Act I, scenes 4 and 5 – the first suggestion of the music which later accompanies the Drum Major's seduction of Marie – seems to revolve around the fixed pitch area associated with the variant of Marie's 'waiting' motive and the notes of cadential chord *A1* at T–O (see Ex. 89).

Ex. 89

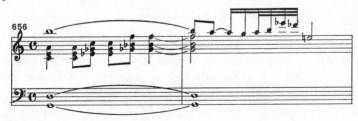

[1] Perle, *Music Review,* 32: 4, 1971, p. 290.

The chromatic progressions and the intervals of a fourth or fifth that characterize the harmonic structure of Marie's music reappear in much of the music associated with the Drum Major. The 'seduction' music itself – which first appears at bar 671 of Act I, sc. 5, and reappears at a number of points in the course of the opera, most noticeably as the music played by the stage band in Act II, sc. 4 – is based melodically on a sequence of fourths and includes the chromatic progressions associated with Marie in its harmonic structure. The rhythm and melodic contour of the opening phrase of the seduction music are reminiscent of the fanfare that introduced the Military March in Act I, sc. 3. Example 90 shows one of the appearances of the seduction music in Act II, sc. 4.

Ex. 90

The upper parts of the opening chords of Ex. 90 are clearly related to the main motive associated with the Drum Major (Ex. 91), and to the melody of

Ex. 91                    667                                    (Act I, sc. 5)

the Drum Major's 'arietta' in Act I, sc. 5, a melody which later produces the Rondo theme of Act II, sc. 5 (Ex. 92).

Ex. 92

The two cadential chords are not the source of all the musical material in *Wozzeck*. Momentary similarities of harmony or contour are also employed as a means of relating apparently independent material to that which is more obviously derived from the two cadential chords. Such a temporary relationship is established between material from Act I, scenes 2, 3 and 4 in the passage at bars 479–86 of Act I. The passage is shown in Ex. 93 below.

The figuration marked $z$ in the opening bar of Ex. 93 is the melodic cell, accompanied by the chromatic harmonic progressions, associated with Marie and discussed earlier (see Ex. 81). This bar (bar 479 of Act I) presents overlapping statements of the cell accompanied, in the bass, by its inversion.

In bar 480 a statement of the chord series which determined the harmonic structure of Act I, sc. 2 ($y$ in Ex. 93) is presented in such a way that it includes the inversion of Marie's melodic cell and overlaps and intersects with a horizontal statement of cadential chord $A_1$ at T–5 (marked $x$ in Ex. 93). The chord series of Act I, sc. 2 is shown in Ex. 94. As has been pointed out earlier,[1] the statement of cadential chord $A_1$ at this point, in the interlude between Act I, scenes 3 and 4, balances the statement of cadential chord $A_1$ at T–O in the interlude between Act I, scenes 2 and 3, which was itself closely related to the statement of cadential chord $B$ which formed the final phrase of Marie's Lullaby at the centre of the scene. The repetition of three notes of this statement of cadential chord $A_1$, with the addition of the note A (the continuation of the chain of fourths in the upper part of bar 481), converts the chord marked $W$ at bar 482 into a four-note segment of cadential chord $A_1$ at T–O, the level at which it appeared in the introduction to the previous scene at bar 317. Chord $V$ at bar 483, formed by the lowest note of chord $W$

Ex. 93

descending a semitone, similarly presents a four-note segment of cadential chord $A$ at T–O.

---

[1] See pp. 60–61 above.

A further lowering of the bass note from F sharp at Chord *V* to F produces, in the grace notes of *U*, the opening notes of figuration *T*; *T* is a reprise of the fanfare introduction to the Military March, which appeared at the beginning of Act I, sc. 3 (see bars 328–32).

Figuration *S* which follows reproduces the rhythm and, to a large extent, the contour and pitch of figuration *T*. The alteration of the three notes marked with an asterisk in *T* to those similarly marked in *S* converts the fanfare introduction of the March into the twelve-note theme of the Passacaglia which is the basis of Act I, sc. 4, which follows.

The statement of cadential chord *A1* at bars 317–8, in the passage which precedes Act I, sc. 3, is also the focal point of a series of relationships established during the course of Act I, scenes 1 and 2. The chord series shown in Ex. 94, which is the source of much of the melodic and harmonic material of Act I, sc. 2, is related to the music of Act I, sc. 1 through its inclusion of the notes E flat and D flat in the first chord of the series and its inclusion of the tritone dyad B–F in chords two and three. The role played by the tritone dyad B–F in Act I, sc. 1 has been discussed above. The note C sharp/D flat is the 'tone centre' of much of the first scene of the opera;[1] the notes D flat and E flat are particularly emphasized in the transition to and the opening bars of the Pavane (bars 27–31 and bars 40–42) and in the reprise of this section at the beginning of the first orchestral interlude.

Ex. 94

Those sections of Act I, sc. 2 not based upon the chord series of Ex. 94 are based on a folk-song like melody, the opening phrase of which is shown in Ex. 95. The opening phrase of the folk melody is composed of a segment of the whole-tone scale 'plus one "wrong" note', a feature which relates it to many of the melodic patterns employed in the opera and to cadential chord *B*. On its first appearance the phrase is accompanied by a flute tremolo on the notes E flat and D flat derived from the first chord of the series of Ex. 94. The origin of these two notes is demonstrated in the preceding bar when they are stated as components of the first chord of the series. The two highest notes of the chord (the fourth E flat–A flat) are stated as a melodic figuration

---

[1] For example C sharp/D flat forms the highest and lowest note of the Captain's motive (bars 4–5, 26–7), is emphasized as a component of cadential chord *B* (at bars 47–50 and bars 168–71) and is the note on which Wozzeck's repeated 'Jawohl, Herr Hauptmann' appears. The role of this note in I/1 is discussed in Perle, *Music Forum*, I, New York, 1967.

on the horn in such a way as to suggest a relationship with the fourth D–G which opens the folk song melody.

The opening phrase of the folk song reappears at its original pitch (as shown in Ex. 95), at which level it has five of its six notes in common with cadential chord *A1*, against the statement of cadential chord *A1* at T–O at bars 320–21 (cf. Ex. 95 and Ex. 77 above).

Ex. 95

*Wozzeck* represents both a summing-up and a development of the technical and stylistic characteristics of Berg's previous music and there are many clear similarities between the compositional procedures employed in the opera and those employed in the earlier works. The handling of the leading motives in *Wozzeck* is a further extension of the techniques of motivic organization and thematic transformation found in all Berg's music from the Piano Sonata op. 1 onwards. In *Wozzeck* the association of important recurring themes with specific pitch levels, which is also a feature of the *Altenberg Lieder*, acquires a large-scale structural significance. Although occasionally transposed in order to facilitate contrapuntal combination or to enhance other structural elements (as in the presentation of the fugue subjects in Act II, sc. 2), the pitch level with which it is associated is usually regarded as an important characteristic of a motive and some kind of hierarchical arrangement of pitch areas and levels is thus established. Since the different motives are usually associated with particular characters in the opera these pitch levels acquire both structural and dramatic significance. Marie's 'waiting' motive, for example, makes only a single appearance at a pitch level other than that shown in Ex. 83 and, as I have already shown, this pitch collection thus functions as a referential tone centre associated with the figure of Marie. The further extension of this technique in *Lulu*, in which the 'centric' organization of pitch levels is fused with a leading motive-like treatment of clearly defined tonal areas, will be discussed in the following chapter.[1] Similarly, although their influence extends over a much greater range and affects other aspects of the musical structure, the two cadential

[1] See pp. 94–100 below.

chords of *Wozzeck* act as a source of motivic and intervallic figurations in
much the same way as does the clarinet phrase which opens the first of the
op. 5 Clarinet Pieces. Even the appearance, in *Wozzeck,* of themes which
contain all twelve notes of the chromatic scale, often cited as the most
forward-looking feature of the opera, is not new; such themes can be found,
used in a very similar fashion, in Berg's previous works. Although occurring
as isolated features and not employed systematically, at least three of the
most basic characteristics of Schoenberg's twelve-note method – the use of
themes which contain all twelve notes of the chromatic scale, the verticalization of linear motives as a means of obtaining harmonic formations and the
assumption that material can be stated in its retrograde, inverted and retrograde inverted as well as its prime form – are present in Berg's music from
the *Altenberg Lieder* of 1912 onwards. The flute theme which appears at
bar 5 of the final Passacaglia of the *Altenberg Lieder* (Ex. 21, *D*) is generally
accepted as the first twelve-note theme written by any of the three composers of the Second Viennese School. Although this twelve-note theme is
employed simply as a melodic element, appearing only in its prime form and
giving rise to no harmonic formations, the five-note figure that opens the
Passacaglia (Ex. 21, *B*) is constantly employed in all its linear aspects and as
a vertical formation throughout the work. The first appearance of this motive
(Song I, bar 14) in the cycle is as a simultaneity and the work ends with a
passage in which repeated vertical statements of this five-note figure act as
an accompaniment to overlapping horizontal statements of its retrograde
form.

The handling of the twelve-note Passacaglia theme in Act I, sc. 4 of
*Wozzeck* is not essentially very different from the handling of the twelve-note
Passacaglia theme in the last of the *Altenberg Lieder*. Although the twelve-note
set of Act I, sc. 4 of *Wozzeck*, unlike that of the *Altenberg Lieder*, is presented
as both dyads and three-note chords during the course of the scene,[1] and
affects the harmonic formations and the melodic pattern employed elsewhere
in the scene, the set always appears at its initial pitch level and is never stated
in any form other than its prime. Similarly the twelve-note series which forms
the consequent of the variation theme in Act III, sc. 1 of *Wozzeck* appears
once (in the first variation) as dyads but is otherwise used as a purely thematic
element and always in its prime form. The presentation of material in its
retrograde or inverted form can be found in the *Altenberg Lieder*, the first of
the op. 6 Orchestral Pieces and is a frequent occurrence in *Wozzeck,* but
such procedures are usually applied to large sections of music rather than
smaller thematic elements.[2] The twelve-note Passacaglia theme and the
twelve-note section of the variation theme of Act III, sc. 1 of *Wozzeck* are,

[1] See I/4, bars 538 and 576–84.
[2] See p. 185f., below.

as George Perle has pointed out, simply 'special' kinds of themes; 'special' in that they happen to contain all twelve notes of the chromatic scale.[1]

The Chamber Concerto is a bridge between Berg's earlier techniques and those employed in the later twelve-note music in that the use of a twelve-note series in all its linear aspects, particularly in the Adagio second movement, represents a bringing together of procedures which, in Berg's previous works, are employed only independently. The bringing together of these procedures is inherent in the structural plan of the concerto as a whole, which is based on the possibility of presenting large complexes of music in their prime, retrograde, inverted and inverted retrograde forms.[2] Much of the material of the concerto results from the systematic application of various methods of organizing the twelve notes of the chromatic scale; only occasionally, however, do these methods correspond to those of the Schoenbergian twelve-note system. This correspondence is most clear in the Adagio second movement of the concerto, each distinct section of which presents repeated horizontal statements of a different twelve-note series. The harmonic formations are derived from the series but are handled freely and do not observe any strict serial ordering. As in Schoenberg's twelve-note system the melodic contour of the series is varied through octave transposition. Ex. 96 shows the different series employed during the course of the movement. Ex. 96a, the opening series, appears three times on the solo violin at bars 241–59. It is accompanied by chords, formed from the row segments indicated by dotted lines in the example, which move in parallel chromatic motion. Segment *IV*, which appears at bar 253, is the basis on which are built two superimposed diminished seventh chords. Statements of the second series of the movement (Ex. 96b, bars 260–71) are accompanied throughout by parallel diminished seventh chords. The eleven-note series shown in Ex. 96c is stated four times from bars 271–82; it is accompanied by a cantus-firmus-like augmentation of the previous series (Ex. 96b) which provides the missing twelfth note of the series. Ex. 96d unfolds on the horn as a countersubject to the final two statements of Ex. 96c at bar 277f.; in the form shown in Ex. 96e, the series is the main melodic material of bar 283f. The series shown in Ex. 96f, accompanied by a chord consisting of its last three notes, appears briefly at bar 322f. where it acts as the bridge back to the first reprise of the opening section.[3]

Whereas the Adagio of the Chamber Concerto is concerned with different twelve-note sets characterized, as they are in Schoenberg's twelve-note method, by note order and interval sequence, the first movement is primarily concerned with twelve-note harmonic areas and melodic patterns which are

---

[1] See Perle, *Music Forum*, I, New York, 1967, p. 251.
[2] See pp. 186–7 below.
[3] See p. 186 below.

Ex. 96

characterized by interval type. The exception is the opening theme of the movement which presents a twelve-note series defined by interval sequence. The movement is preceded by a five-bar 'motto' derived from the musical equivalents of the letters of the names 'Arnold Schönberg',[1] 'Anton Webern' and 'Alban Berg'. The Schoenberg motto appears on the piano, 'Webern' on the violin, 'Berg' on horn. The eight notes of the 'Schönberg' figuration includes all the notes of the 'Webern' and 'Berg' figurations (Ex. 97).

Ex. 97

The main 'Thema scherzoso', which begins the movement proper, pre-fixes the eight-note 'Schönberg' figure with its four missing notes to form a complete twelve-note series. The last six notes of the 'Schönberg' figure, arranged as dyads, provide the accompanying clarinet chords (see Ex. 98).

---

[1] This spelling, as opposed to that employed elsewhere in the book, is adopted here because the substitution of the 'oe', which Schoenberg adopted in America, for 'ö' would necessitate the addition of another note to Berg's motto.

Ex. 98

The characteristic ordering of this opening phrase of the 'Thema' is broken down in the following bars in which a number of melodic patterns are derived from the twelve-note series by rearranging its constituent segments. Exx. 99a and 99b illustrate the derivation from the series of the cor anglais figure and the bassoon figure at bars 4–5. The final notes of the cor anglais figure form the 'Webern' part of the motto; the last notes of the bassoon figure, which include the three notes of the 'Webern' figure, overlap with a statement of the 'Berg' part of the motto which begins the subsequent

Ex. 99

flute phrase. This flute phrase and its derivation from the constituent elements of the previous bassoon figure is shown diagrammatically in Ex. 99c.
The arrangement of these elements into chains of ascending thirds, and the
maintenance of the three-note collection E–G–B flat from the motto, anticipates later melodic patterns.

Four kinds of 'interval fields' – total chromatic areas each of which concentrate on a specific interval class – form the basis of the material employed
in the rest of the opening 'Thema' section: fields consisting of superimposed
major thirds, of minor thirds, of perfect fourths and of whole tones. Bars
8–11 are dominated by harmonic and melodic formations based on the four
possible collections of major thirds which together cover all twelve notes of
the chromatic scale. At bars 8–10 a clarinet melody, derived from, and begin-

Ex. 100

ning as a retrograde of, the flute figuration at bars 5–7, is accompanied by a
chain of descending thirds formed from *a* and *b* in Ex. 100; each note of *a*
and *b* is prolonged so as to produce, at bar 10, a six-note chord of superimposed thirds. The same hexachord (*a* and *b*) is stated in reverse as a
melodic figuration on bass clarinet at the completion of the chord at bar 10.
Bars 10–11 present a complementary chain of descending major thirds
derived from *c* and *d* in Ex. 100.

On each of the two major third hexachords, *a–b* and *c–d*, is superimposed
a figuration based on one of the other interval-fields. The bassoon statement
of *a–b* is accompanied by a clarinet statement of the minor third collection
E–G–B flat which leads to two chords of superimposed minor thirds at bar
10. This minor third collection derives from the motto theme which opens
the movement where the notes E–G–B flat appear as adjacencies in both the
Schoenberg and Berg segments. At bar 11 chords of superimposed perfect
fourths are presented above the statement of *c–d* (Ex. 101). Interval-fields
based on the minor third and the perfect fourth dominate the opening of the
second section of the 'Thema' at bars 16–19. At bars 16–19 a complete

Ex. 101

circle of descending perfect fourths on trombone and bassoon forms the accompaniment to the gradual unfolding on clarinet and oboe of the three distinct collections of superimposed minor thirds which, together, cover all the notes of the chromatic scale. Each of these three collections (*i*, *ii* and *iii* in Ex. 102a) forms a diminished seventh chord. The clarinet and oboe first (bar 16) present a figuration which employs two notes of each collection, then a figure employing three notes of each (bar 18) and finally (bar 19) a figuration employing all four notes of each.

Ex. 102

(other parts omitted)

The remaining allargando part of the central section of the 'Thema' (bars 20–24) extends the minor thirds of collection *ii* against a background of repeated chords based on a single whole-tone hexachord (Ex. 103).

Ex. 103

The third and final section of the 'Thema' (bars 25–30) returns to the figurations based on the major third collection of Ex. 100, which earlier dominated bars 8–12. The collections are not, this time, employed to create a totally chromatic area but as melodic details against a harmonic background with strong tonal connotations. The segments of these four major third collections are indicated in Ex. 104.

Ex. 104

In his 'Open Letter' to Schoenberg on the Chamber Concerto Berg speaks of three kinds of harmony: 'long stretches of completely dissolved tonality, . . . shorter passages with a tonal flavour and also passages that correspond to the laws . . . for "composition with twelve notes relating only to one another"'.[1] Each of these three kinds of harmony is represented in the 'Thema scherzoso', the overall harmonic plan of which may be represented thus:

| bars 1–8 | bars 8–12 | bars 16–20 | bars 20–24 | bars 25–30 |
|---|---|---|---|---|
| Twelve-note series (based on 'Schönberg' motto) and its derivations. | Chromatic 'field' of major thirds (bars 8–10) plus minor thirds (bars 10–12) plus perfect fourths. | Chromatic 'fields' of minor thirds and perfect fourths. | Whole tone hexachord plus minor thirds. | Melody on major thirds. |

⌐ Serial ┘   ⌐ Dissolved tonality ───── – – – – → Tonal ┘

As well as showing clear links with the procedures employed in his earlier music, the handling of the twelve-note series of both *Wozzeck* and the Chamber Concerto anticipate many of Berg's practices in his later twelve-

[1] Reich, *Alban Berg*, London, 1965, p. 147.

note works. Like the series of the Passacaglia of *Wozzeck* (Act I, sc. 4) and the Adagio of the Chamber Concerto, the sets of many of Berg's later works are, as Perle has pointed out, usually regarded as themes and associated with a specific melodic contour and rhythmic pattern.[1] The use of a number of different twelve-note series, as in the Adagio of the Chamber Concerto, or of sets characterized by elements other than linear order, as in the first movement of the same piece, is a feature of many of the later works. Equally characteristic is the Chamber Concerto's mixture of serial, atonal and tonal elements; the plan of the orchestral Variations in Act III of *Lulu* follows, in reverse, the same progression from serial to tonal via free atonal music as that shown in the above diagram of the 'Thema' of the first movement of the Chamber Concerto.

Neither Berg's characteristic musical style nor his preoccupation with certain kinds of formal and organizational procedures changed with his adoption of the twelve-note method. In many respects the twelve-note system was simply a codification of some of the techniques which had been a feature of Berg's music from the period of the *Altenberg Lieder* onwards. What this codification did afford him, however, was, as I shall attempt to show in the following chapter, some indication of the ways in which his already established technical procedures could be extended so as to include both the largest and smallest pitch elements and, thus, a further and more rigorous means of organizing the total musical structure.

[1] See Perle, *Serial Composition and Atonality*, 2nd edn., London, 1968, pp. 76–7.

# III

# Twelve-note Techniques

Of Berg's works only the last five – the song 'Schliesse mir die Augen beide', the *Lyric Suite, Der Wein,* the Violin Concerto and *Lulu* – are composed using the twelve-note method. Berg's handling of the method in these works, however, differs radically from that of Schoenberg and Webern; many of the procedures employed are peculiar to Berg's music and are not sanctioned by the accepted conventions of row-handling.

The most generally accepted set of 'rules and directions for twelve-note composition'[1] are those given by Josef Rufer in his 'Composition with twelve notes related only to one another', a work which is usually regarded as the 'authoritative exposition'[2] of Schoenberg's methods. The basic postulates of the twelve-note system, as given by Rufer, may be summarized as follows:

(i) A twelve-note series consists of all twelve notes of the chromatic scale arranged in a specific order.
(ii) No note is repeated within the series.
(iii) Each series can be used in four forms: the original form, its inversion, retrograde and retrograde inversion.
(iv) The series, or segments of the series, can be stated horizontally or vertically.
(v) Each of the four forms may be transposed to begin on any note of the chromatic scale.[3]

Although Rufer does not elevate it to the status of a 'rule', it is also a generally accepted convention of twelve-note composition that only one series should be used in a work. In fact, as George Perle has pointed out,[4] of the music of the three composers of the Second Viennese School only that of Webern conforms to this 'convention' for, although Rufer quotes Schoenberg as saying that 'it does not seem right . . . to use more than one series',[5] Schoenberg himself breaks this edict in both the String Trio and the *Ode to Napoleon.*

[1] Rufer, *Composition with twelve notes* (transl. Humphrey Searle), London, 1955, p. 84.
[2] Ibid., Translator's Preface, p. v.
[3] c.f. Rufer, op. cit., pp. 84–6.
[4] Perle, *Serial Composition and Atonality,* 2nd edn., London, 1968, p. 2, footnote 3.
[5] Rufer, op. cit., p. 106.

The first and second episodes of the String Trio present two new orderings of the series; the *Ode to Napoleon* uses a series which is consistently employed as two six-note segments and, although the total content of each hexachord is unchanged throughout the work, the note order within each is constantly varied. The procedures employed in the *Ode to Napoleon* have more in common with those suggested by the twelve-note method of J. M. Hauer than they have with the techniques of row-handling laid down by Rufer in his description of the Schoenbergian method. In Hauer's twelve-note method[1] the twelve-note set can be defined only in terms of the total content of its two constituent hexachords. The note succession within the two hexachords which make up the set can be changed at will and has no referential importance, other than that with which the composer chooses to invest it in the course of the composition. Hauer calls such a set a 'trope' and I shall adopt this term to denote a segmented set in which the note succession is unordered.

Although characteristics of both Schoenberg's and Hauer's systems can be found in Berg's music, none of his works employs either method exclusively.

The Schoenbergian series is regarded as a self-sufficient succession of intervals, from which all the melodic and harmonic formations in the piece are derived and which is assumed to maintain its identity regardless of its direction and of how it is compositionally projected. The interval sequence thus functions, in theory at least, as the basic – and, indeed, the sole – referential element of the work. Berg's twelve-note music, on the other hand, frequently suggests criteria outside those of the set and the set itself is regarded as having other characteristics in addition to those of interval succession. Thus, rather than being regarded as an abstract self-sufficient interval sequence, the Bergian set is usually associated with a particular melodic contour. Berg also chooses sets that include formations of a kind reminiscent of tonal music and employs these sets in a way that emphasizes these traditional associations. While these characteristics have their origins in the set, the interval succession does not in itself form the sole referential element in the piece. The melodic contour or the tonal implications of the set (or any other characteristic of, or compositionally derived from, the set during the course of the work) are assumed to be as important a feature of set identity as the interval succession and may, on occasions, be regarded as more important and take precedence over interval succession. Because of this, the exact nature of the frame of reference which the Bergian set provides may vary during the course of a work, the set being employed in a traditional Schoenbergian manner (in which the interval sequence is regarded as being of paramount importance) in some passage while elsewhere the interval

[1] See Hauer, *Vom Melos zur Pauke* and *Zwölftontechnik*, Vienna, 1962.

succession may be altered in order to enhance the tonal or harmonic implications of the set or to emphasize important contour relationships.

In the third movement of the *Lyric Suite,* for example, Berg employs the
set as an abstract intervallic structure, his choice of rows being determined
by the desire to enhance a structural peculiarity of the series – the fact that
the four notes B, B flat, A and F (marked *z* in Ex. 105 below) appear, in
different permutations, as adjacencies at four different transpositional levels.
The four forms of the series are cyclically permuted so that each one begins
with the four-note group *z*. The significance of this four-note collection in
the work as a whole has been discussed in the previous chapter.[1] Throughout
the movement these four forms are superimposed and stated canonically in a
variety of different ways, the different time intervals between canonic entries
being determined by the desire to ensure that at no point is the same note
stated simultaneously in two or more parts.[2]

Ex. 105

In the first movement of the *Lyric Suite,* on the other hand, the most
important characteristic of the set is not the interval sequence but its harmonic and tonal implications. The basic set of the first movement of the
*Lyric Suite* (which differs slightly from that of the third movement shown in
Ex. 105)[3] is shown in Ex. 106. A feature of the set is the contrast between the

Ex. 106

harmonic and tonal areas defined by the first 'white-note' hexachord and
the second, predominantly 'black-note', hexachord. This hexachordal
division is implicit in the rhythmic and melodic articulation of the first
violin's opening statement of the set. Throughout the movement Berg con-

[1] See pp. 27–9 above.
[2] See J. Maegaard, 'Ein Beispiel des Atonalen Kontrapunkts im Frühstadium' (*Zeit-
schrift für Musiktheorie*) translated as 'Berg's Seventeen Four-part Canons' in the *International Alban Berg Society Newsletter* No. 3, Jan., 1975.
[3] See pp. 125–7 below.

centrates on those transpositions which reproduce the contrast between the two harmonic areas of the set at P–O.[1]

In both the 'Nine pages on the *Lyric Suite*',[2] which he wrote for the Kolisch Quartet, and a letter written to Schoenberg while working on the *Lyric Suite*[3] Berg draws attention to the tonal implications of the two hexachords, observing that the set has 'two symmetrical halves separated by a diminished fifth (which plays a big role in general): first half in F major, the second half in B or C flat major'.[4]

Two other sets are employed during the course of the first movement. These are shown in Exx. 107a and 107b. Both sets are produced by reordering the notes within the two hexachords of the original set. Not only is the contrast between the areas defined by the two hexachords of the original set thus maintained, but the tonal implications of the two harmonic areas are enhanced by reordering their contents to form two scale segments (Ex. 107a)

Ex. 107

Set A¹    Set A²

and a sequence of fifths (Ex. 107b). The tonal connotations suggested by this handling of the basic set are further emphasized by the fact that, for much of the movement, Berg chooses to employ triadic and other chord formations that are deliberately reminiscent of traditional music. Such harmonies are implicit in the interval succession of the basic set; notes 1 to 4[5] of the set at P–O, for example, produce an F major[7] chord, notes 2 to 5 an A minor[7], notes 8 to 11 a G flat[6] chord and notes 9 to 11 an E flat triad. In addition, the tritone at the centre of the set and that between notes 12 and 1 together form a diminished seventh chord, a harmonic formation which is employed at a number of points as a means of vertically aligning set forms. At the end of the movement, for example, statements of the scale-like subsidiary set shown in Ex. 107a are superimposed in such a way as to produce a sequence of diminished seventh chords (Ex. 108).

The techniques employed in the first movement of the *Lyric Suite* include features that are reminiscent of both Schoenberg's and Hauer's twelve-note systems. The internal permutation to which the two hexachords

[1] The method employed to denote set forms and transpositional levels is explained in the Preface, p. x.
[2] In Rauchhaupt (ed.), *Schoenberg – Berg – Webern : The String Quartets*, a documentary study, Hamburg, 1971, pp. 102–113.
[3] See the *International Alban Berg Society Newsletter*, No. 2, pp. 5–7.
[4] 'Nine pages on the *Lyric Suite*', op. cit., p. 104.
[5] The method employed to denote the position of notes within set forms is explained in the Preface, p. x.

of the basic set are subjected suggests the trope system of Hauer. These permutations, however, produce only two subsidiary sets both of which are

Ex. 108

employed only as incidental melodic details[1] and both of which are allotted specific and limited structural roles in the overall design of the movement, the set shown in Ex. 107a appearing only in the codetta sections (bars 33–5 and 62–9) and that shown in Ex. 107b only in the codetta and the approach to the bridge passage (bars 7–12 and 42–8). Elsewhere the basic set has priority and is handled in a way that is consistent with the postulates of the Schoenbergian twelve-note method. Yet, although the triadic and other chord formations and the contrast between the harmonic areas defined by the two hexachords are implicit in the set structure, these characteristics attain an identity over and above their identity as set elements; they create a harmonic and melodic atmosphere which, because reminiscent of traditional music, deliberately invites interpretation according to traditional tonal criteria. The handling of the set not only combines characteristics of the twelve-note systems of Schoenberg and Hauer but balances the demands of these twelve-note systems and those of the tonal system.

A similar technique to that employed in the first movement of the *Lyric Suite* forms the basis of some of the procedures employed in *Lulu*, where many of the different sets are related through their common hexachordal or segmental content. Ex. 109 shows the most important of the sets employed in *Lulu*. With the exception of Ex. 109a, which is the basic series of the whole opera, and Exx. 109b, 109c, and 109d, all the sets shown are associated with particular characters or with particular objects which appear in the drama. The character or object with which each set is associated is indicated in the example.[2]

The sets shown in Exx. 109b and 109d are based on two of the three basic cells shown in Exx. 110a, 110b and 110c. All three cells are announced in the opening bars of the work and recur constantly throughout the opera. A fourth cell, which marks important entrances and exits, is shown in Ex.

[1] Though not directly derived from it, the chains of fifths which characterize the set shown in Ex. 107b are, however, reflected in many of the chord formations.
[2] The terms used to denote these sets and my descriptions of and comments on the thematic material of *Lulu* are based on the work of Perle. (See in particular Perle, 'Lulu: thematic material and pitch organization', *Music Review*, 26, 1965, pp. 269–302, and *Serial Composition and Atonality*, 2nd edn., London, 1968, pp. 141–51.)

Ex. 109

a) Basic series

b) Trope I

c) Trope II

d) Trope III

e) Dr. Schön's series

f) Alwa's series

g) Countess Geschwitz's trope

h) Athlete's trope

i) Athlete's series

j) Schigolch's serial trope

k) Schoolboy's serial trope

l) Marquis' series

m) Medical specialist's dyads

n¹) Painter's dyads

n-1) Painter's chords

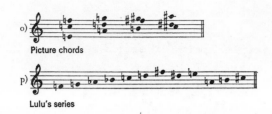

Picture chords

Lulu's series

100d; this cell is frequently superimposed upon basic cell *III* to produce the composite cell shown in Ex. 110e. Of the three tropes shown in Exx. 109b, 109c and 109d, trope *I* consists of three statements of basic cell *I*, trope *II* of three statements of basic cell *III*, trope *III* of two statements of basic cell *I* (one prime and one inverted statement) and one of basic cell *III*. Like the basic cells themselves these tropes are independent of any association with particular characters or objects in the opera but occur throughout the work as a means of marking significant lines of text or important dramatic events.

Ex. 110

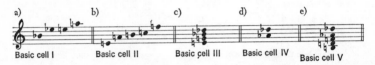

Basic cell I    Basic cell II    Basic cell III    Basic cell IV    Basic cell V

The remaining sets in Ex. 109 are associated with different figures or objects in the drama. Ex. 109 shows these sets in their most characteristic form, at their most important transpositional level and with the melodic contour with which they are most consistently associated. The Athlete[1] is associated with both the trope shown in Ex. 109h and the series shown in Ex. 109i. Exx. 109m to p shows four sets which are directly derived from the basic series.[2] Exx. 109m and 109n are associated with the figures of the Medical Specialist and the Painter, both of whom play only minor roles in the work and are thus deemed unworthy of having their own individual series; both Exx. 109m and 109n are derived from the basic series stated as a sequence of dyads. The Medical Specialist is represented by the series of dyads shown in Ex. 109m, produced by extracting and sustaining two notes of the basic set and stating the remaining notes as two-note chords. The Painter is represented by the series of dyads shown in Ex. 109n, produced by superimposing the two hexachords of the basic set. This sequence of dyads generates the chords shown in Ex. 109n-1, which are obtained by stating adjacent pairs of dyads (bracketed in Ex. 109n) simultaneously. Neither

[1] Berg's intentions regarding the names of the characters in *Lulu* are discussed below, pp. 198–200.
[2] The extent to which the other sets shown in Ex. 109 are derived from the basic series is considered below, p. 112f.

Ex. 109n nor Ex. 109n–1 is exclusively associated with the Painter. Whilst playing an important role in numbers such as the Arioso in Act I, sc. 1 – where it has an obvious association with the Painter – Ex. 109n–1 also acts as an independent harmonic trope, appearing in numbers where its association with the Painter has no special relevance. Ex. 109n–1 is prominent in much of Act III, sc. 1. The most important of the harmonic tropes derived from the basic set is that shown in Ex. 109o. This trope, which is obtained by dividing the basic set into three-note segments and stating each segment as a chord, becomes associated with the portrait of Lulu which we see being painted at the beginning of the opera and which acquires an important symbolic meaning during the course of the work. I shall refer to this trope as the 'Picture trope'. Lulu herself, in accordance with her role in the drama,[1] is not characterized by her own individual series but is associated with the basic series and the series shown in Ex. 109p which is composition-ally derived from the basic series. This series, which is invariably presented as an incidental melodic detail in the form in which it appears in Ex. 109p, is obtained by stating each of the three horizontal voices of the Picture trope (Ex. 109o) in succession. The relationship of this series (which I shall call 'Lulu's Series') to the basic series demonstrates an unorthodox and peculiarly Bergian twelve-note procedure: the development of new material through the compositional unfolding of a chain of relationships in which each step forms an audible link between otherwise unrelated figurations. Other ex-amples of this procedure appear in *Lulu* and Berg's other twelve-note works and I shall discuss it in greater detail later in this chapter.

Most of the sets associated with individual characters in *Lulu* are employed as a means of differentiating between the various figures in the opera. With the exception of the series associated with the Marquis, which is usually accompanied by harmonies derived from other sets and will be discussed in greater detail later,[2] these sets give rise to a number of individual harmonic and melodic formations which, along with the characteristic contour asso-ciated with each set, act as leading motives throughout the opera. Schön's set in its prime form, for example, is characterized by its opening major triad; Alwa's by its opening minor triad. Schigolch is characterized by chromatic figurations, the Athlete by chord clusters and Countess Geschwitz by pentatonic harmonic and melodic figurations. The harmonic and melodic differences between sets are exploited throughout the work as significant dramatic devices. The difference between Alwa's characteristic minor and Schön's major triad, for example, forms the basis of the passage in Act II, sc. 1, when Schön overhears Alwa declare his love for Lulu. Similarly the move from the A major triad, which forms part of the repeated chord which

[1] See p. 237 below.
[2] See pp. 109–11 below.

opens Act II, to the A minor triad which forms part of the closing chord of
the act both summarizes the dramatic shift that has taken place during the
act (in the course of which Alwa has usurped his father's position as Lulu's
lover) and points forward to Alwa's fate in Act III.

While giving rise to characteristic harmonic and melodic figurations
which serve to distinguish between the different figures in the opera, however, the most important of the sets shown in Ex. 109 also have a number of
harmonic and melodic elements in common. In particular, the sets associated
with Schön, Alwa, the Athlete and Countess Geschwitz are, like the different sets in the first movement of the *Lyric Suite,* related through their
common segmental content. Ex. 111 shows the series associated with Dr.
Schön (a) and Alwa (b), Countess Geschwitz's trope (c) and the Athlete's
trope (d). Dr. Schön as an individual is usually represented by the prime
form of his series; Ex. 111a shows the inverted form, through which the figure
of Schön is associated musically with the other characters in the opera.
Alwa's set is shown in its prime form, in which form it is usually employed.

Ex. 111

As can be seen from Ex. 111, the two hexachords of Schön's series at I–O are
identical in content with that of the two equivalent hexachords of Alwa's
series at P–O. The relationship between the two series is particularly close
since they are not only related through their hexachordal invariance – that is
to say that (as in the case of the basic set and the two subsidiary sets of the
first movement of the *Lyric Suite*) either set can be derived from the other
by internally permuting the two hexachords – but are also related at an even
more basic level through the fact that each can be partitioned into three-note
segments of identical order and content. These three-note segments are
marked by brackets in Ex. 111. George Perle, who first remarked on the
significance of the interrelation of the different sets in *Lulu,* has suggested

that this set association is intended to symbolize the father-son relationship of Dr. Schön and Alwa.[1] Here, as in the *Lyric Suite*, the two series at their most important associative level emphasize the harmonic contrast between a 'white-' and a predominantly 'black-note' group and this feature is maintained by other sets employed in the opera.

The trope associated with Countess Geschwitz consists of three segments (marked *A, B* and *C* in Ex. 109g). At the pitch level shown in Ex. 109 the first segments (*A* and *B*) are together equivalent to the first ('white-note') hexachord of Schön's series at I–O and Alwa's at P–O, with the addition of the single 'white-note' from their second hexachord. The third segment (*C*) consists of the 'black-notes' of the second hexachord of Schön's series at I–O and Alwa's at P–O. In the opera itself segment *A* of the Countess's trope is usually sustained while segments *B* and *C* are presented as melodic figurations. Segment *B* of the Countess's trope, which is identical in content with the first five notes of Schön's series at I–O, is also identical to one of the basic cells of the opera (see Ex. 110b).

The Athlete's trope (Ex. 112) consists of two chord clusters, the first on the white notes of the piano (corresponding to segments *A* and *B* of the Countess's trope), the second (corresponding to segment *C* of the Countess's trope) on the black notes. Notes 10 to 12 and 1 to 3 of the Athlete's series at P–4,[2] in a cyclically permuted version, produce a six-note group identical with that of the first hexachord of Alwa's series at P–O and Schön's at I–O, in which is embedded a statement of basic cell *II* (and, therefore, of segment *B* of the Countess's trope).

Ex. 112

10  11  12)  1    2    3    4    5    6    7    8    9
Athlete's series, P-4

The common segmental content of the sets associated with Schön, Alwa, Geschwitz and the Athlete is exploited, throughout those scenes in which the characters appear together, as a means of relating the different series and providing harmonic continuity,[3] the two harmonic blocks defined by the 'white-' and 'black-note' segments of the different sets functioning as referential areas similar to the harmonic-tonal blocks defined by the sets of the first movement of the *Lyric Suite*.

The four sets discussed above are related not only to one another but also to the basic series of the opera. The similarities between the harmonic and tonal relationships of these sets and those employed in the opening movement of the *Lyric Suite* are particularly noticeable when one compares the basic

[1] See Perle, *Music Review*, 26, 1965, p. 282.
[2] The Athlete's series is employed only in its prime form.
[3] The elements which these sets have in common also serve to associate these characters dramatically. I shall discuss the dramatic implications of this association in Ch. VI.

set of *Lulu* with that of the first movement of the earlier work, for the two
sets are hexachordally invariant and thus define the same two harmonic and
tonal areas. Although the basic series of the opera at P–O, Schön's series at
I–O and Alwa's at P–O all consist of a 'white-' and a predominantly 'black-
note' hexachord, the three sets are not related through total hexachordal
invariance. As Ex. 113 shows, Alwa's and Schön's series have five notes in
each hexachord in common with the basic set of the opera. Total hexachordal
invariance between these series and the basic series is impossible and the
levels shown in Ex. 113 represent the maximal invariance that can be
achieved. Maximal invariance can also be achieved between the basic series
at P–O and Alwa's and Schön's series at P–5 and I–5 respectively; since, at
this level, the identity of the first hexachord of each series as a 'white-note'
group is destroyed, this transposition is less important compositionally.

Ex. 113

Schön's series, I-0

Alwa's series, P-0

Basic series, P-0

    The first hexachord of the basic series at P–O is, of course, contained in
the 'white-note' cluster of the Athlete's trope and segments *A* and *B* of the
Countess's trope. Thus, although the two hexachords of the basic set do not
outline precisely the same harmonic-tonal areas as those which relate the
four sets discussed above, all have in common the contrast between a
'white-' and a predominantly 'black-note' hexachord. The sets associated
with Schön, Alwa, the Athlete and Countess Geschwitz are thus linked to
one another through one group of harmonic relationships and to the basic
set of the opera through a different but interconnected group. The opening
bars of the 'Circus Music',[1] which appears at bars 9–10 of the Prologue, are
based on notes 1, 2, 3 and 6 of the basic set at P–O, the four 'white notes'
which the first hexachord of the basic set has in common with that of Schön's
series at I–O, Alwa's at P–O, the white-note cluster of the Athlete's trope,
segment *B* of the Countess's trope at P–O and basic cell *II*. The significance
of this pitch collection, and of the 'Circus Music' as a whole, becomes clear
in Act III, sc. 1 of the opera where it forms the introduction to, and the basis
of, the three large ensemble numbers. In *Lulu* the characteristic contour of

[1] The term 'Circus Music' is adopted from Redlich, *Alban Berg,* London, 1957 (see
p. 198).

each set, like the harmonic characteristics to which the set gives rise, affords a means of relating and differentiating between the various sets. In the ensemble scenes of Act II, for example, Berg is able to relate the figures of Schön, Alwa, the Countess and the Athlete through the harmonic elements which their respective sets have in common while at the same time employing the melodic contour as a means of identifying individual figures. The melodic contour also provides a means of forming moment to moment relationships between sets. Most of the sets of *Lulu* are related to one another, and to the basic series, not only through the similar harmonic content of their constituent segments but also through commonly held horizontal details. These common horizontal figures are indicated by brackets in Ex. 114.[1] In addition each of

Ex. 114

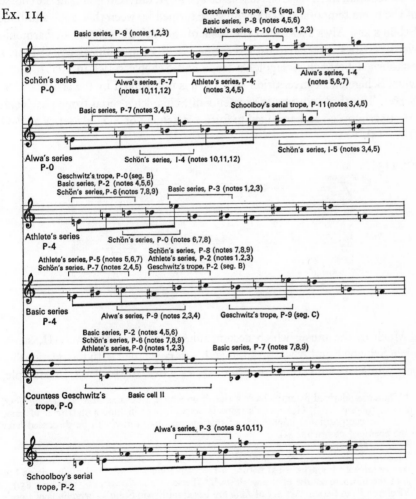

[1] I am indebted to Ex. 48 of George Perle's '*Lulu*: Thematic Material and Pitch Organization' (*Music Review*, 26, 1965, p. 301) for certain aspects of Ex. 114.

the sets shown in Ex. 114 (with the exception of Countess Geschwitz's trope)[1] has embedded in its characteristic melodic contour a statement of basic cell *I*, as indicated by the beamed notes in Ex. 114. This feature is particularly exploited in the 'Film Music' interlude between Act II, scenes 1 and 2, where the different sets are superimposed.[2]

On occasions the set associated with one figure may be compositionally projected in such a way that it assumes the melodic contour or acquires some of the harmonic characteristics associated with another figure in the drama, so that a temporary dramatic relationship between the two is formed. Schigolch's chromatic serial trope, by virtue of Schigolch's own special dramatic and symbolic function in the opera,[3] lies outside the network of harmonic and tonal relations discussed above. At different points in the course of the opera temporary relationships are formed between this trope and both Schön's and Alwa's series on the basis of the melodic contour or harmonic characteristics associated with these series. A compositional association is established between Schigolch's trope and Schön's series in Act I, sc. 2, when Schigolch's conversation with Lulu is interrupted by the arrival of Dr. Schön. The three chromatic segments of Schigolch's serial trope (Ex. 109j) are superimposed and arranged to form a statement of Schön's series at P–O (Ex. 115).

Ex. 115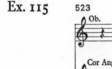

Much of the music which accompanies those scenes in Act III, sc. 2, when Schigolch and Alwa are left together, is concerned with the relationship between Schigolch's serial trope and Alwa's series. At bar 820,[4] for example,

---

[1] The series, derived from the basic series, from which, according to Reich (*Alban Berg*, London, 1965, p. 163), Geschwitz's trope is derived, does include a statement of basic cell *I*. The compositional importance of this intermediary series will be discussed later in the chapter (see pp. 121–3).

[2] See p. 158 below.

[3] George Perle has said that 'Schigolch's serial trope, a symbol of Lulu's background, is consistent with his primordial nature, a representation not only of Lulu's origins but also of the ultimate source of the work itself.' (Perle, *Music Review*, 26, 1965, p. 285.)

[4] References to bars in Act III of *Lulu* are based on Erwin Stein's corrections of Berg's own bar numbers as published in Perle, *Journal of the American Musicological Society*, 17: 2, 1964.

their conversation is accompanied by an ostinato pattern built of overlapping chordal statements of Alwa's series.[1] This ostinato is based on a sequence of four three-note chords derived from a cyclically permuted version of Alwa's series at I–O arranged in such a way that the horizontal voices form figurations similar to those that characterize the chromatic figurations associated with Schigolch (see Ex. 116). Since many of the most important figures in

Ex. 116

Alwa's series, I-O

*Lulu* are associated with characteristic rhythmic or metric patterns and instrumental timbres[2] as well as characteristic sets, harmonic formations and melodic shapes, Berg is able to relate the different figures in the opera in a variety of ways.

Like the divisions of the basic set of the *Lyric Suite* into 'white-' and predominantly 'black-note' hexachords, the 'white' and 'black' note collections which the sets of *Lulu*, shown in Ex. 111 above, have in common have quasi-tonal associations. *Lulu*, like *Der Wein* and the Violin Concerto, also includes passages which centre around specific tonal areas and have more explicit tonal connotations. In these works such passages are far more extensive and seem to operate according to traditional tonal criteria far more than do those momentary tonal allusions in the pre-twelve-note works which were discussed in Chapter II. Here again, traditional music theory has no word or phrase that adequately describes the way in which these 'tonal areas' function in Berg's music. They do not give rise to a completely ordered hierarchy of subsidiary tonal areas, a hierarchy which governs every harmonic and melodic formation and to which every note in the work can be referred. Nor do they, except over very limited periods, exert any sense of 'pull' towards themselves; they do not, therefore, have the same kind of large-scale functions as has a tonic in traditional tonal music. At the same time, these tonal areas do, in those passages in which they operate, suggest some kind of hierarchy of relationships amongst the notes of the set and frequently amongst the different set forms and transpositional levels as well.

In much non-tonal music a note or a collection of notes – whether the collection be a two- or three-note cell, a theme or a twelve-note set – acquires

[1] Since tri-chordal statements of Alwa's series at I–O and Schön's series at P–O produce identical chord sequences, Ex. 116 can be regarded as being derived from Schön's rather than Alwa's series. Perle has suggested (*Music Review*, 26, 1965) that Schön's series is the most likely source since Alwa's series is 'invariably' employed in its prime form.

[2] See pp. 171f. and 215f. below.

particular significance at a specific, fixed pitch level. The recurring themes of
the *Altenberg Lieder* and the four-note collection of the *Lyric Suite,* discussed
in the previous chapter,[1] are examples of such. The function of the tonal
areas of *Der Wein, Lulu* and the Violin Concerto may be regarded as an
extension of that of such referential pitch collections. By analogy with such
fixed pitch collections, which I have previously termed 'tone centres', I shall
term these referential areas 'primary tonal centres'. In *Lulu* the figure of Dr.
Schön, in particular, is specifically associated with the primary tonal centre
of D flat major. The most unambiguous statement of this tonal centre
appears in the coda to Schön's Act I Sonata movement; the opening bars of
this coda are shown in Ex. 117. As can be seen from Ex. 117, both the move-

Ex. 117

ment of the parts and the handling of notes which would traditionally be
regarded as 'dissonances' follow tonal practices. Thus, the 'dissonant' E in
the opening D flat chord is prepared in the previous bar and is treated as an
appoggiatura moving to its resolution on the following, consonant F.
Similarly, the dissonant A in the bass on the first beat of bar 2 of Ex. 117 can
be regarded as an accented passing note, moving from the consonant A flat
of the previous bar to the consonant B flat on the third quaver of bar 2.

On its first important appearance in Act I, sc. 2 (bars 615–24) the harmonic
structure of the first eight bars of the coda theme follows a traditional
progression away from, and back to, the opening D flat triad. In the extended
version of the coda which forms the orchestral interlude between Act I,
scenes 2 and 3, the range of the D flat tonal centre is extended in such a way
that the whole interlude has an ABA structure, the opening and closing
passages in D flat major being separated by a passage not on this tonal
centre. Both the original coda section and the extended version of the coda
which forms the interlude between Act I, scenes 2 and 3 reappear at a number
of points in the opera and always on their original D flat tonal centre which
thus acts as a stable and fixed reference point throughout the work.[2] The
opening thematic figuration of the coda theme appears as an independent

[1] See pp. 27–9 above.
[2] See pp. 210–11 below.

leading motive at a number of points and, even when divorced from its
original harmonic support, always does so at its original pitch level.[1] The
unambiguous D flat tonal centre of the Sonata coda theme is the logical
outcome of certain aspects of both the structure and Berg's handling of
Schön's series elsewhere in the opera. The first phrase of the main theme of
the Sonata movement opens with Schön's series at P–4, at which level the
first three notes form a D flat major $^6_4$ chord, and ends with the notes G
sharp and C sharp, the enharmonic equivalents of A flat and D flat respectively. Schön's theme at P–4 accompanies many of the most significant lines

Ex. 118

of text elsewhere in the opera. It is at this level that Schön's series forms part
of the Prince's chorale theme in Act I, sc. 3,[2] originally appearing when Alwa
refers to his father's sponsorship of Lulu's career (bar 1119). When Lulu,
having murdered Schön in Act II, sc. 1, refers to him as 'the only man I ever
loved', her words are set to Schön's series at P–4. The consequent of the
opening phrase of the Sonata theme also begins with the notes D flat and
A flat, the notes which opened the antecedent. As can be seen from Ex. 119
the two notes are stated simultaneously, the D flat being the opening note of
Schön's series at P–9, the A flat the opening note of its inversion at T–11.[3]

Ex. 119

Together the two set forms produce the series of dyads shown in Ex. 120.
Although these dyads, centring on the dyad D flat–A flat, occur only a few
times in the Sonata movement itself, they become the basis of Schön's

[1] See, for example, the reappearance of this opening figure at II/1, bars 393–4, to the
words, 'You, my unavoidable destiny' (Du unabwendbares Verhängnis), at bars 472–4, to
the words, 'Divorce you!' (Ich mich scheiden lassen!) and at bars 608–9, the moment
of Schön's death.

[2] See pp. 108–11 below.

[3] The following section is adapted from my article 'Dr. Schön's Five-strophe Aria: Some
notes on Tonality and Pitch Association in Berg's *Lulu*' (*Perspectives of New Music*, 8:
2, Spring/Summer, 1970, pp. 23–48) to which the reader is referred for a more comprehensive discussion. The article and the above section should be read in the light of Perle's
more recent work on the important structural functions of the kind of P and I set form
pairing discussed here. (See Perle, *Serial Compostition and Atonality*, 3rd edn., Univ. of
California Press, Los Angeles, 1972, pp. 147–81.)

Five-strophe Aria in Act II, sc. 1. Throughout the Five-strophe Aria the
main orchestral melody is accompanied by its inversion in such a way that

Ex. 120

the two lines together form, in the first two strophes and at the very end of
the Aria, the invariant dyads shown in Ex. 120. In the third, fourth and fifth
strophes, the P and I set forms in the orchestral parts are paired in such a
way that they produce the dyads shown in Ex. 121 below. These two series
of dyads affect the whole Aria, organizing all the sections and subsections,
determining the presentation of material associated with characters other
than Dr. Schön and also influencing the presentation of other independent
details.

Ex. 121

  The most important of these dyads are dyad I of the sequence shown in
Ex. 120 and dyad I of the sequence shown in Ex. 121, the first of which
consists of the fourth dyad D flat–A flat (the root and fifth of the 'tonic'
triad of the D flat primary tonal centre associated with Dr. Schön), the second
of which also includes the note D flat. The first and second strophes of the
Aria begin and end with statements of the D flat–A flat dyad of Ex. 120; the
third, fourth and fifth strophes begin with statements of the D flat–G flat
dyad of Ex. 121. Two characteristics of these sets of invariant dyads have a
particularly important effect on some of the harmonic and melodic formations
which appear during the Five-strophe Aria. Firstly, either set of dyads can be
arranged symmetrically as a sequence of fourths around their two respective
fourth dyads. Ex. 122 shows how (a) such a sequence of fourths can be
produced by arranging the dyads of Ex. 120 around the 'tonic' D flat–A flat
dyad and (b) a sequence produced by a similar arrangement of these dyads
around D–G, the other fourth dyad of Ex. 120.

Ex. 122

Secondly, either set of dyads can be arranged symmetrically around its two respective semitone dyads to produce a sequence, the outer notes of which expand chromatically by semitone step. Exx. 123a and 123b show how these semitone sequences can be produced by such an arrangement centred on the two semitone dyads of Ex. 120.

Ex. 123

At a number of points in the Aria Berg exploits both of these possibilities simultaneously by superimposing fourth chords which progress in contrary motion by steps of a semitone (Ex. 124).

Ex. 124

Some indication of the far-reaching structural significance of these invariant dyads, and, thus, some indication of the extent to which the primary tonal centre of D flat, embodied in the coda of Dr. Schön's Sonata movement, is linked to the other material of the opera, can be gathered from a consideration of the way in which these dyads relate to basic cells *I* and *II*.[1] Together the two fourth dyads of Ex. 120 (A flat–D flat and D–G) form a statement of basic cell *I* at a pitch level at which it has acquired particular significance during the course of the opera. The Painter's despairing cry of 'All lies' ('Alles Lüge') immediately before his suicide in Act I, sc. 2 (bar 724) is set to a descending version of basic cell *I* at this pitch. Since the Painter is Lulu's husband at that point in the opera, the reappearance of basic cell *I* at this same pitch level at bars 1142–5 of Act I, sc. 3 forms a suitably pointed comment on the Prince's words in those bars – 'As a wife she would make a

[1] See Ex. 110 above.

man superbly happy'.[1] Basic cell *I*, again on the notes C sharp–G sharp–D–G, accompanies Lulu's words 'I, I married you' in the Cavatina of Act II, sc. 1 (bar 77). The reappearance of basic cell *I* in the form of the two fourth dyads which lie at the heart of the organizational procedures employed in the Five-strophe Aria, which culminates in Lulu's murder of Dr. Schön, is thus bitterly ironic. The first strophe of the Aria begins with two chords built of superimposed fourths, the basis of which are the two fourth dyads of Ex. 120; the voice part simultaneously states a horizontal version of these two fourth dyads in the form of basic cell *I* (Ex. 125).

Ex. 125

The series of dyads illustrated in Ex. 120 also relates to the five-note 'white-note' collection A–E–C–B–F, the first five notes of Schön's row at I–O, which formed the basis of the vocal part of Schön's Ballade[2] 'Das Mein Lebensabend' at the beginning of Act II (bars 40–60) and which, as a simultaneity, accompanied his prophetic words 'One cannot even be sure of one's life' at bars 48–50 of the Ballade. Bars 48–50 of the Ballade reappear as the Introduction to the Five-strophe Aria. This five-note 'white-note' collection is identical with basic cell *II* and thus, as has been pointed out above,[3] with the collection common to many of the different sets employed in the opera. The five-note collection consists of two of the dyads of Ex. 120 arranged symmetrically around the semitone dyad B flat–B natural of that collection. When, in the passage immediately preceding the Introduction to the Five-strophe Aria, basic cell *II* is stated as a melodic figuration at the pitch at which it consists of the five notes A–E–C–B–F, the note B flat, which converts the five-note collection into the six notes of dyads *III*, *IV* and *V* of Ex. 120, appears as a pedal note in the bass. This passage (bars 362–76), which compositionally demonstrates the relationship between basic cell *II* and the invariant dyads of the following Aria, is shown in Ex.126.

The first two, and last four, bars of the example present ascending and

---

[1] See Perle, *Music Review*, 26, 1965, p. 271.
[2] See p. 202 below.
[3] See p. 89–90 above.

descending statements of basic cell *II* over a pedal B flat. In the seven central bars the outer notes of the figuration are extended by successive semitone steps to exhibit the symmetrical arrangement of dyads illustrated in Ex. 123. Bars 543–7 at the end of the Aria demonstrate the same relationship. In bars 416–7 basic cell *II* is accompanied by its inversion at the minor third below, a pairing of row forms which results in vertical statements of five of the six dyads of the sequence illustrated in Ex. 121.

Ex. 126

Like the D flat primary tonal centre associated with Dr. Schön, the unambiguous F sharp minor centre associated with the first statement of the most memorable of the versions of Alwa's Rondo theme also acts as a reference point. At bar 319 of Act II, sc. 1, the F sharp minor tonal centre occurs at the words 'Eine Seele, die sich am Jenseits den Schlaf aus den Augen reib' ('A soul, in the beyond, who rubs the sleep from her eyes'), a line which Berg regarded as being particularly important to the listener's understanding of both the drama and Lulu herself.[1] It was his setting of this line which Berg quoted in his tribute to Karl Kraus on his sixtieth birthday.[2] The Rondo material of Act II, sc. 1 reappears at its original pitch in Act II, sc. 2. In Berg's operas a musical repetition always underlines some verbal or dramatic link; the F sharp minor tonal centre is associated with Alwa's recurrent references to Lulu's eyes, the music which originally accompanied the words 'Eine Seele, die sich am Jenseits den Schlaf aus den Augen reib' reappearing to the words, 'In deinem Augen schimmert es, wie der Wasser-spiegel' ('Your eyes shimmer like the surface of water') (bar 1037) and the words 'Wenn Deine beiden grössen Kinder-augen nicht wären' ('Were it not for your large child-like eyes') (bar 1076).

The musical material of *Lulu* can be considered as falling into three groups defined by their respective harmonic and tonal characteristics. The first group consists of those passages which exploit the harmonic and melodic differences between the various sets. These passages are based on harmonic and melodic formations associated with particular characters or events in the opera. The second group of material consists of those passages based on the harmonic, melodic and tonal characteristics which certain sets have in common and particularly on the contrast between 'white-note' and 'black-note' segments which is a feature of a number of sets. The third group consists of those overtly tonal passages which invite a traditional interpretation. These three groups of material are not mutually exclusive. A set may be handled in different ways at different points in the work. Schön's set at P–O, for example, with its characteristic opening major triad, is used as a means of identifying Schön as an individual, at I–O it is employed as a means of relating him to other characters in the opera through the harmonic and tonal areas which it holds in common with other sets whilst the D flat defined by the opening triad at P–4 acts as a leading-motive-like 'tonic' associated with his music for much of the opera.

The distinction between these three groups of material acts as a large-scale formal device, the move from one harmonic-tonal group to another articulating the overall structure of the work, in a way that I have discussed in the previous chapter.[3] The tonal centres associated with Dr. Schön and Alwa are important in this respect, each acting as a point of resolution of the tonal ambiguity of the preceding sections. The dramatic significance of the coda of Schön's Sonata movement, perhaps the most memorable and immediately

---

[1] See Reich, 'An der Seite von Alban Berg', *Melos*, 27, 1960, pp. 74–5.
[2] It was Kraus who first produced *Pandora's Box* in Vienna and whose speech at the première had a deep influence on Berg's conception of the work. (See Reich, *Alban Berg*, London, 1965, p. 156.)
[3] See p. 17 above.

striking passage in the work, will be discussed later.[1] The only other passage
in the opera which has a similar effect on the listener is Lulu's great cry on
her return from jail in Act II, sc. 2 ('Oh Freiheit', bar 1001), when the music
moves into a clear G flat major. In its immediate context this passage serves,
both musically and dramatically, as the resolution of the Melodrama of the
preceding 48 bars; on a larger scale it acts as the resolution of the whole of
Act II, sc. 2 up to this point. The significance of Lulu's cry of happiness on
regaining her liberty becomes clear in the great duet between Lulu and the
Marquis in Act III, sc. 1, when her freedom – which she describes as 'the
only thing I have ever owned' – is again threatened.[2]

Although the interlinking of different sets through their common hexachordal or segmental content, as in the opening movement of the *Lyric
Suite*, plays an important structural role in *Lulu*, it is only one of a number
of interrelated elements which form the basis of the harmonic and melodic
language of the opera. Together these elements create a certain kind of all-
pervasive quasi-tonal harmonic and melodic atmosphere to which, as Perle
has pointed out, the 'sets themselves are subordinate'.[3]

Whereas in *Lulu* and the *Lyric Suite* the different harmonic and melodic
elements create and are absorbed into 'some kind of tonality',[4] the harmonic
and melodic language of *Der Wein* and the Violin Concerto have overtly
tonal implications. The basic sets of *Der Wein* and the Violin Concerto are
shown in Exx. 127a and 127b. Both sets have clear tonal connotations and the
desire to enhance these tonal connotations is one of the main considerations
governing Berg's choice and handling of set forms and transpositional levels
in the two works.

Ex. 127

The first six notes of the set of *Der Wein* at its primary level (P–O) outline
part of an ascending D minor scale.[5] D minor is emphasized throughout as a

---

[1] See p. 202f. below.
[2] See Perle, 'The Character of Lulu: A Sequel', *Music Review*, 25, 1964.
[3] Perle, *Music Review*, 26, 1965, p. 275.
[4] Perle, *Serial Composition and Atonality*, 2nd edn., London, 1968, p. 89.
[5] Redlich ('Bergs Konzertarie *Der Wein*', *Österreichische Musikzeitschrift*, 21, 1966) has
drawn attention to the fact that, although all commentators on the work have regarded the
form shown in Ex. 127a as being the primary form of the set, Berg's own sketch of the set
(reprinted in Reich's *Alban Berg*, London, 1963) shows the inverted form. While the single
sketch-sheet for *Der Wein* in the Stadtbibliothek, Vienna, confirms that Berg regarded
this as being the primary form of the set, a sketch headed 'the Twelve-note row of *Der
Wein*' which Berg wrote in the guest book of Růžena Herlinger shows the ascending form

'primary tonal centre' appearing at all the important structural points of the work. *Der Wein* can be divided into three sections, each section corresponding to one of the three poems which form the text of the work. The third poem is set as a varied reprise of the first while a large part of the central section is palindromic. The opening bars of the work (bars 1–7) are based upon row forms P–O, I–3, P–7, I–8 and R–O, all of which include the three-note figure D–E–F or F–E flat–D; these figures are extracted from the different row forms and act as a bass ostinato pattern (see Ex. 128). The same D area

Ex. 128

appears at the end of the first section, the closing group of which is approached (bars 69–72) by a series of descending D major and minor scale figures in the bass produced by juxtaposing and overlapping similar segments from the inverted form of the set at different transpositional levels. The third and final section of the work begins and ends with the D minor figurations which opened the Aria. It is significant that at the opening of the second song, the central section of the work, particular prominence is given to the triad of A major, the notes of which are extracted from a number of different row forms and form a held pedal chord on the horns. The opening of the central section thus implies a dominant relationship to the first and third sections.

The tonal implications of the set of the Violin Concerto, which at its primary level (Ex. 127b) begins with a G minor triad followed by a D major triad, have a similar long-term structural effect on the overall plan of the work. The opening bars of the piece juxtapose the G minor area of the opening notes of the set at P–O and a tonal area around B flat, the relative major of G minor. This juxtaposition (which is, to some extent, implicit in the structure of the set, since notes 12, 1, 2 and 3 of P–O together produce a B flat major added-sixth chord which incorporates both a B flat major and a G minor triad) reappears in the chorale of the second movement and runs through the whole concerto. In the Bach harmonization which Berg uses, the chorale starts in B flat major and ends in G minor. The beginning of almost

---

illustrated in Ex. 127a. I shall regard the set form and level shown in Ex. 127a, which acquires a particular prominence during the course of the work, as being the primary form of the set of *Der Wein* and shall designate it P–O.

every main section of the piece is marked by a passage which opens on one of these 'tonic' triads or on triads on D or F, the 'dominants' of the original G and B flat triads.[1] The work ends on the ambiguous B flat⁶ chord.

I have said above that in Berg's music a twelve-note series is usually regarded as having other characteristics in addition to that of interval succession. In many passages of *Der Wein* the tonal implications of the series and the melodic contour with which the series is most frequently associated is often regarded as being of more importance than the interval succession. The series is frequently altered and submitted to cyclic and other forms of permutation as a means of enhancing the tonal and thematic similarities between row transpositions. A simple example of cyclic permutation, employed in order to emphasize such similarities, can be found at bars 11–12 of *Der Wein* where a statement of P–7 is fused with a cyclically permuted statement of RI–5 beginning on note 8. Notes 8–12 of RI–5 and notes 1–5 of P–7 are juxtaposed to form a single C major scale on harp; the remaining notes of the two forms of the series appear as similar three- and four-note figures on harp and pizzicato violins (Ex. 129).

Ex. 129

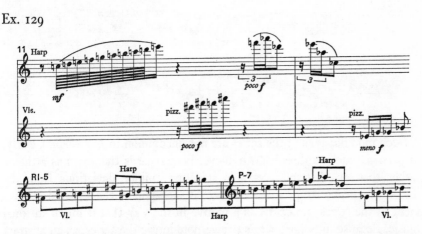

An example of the interval structure of the series being altered in order to emphasize the tonal and melodic similarities of two transpositional levels can be seen at bars 69–70, where the first hexachords of P–6 and P–8 are juxtaposed in the first horn part; the similarities between the two hexachords are

[1] The following plan shows the main tonal centres at the beginning of each of the main sections in the first movement of the Violin Concerto:

| bar | | |
|---|---|---|
| 11 | a tempo | G minor |
| 84 | Tempo primo | G minor |
| 104 | Allegretto (Trio I) | D minor |
| 114 | Rustico | B flat |
| 132 | Tempo primo | D minor (reprise of Allegretto) |
| 155 | Trio II | G major/minor |
| 173 | Quasi Trio I | D minor |
| 257 | Final bar | G minor |

enhanced by the appearance of an additional note between notes 5 and 6 of
P–6 and by the alteration of the second note of P–8 from C to B. A more
complicated passage at bars 52–6 includes both permutation and an alteration
of the interval sequence. Interrelated fragments from four different forms of
the series – R–11, I–6, P–O and I–8 – are brought together in a single melodic
line on the saxophone; the remaining notes of each form of the series are
shared between the strings and the glockenspiel. As can be seen from Ex. 130,
a statement of R–11 at bar 52 is followed by a statement of I–6, the first
hexachord of which is presented by the saxophone in a permuted version
(notes 4 and 5 of I–6 are the same as, and overlap with, notes 11 and 12 of
R–11); then follow (bar 54) statements of the first hexachords of P–O and
I–8, the fifth note of P–O being changed from A to A flat so as to emphasize
the similarity between the two hexachords. The second hexachords of I–6,
P–O and I–8 are presented as melodic figurations on the glockenspiel and
form the basis of the accompanying string chords.

Ex. 130

Such modifications of the series are not uncommon in *Der Wein*. Clearly,
in passages such as those shown above, Berg regards the series as a theme
rather than an abstract intervallic structure; minor deviations from the
interval sequence are permissible since, at such points, the series, or a fragment of the series, functions as a motive in the way that it might in tonal
music. Because in Schoenberg's twelve-note music the series, as an abstract
interval sequence, provides the basic referential element of the work, twelve-
note theory recognizes only 'real' inversions and 'real' transpositions. In
tonal music, where the thematic elements are working within a larger referential framework, other forms of inversion and transposition, such as tonal
inversion or a tonal answer in a fugue, are also permitted. In certain passages
of *Der Wein*, as in traditional music, considerations of key-feeling take precedence over those of melodic exactitude.

Berg's habit of associating his sets with a particular melodic contour and
of avoiding retrograde forms of the series, which would destroy the recogni-
zability of this melodic contour, is further evidence of his tendency to regard
the series as much as a thematic formation as a sequence of intervals. With

the exception of those large-scale palindromes of which Berg is especially fond – when whole sections of music, and thus the individual statement of the sets of which they are composed, run backwards – Berg usually employs retrograde forms only for special 'effects' and as a clearly indicated conceit. In such cases a short passage, or a series, and its retrograde are usually juxtaposed and articulated in a way that will make the relationship clear. Thus, in *Lulu*, Dr. Schön's statement (Act I, sc. 2, bars 680–1), 'Ich komme nicht hierher, um Skandal zu machen. Ich komme, um Dich vor dem Skandal zu retten' ('I didn't come here to make a scandal, I came to save you from one') has two complementary halves; the second half of the sentence, which contradicts the first, is set as a retrograde of the first half, the whole forming a short two-bar palindrome (Ex. 131).

Ex. 131

Similar examples can be found in Act I, sc. 2, bars 489–91 (Schigolch: 'Die Strassen werden immer länger und die Beine immer kürzer', 'the streets get longer and my legs shorter') and bars 708–9 ('Bei einer Herkunft, wie sie Mignon hat, kannst Du unmöglich mit den Begriffen der bürgerlichen Gesellschaft rechnen', 'With a background like Mignon's you can't judge by the usual bourgeois standards'). In all these cases the use of the retrograde is associated with an implied negation in the text. A retrograde row, again juxtaposed with its prime form so as to make a short palindrome, appears at bar 23 of the last movement of the *Lyric Suite* where, as I shall show later, it also seems to have an extra-musical significance. Comparable short, though non-dodecaphonic, palindromic figurations appear at important points in *Wozzeck*. I shall discuss the significance of palindromic structures in Berg's music in the final chapter.[1]

It is noteworthy that even in the large-scale palindromes of the 'Allegro misterioso' of the *Lyric Suite* and the Sextet of Act I, sc. 3 and the 'Film Music' Ostinato of *Lulu*, Berg takes care to employ thematic material the retrograde of which is identical with, or similar to, its inversion. The characteristic method of dividing the set of the 'Allegro misterioso' third movement of the *Lyric Suite*,[2] for example, produces the two figurations shown in Ex. 132a: one of these figures is a chromatic scale, the retrograde of which is identical with its inversion. The similarity between the retrograde form of these figurations, as they are employed in the second half of the 'Allegro misterioso', and their transposed inversions can be seen by comparing Exx. 132b and 132c.

Ex. 132

The first half of the Sextet (bars 1177–1203) of Act I, sc. 3 of *Lulu* also employs figurations which progress, in the main, by ascending chromatic steps; their retrograde in the second half of the Sextet consists (as would their inversion) of descending chromatic steps. Two of the three most important of the thematic cells of the 'Film Music' interlude between Act II, scenes 1 and 2, of *Lulu* have retrogrades which are identical with their inversions (Exx. 133a and 133b), whilst the third cell has a retrograde which differs from

Ex. 133

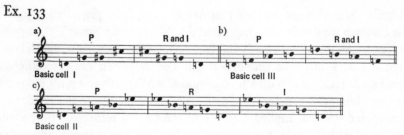

[1] See pp. 237–9 below.
[2] See p. 130 below.

its inverted form by only one note (Ex. 133c). Apart from such large-scale palindromes, or short passages in which palindromes are specifically employed as conceits, the melodic contour is, as Perle has pointed out, 'assumed to retain its identity when it is inverted but never when reversed'.[1]

The appearance of a number of retrograde forms of the series in *Der Wein* and the Violin Concerto is something of an exception to this general rule. In both works, however, the series is such that the most characteristic features of the prime are maintained in the retrograde form. Thus, the R and RI forms of the series of the Violin Concerto, for example, respectively present cyclically permuted statements of the I and P forms. Similarly, the retrograde forms of the series of *Der Wein* do not destroy the thematic contour of the scale figure which is the most characteristic feature of the series, any more than the retrograde of a major scale makes its relationship to the original pattern unrecognizable. RI–7 of the series of *Der Wein*, for example, begins with the four-note pattern that ends P–O; the first six notes of P–O consist of an ascending D minor scale figure whilst the last six notes of RI–7 consist of an ascending D major scale figure. Clearly, the abstract intervallic relationships between these two forms of the series are less important than their tonal and thematic similarities, RI–7 being understood by the listener as a 'major' version of P–O with the order of various segments rearranged in relation to one another. Retrograde forms are, therefore, employed freely throughout *Der Wein* since they do not, in this instance, destroy the characteristic contour of the series; the thematic features of the series are maintained, the retrograde forms – like the various permutations and modifications of the series discussed above – merely introducing slight deviations.

Because Berg regards the thematic characteristics of the set as being of importance in their own right, set-fragments frequently acquire an identity as motivic elements and function independently of the set from which they originate. The scale-like fragment of the set of *Der Wein* often appears independently of the remaining notes of the series. At bars 56–8, for example, a climax is gradually built up from sequential statements of the first hexachords of different P and I forms of the series: the scale figures are here used purely as motivic elements and the second hexachords of the set remain unstated. Such independent thematic fragments are a common feature of *Lulu* where many figurations, initially derived from a twelve-note set but characterized by specific rhythmic and melodic shapes, become associated with certain events in the drama and reappear as independent motives at significant dramatic points later in the opera.[2]

Figurations which acquire an independent existence of this kind are not

---

[1] Perle, *Music Review*, 26, 1965, p. 274.
[2] See, for example, the appearance of the theme of Dr. Schön's Sonata movement at bars 82 and bars 609 of II/1.

always as clearly implicit in the structure of the series as is the scale-figure of *Der Wein*. One of the most important harmonic and melodic figurations in *Der Wein* consists of a sequence of tritones which is in no way suggested by the structure of the series itself. The way in which this tritone figure is generated is of some interest, since it affords a further example of one of Berg's most characteristic, and most theoretically unorthodox, techniques. As a harmonic phenomenon the figuration appears as three chromatically descending or ascending tritone dyads (Ex. 134).

Ex. 134

One of Berg's sketches for *Der Wein*[1] suggests that these tritones are derived by extracting three pairs of adjacent notes (notes 3 and 4; 7 and 8; 10 and 11 of P and I forms) from a cyclically permuted version of the series in the manner shown in Ex. 135a; these notes then form the tritone figurations (hexachord *A* of Ex. 135b) whilst the remaining notes form the second hexachord (*B*) of the set.

Ex. 135

Since the chromatic tritone figurations of Ex. 134 can only be produced by subjecting the basic set to some kind of permutation, any one version of these tritone dyads can be obtained by applying the same procedure to eight different forms of the set; in the case of the dyads shown in Ex. 134 from P–I, P–7, I–3, I–9 or their retrogrades. The set form, from which a statement of these dyads is derived, is thus indicated neither by the pitch nor the order of the tritones themselves but by the order in which the remaining notes of the series (those shown in hexachord *B* of Ex. 135b) are presented.[2] On the first appearance of this tritone figuration (bar 15) Berg is careful to suggest its derivation by presenting, at the same time as the tritones themselves, the remaining notes of the sets (hexachord *B* in Ex. 135b) on the first horn in an order that can be related to the series at I–7 or, cyclically permuted,

---

[1] Reproduced in Reich, *Alban Berg*, London, 1965, p. 154.
[2] Even so, the ordering of the notes in hexachord *B* cannot positively identify a single set form as the source of these tritone dyads since any one ordering is common to two set forms.

P–7. In later statements, however, the notes of hexachord *B* are presented in such a way that it is impossible to identify the set form or forms from which the tritone figure is derived. The set shown in Ex. 135b, though derived from the basic set, thus functions as an independent trope.

Although the two similar three-note cells (marked *i* and *ii* in hexachord *B* of Ex. 135b) are usually stated as melodic units, they are occasionally superimposed and arranged to form chromatically ascending or descending tritone dyads similar to those of hexachord *A*. The complex pattern of superimposed tritones at bars 24–6 is produced by stating two levels of the set shown in Ex. 135b – which I shall henceforth term a 'subsidiary trope' – simultaneously, both hexachords of each form being presented as tritone dyads. Similarly, the dyads of hexachord *A* of the subsidiary trope are sometimes presented in a melodic form. Horizontalized versions of this hexachord play a particularly important role in 'Der Wein der Liebenden', the central section of the work.[1] At bars 97–9, for example, the three tritone dyads of hexachord *A* appear as a melodic figuration on the glockenspiel whilst one of the three-note cells of hexachord *B* appears on the horn and the other, in a reordered version, on the violin. Elsewhere melodic statements of these tritone figures derived from the trope attain a completely independent existence. Bars 123–5 present a number of overlapping tritone figures in which both the chromatic movement associated with hexachord *A* and the identity of the three-note cells of *B* are destroyed.

The gradual evolution of these tritone figures during the course of the work depends upon a chain of relationships similar to that which produces the series which I have earlier called 'Lulu's series' (Ex. 109). At its first appearance at bar 15 of *Der Wein,* the derivation of the tritone figuration from the basic set is suggested by the unfolding of the remaining notes of the set in the horn part. Once this relationship has been established, however, the two resulting six-note groups are regarded as forming an independent subsidiary trope which can be subjected to procedures which obscure the relationship between the trope and the basic set from which it sprang. The order of the notes in hexachord *B* is permuted to form tritone figures similar to those which characterize hexachord *A*. The interval of a tritone is then assumed to be the most important characteristic of the trope and eventually attains complete independence as a self-sufficient motive.

A similar, though more complicated, chain of relationships generates the material which forms the basis of the Chorale Variations in Act III, sc. 1 of *Lulu.* The series which is associated with the Marquis in Act III is also associated with the Prince in Act I, sc. 3, and the Manservant in Act II, sc. 1.[2] The derivation of this series is compositionally unfolded in Act I,

[1] See p. 186 below.
[2] See p. 198f. below.

sc. 3, when the Prince first appears. It is obtained by partitioning successive statements of Alwa's series, the basic series of the opera, and Schön's series into groups of 1, 2, 3, 4, 5, 6, 5, 4, 3, 2, and 1 notes in the manner shown in Ex. 136. The final notes of each group, with addition of the missing twelfth note at either the beginning or end, together form the Marquis's series. When the derivation of this set is first unfolded at bar 113f. of Act I, sc. 3, the generative process appears in the orchestral part while the complete Marquis's series appears simultaneously in the vocal part.

Ex. 136

Alwa's series                                   Basic series

Schön's series

At this first appearance, statements of the three series from which the Marquis's series is derived are accompanied by chords derived from the Picture trope (Ex. 109o), the Painter's chords (Ex. 109n), the basic series and other harmonic tropes. The final note of each group, the notes which form the Marquis's series, are prolonged. The chords with which these notes are first associated in this generative passage form the harmonized version of the chorale theme which is the basis of the Chorale Variations in Act III, sc. 1. Thus, although initially presented as a sequence derived from various twelve-note harmonic tropes, the chords which finally appear as the chorale theme resulting from this procedure are not themselves twelve-note chords. Ex. 137a shows the harmonized chorale theme. Ex. 137b shows the first

Ex. 137

ten notes of Alwa's series as presented at bars 113–5 of Act I, sc. 3, in the passage during which the chorale theme is initially generated. The harmonies accompanying these notes are derived from the Painter's chords (marked *i* in Ex. 137b), the basic series partitioned into three-note segments and superimposed (*ii*), and the Picture harmonies (*iii*). The first four chords of the harmonized chorale theme of Ex. 137a are obtained by extracting notes 1, 3, 6, and 10 of Alwa's series and their respective chords from Ex. 137b. As can be seen from Ex. 137a, the note E appears in the second, third and fourth chords of the chorale theme, chords two and three having the notes E and D in common and chord four having E and F sharp in common with chord three as well as the note G in common with chord one. The chords of the chorale theme themselves give rise to new figurations in the Chorale Variations of Act III, sc. 1, when the chords are stated in the orchestral parts and the notes of the chords permuted to form the basis of new melodic, non-dodecaphonic, patterns in the vocal line (Ex. 138).

Ex. 138

(Marquis' series P-7)

A similar technique can be seen at bar 389 of Dr. Schön's Five-strophe Aria in Act II, sc. 1 of *Lulu,* where a statement of the Picture chords, derived from an inversion of the basic series, is presented on the wind and brass instruments while the voice presents a permuted version of the notes that make up the chords; the vocal part thus presents a horizontal figuration which, while derived from the basic series through the Picture chords, has no direct relation to the linear ordering of the basic series itself (Ex. 139).

Ex. 139

Basic series I-1

I have hitherto referred to most of the series employed in *Lulu* as though they were distinct, independent sets. Whether the different series of *Lulu* are independent, rather than derived from a single source set, has been the cause of much controversy.

In his first article on *Lulu*,[1] written a year after Berg's death, and in all his subsequent writings on the opera, Berg's friend and biographer Willi Reich put forward the view that the work was based on a single twelve-note series and that the other sets employed in the work were derived from this source set in a variety of ways. Until recently this view has been accepted by almost all writers on the work.

Doubts as to whether this method of analysing the work had any relevance to the actual auditory experience were first expressed by Hans Keller in 1953[2] and Reich's analysis of the opera has been strongly contested in a series of articles by George Perle.[3] Although other writers have since become involved in the controversy – most notably, perhaps, Manfred Reiter in his book supporting and amplifying Reich's analysis[4] – the conflict of opinions is best expressed by Reich and Perle and it will be useful to summarize their argument before dealing with the topic.

Reich argues that 'the work's thematic unity is guaranteed by the fact that a single twelve-note series . . . determines the whole musical action of the opera. Berg used special methods to derive all the most important musical figures from this series.'[5] The single twelve-note series is that which I have previously referred to as the 'basic series'. In Reich's analysis all the sets in the work, other than the basic series itself, are obtained by extracting notes from the basic series, the notes extracted being determined by a variety of precompositionally established numerical sequences. In some cases the resulting series is also subjected to other operations before achieving its most characteristic form. Thus, Alwa's series is derived by extracting every seventh note from successive statements of the basic set (Ex. 140).

Ex. 140

Schön's series is derived by extracting the first note and then omitting notes from successive statements according to the sequence 1, 2, 3, 3, 2, 1 in the manner shown below (Ex. 141).

[1] Reich, 'Alban Berg's *Lulu*', *Musical Quarterly*, 22, 1936.
[2] Keller, 'Lulu', *Music Review*, 14, 1963.
[3] See, in particular, Perle, *Journal of the American Musicological Society*, 12, 1959, and *Music Review*, 26, 1965.
[4] See Reiter, *Die Zwölftontechnik in Alban Bergs Oper 'Lulu'*, Regensburg, 1973.
[5] Reich, *Alban Berg*, London, 1963, pp. 161–2.

Ex. 141

The derivation of the trope associated with Countess Geschwitz will be discussed later.[1]

Perle, on the other hand, argues that 'the music of *Lulu* is not referable to a single twelve-note set' and that the operations which Reich describes are 'either invalid, or, as supposedly demonstrating the priority of the basic series and significant precompositional relationships between it and the "derived" sets, irrelevant'.[2] Perle also points out[3] that Reich ignores the existence of many sets, a deficiency which Manfred Reiter has attempted to correct in his recent book on the twelve-note techniques in *Lulu* where he has demonstrated how those sets which Reich overlooks can be derived from the basic series by operations similar to those which Reich describes.[4] Thus, the Athlete's series is derived by extracting alternate notes from the basic series (Ex. 142).

Ex. 142

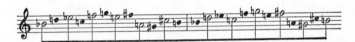

The Schoolboy's series is derived by extracting every third note (Ex. 143).

Ex. 143

Reich shows how the fourth-patterns of basic cell *I* are derived by extracting certain notes from the basic series and how this and other figurations, obtained by applying a similar process of selection to the remaining notes of the series, produce trope *III* (Ex. 144).

Ex. 144

[1] See pp. 121–3 below.
[2] Perle, *Music Review*, 26, 1965, p. 294.
[3] Ibid., p. 295.
[4] Reiter, *Die Zwölftontechnik in Alban Bergs Oper 'Lulu'*, Regensburg, 1973, pp. 57–60.

Reiter extends this process to trope *I* which, he argues, is derived by re-ordering the two hexachords of the basic series to form the sequence of fourths shown in Ex. 145b and then stating dyads from each of the two new hexachords alternately in the manner shown below.[1]

Ex. 145

Reiter ignores trope *II* although he discusses the derivation of the dimin-ished seventh chord (basic cell *III*) on which it is based. It is clear, however, that trope *II* can be obtained by a further extension of the kinds of procedures which Reich and Reiter describe.

The argument between the two opposing schools of thought has become confused by personal loyalties and by the lack of any real agreement about the exact nature of the problems being discussed. For much of the time the protagonists have been arguing at cross purposes. The essential argument between Reich and Perle is not, as Reich has suggested,[2] about the ways in which Berg initially arrived at the different sets in *Lulu*. A recently published letter from Berg to Schoenberg, and a number of letters to Webern in which Berg discusses his intentions of employing a variety of subsidiary sets, make it quite clear that Berg originally obtained these subsidiary sets from the basic series by employing the derivative procedures which Reich describes.[3]

---

[1] Ibid., p. 37.

[2] See Reich, 'Drei Notizblätter zu Alban Bergs *Lulu*', *Schweizerische Musikzeitung*, Nov.–Dec., 1966.

[3] Berg's letter to Schoenberg is published in Carner, *Alban Berg*, London, 1975, p. 205. In a letter to Webern dated 20.9.1929 Berg remarks:

> I think that I have recently found a good solution to the problem of using the rows for such a lengthy work. (Apart from the different forms which I have long since already derived from them.) You'll see what I have discovered from the attached sheet of paper. From the mathematical point of view it is something that is self-evident. But in the musical technique of row composition it is something that, perhaps, no-one has yet discovered and that – as said – can be applicable to any twelve-note row. . . .

Webern's reply is dated 28.9.1929:

> Your discoveries in the field of 'row-construction' seem very significant to me for the possibilities of obtaining from the basic row through permutation (I believe that that is what one calls, in mathematical terms, the kind of derivations that you have proposed) rows which seem to be new and yet stand in demonstrable relation with it (the basic row). In cases where the four forms of the row and its transpositions don't answer the purpose – as they clearly don't with you – to be able to obtain such through derivation seems to me to present possibilities for connections which have far reaching use. . . .

The sheet of paper (presumably manuscript paper) which Berg mentions is lost.

The latter, together with Reiter's further description of the procedures which generate the Athlete's series and the Schoolboy's trope – two sets ignored by Reich – are further confirmed by the many sketches and row charts which Berg made while working on the opera.[1] Such procedures are quite consistent with Berg's handling of the twelve-note method in his other works and, indeed, the most curious feature of the letter from Berg to Webern quoted above is that Berg discusses these procedures as though they were novel and employed in his music for the first time in *Lulu*. As I shall show many of Berg's earliest twelve-note works employ derivatives similar to those employed in *Lulu*.

Mosco Carner has suggested[2] that the publication of Berg's own description of these derivative procedures settles 'once and for all the much debated question of whether he used a single row or several other rows', but the ways in which Berg originally arrived at these subsidiary sets is not the subject of the argument. Nor is the argument, essentially, about the validity of these derivative procedures. Perle has shown[3] that the procedure which generates Countess Geschwitz's trope is rendered 'superfluous by the derivation of another one of the auxiliary sets employed in *Lulu* from every seventh note of the basic series, of which the derived set consisting of every fifth note is merely the retrograde (cyclically permuted so that the order numbers are 11, 0, 1, . . . 10)',[4] and that the same trope can be more easily derived from many other sets, including that of the first movement of the *Lyric Suite*. Yet this does not, in itself, invalidate the operations which are supposed to generate the Countess's trope for, as Perle himself elsewhere observes, 'though a given operation may be irrelevant as a pre-compositional means of establishing connections between the basic series and other sets it may be valid as an explicit compositional event'.[5]

The real difference between the two views is about the extent to which the 'unity of the opera'[6] depends upon the fact that the different sets are derived from the basic series by means of these procedures and the extent to which the listener is able, consciously or subconsciously, to perceive these relationships. That many melodic and harmonic relationships exist between the subsidiary sets themselves, and between these sets and the basic series, has already been demonstrated; the debate centres on whether the 'unity of the opera' depends upon the exploitation of such relationships between

[1] A photograph of one of Berg's row charts appears in Scherliess, *Alban Berg*, Hamburg, 1975, pp. 116–7.
[2] Carner, *Alban Berg*, London, 1975, p. 205.
[3] Perle, *Serial Composition and Atonality*, 2nd edn., London, 1968, pp. 74–5.
[4] Perle adopts a different system of numbering the notes in a series from that adopted in this book, the first note of the set being designated order number 0 and subsequent notes numbered from 1 to 11.
[5] Perle, *Music Review*, 26, 1965, p. 294.
[6] Reich, *Alban Berg*, London, 1965, p. 161.

independent sets or, as Reich claims, upon the fact that these subsidiary sets are not independent but derived from the basic set.

Manfred Reiter has discussed many of those passages in the opera in which he believes that the operations described by Reich (and similar operations which produce the sets which are ignored by Reich) are compositionally unfolded. But since (as I shall show later) the procedures which are supposed to generate many of the sets of *Lulu* are not unfolded at any point in the work, Reiter also argues that the listener will feel the relationship between the basic set and a derivative set irrespective of whether the procedure is unfolded. In support of this view Reiter quotes Stein's statement that 'It is absolutely superfluous – and also quite impossible – that the ear should be able to follow it (the series) in all its combinations . . . the unity is felt even if it is not understood'[1] and says of Reich's approach that 'it is self-evident to Reich that a knowledge of these technical procedures is superfluous to an instinctive understanding of the composition.'[2]

There are a number of flaws in such a defence of Reich's approach. Stein's statement is concerned with the problem of whether, in a work that is based on a single series, the listener is consciously aware of the series. Even if Stein's comments are correct when applied to such music it cannot be assumed that they are equally applicable to the listener's appreciation of the relationship between the basic series and the different sets of *Lulu*.

The problem is not, as Reiter suggests, whether the series itself is perceived but whether the kind of relationships which he and Reich describe are capable of being perceived. The kind of procedures which Reich and Reiter describe could be employed to derive almost any twelve-note set from any other. For example, Reiter describes the four consecutive triads which appear at Act I, sc. 1, bar 92 of *Lulu* as being derived from the basic set of the opera in the manner shown in Ex. 146.[3]

Ex. 146

A similar procedure applied to the RI form of the series of Webern's Concerto op. 24 will produce exactly the same sequence of triads (Ex. 147).

Since similar derivative methods to those described can be employed to produce quite different subsidiary sets from the basic series of *Lulu*, and to

[1] Stein, quoted in Reiter, *Die Zwölftontechnik in Alban Bergs Oper 'Lulu'*, Regensburg, 1973, p. 63.
[2] Ibid., p. 7.
[3] Ibid., p. 16.

produce the subsidiary sets of *Lulu* from a quite different basic set, it can hardly be claimed that such methods ensure the thematic unity of the work. Such methods, in themselves, ensure nothing. It is not enough to assume

Ex. 147

that 'the unity is felt even if it is not understood'. While it may be generally agreed that 'a knowledge of the technical procedures is superfluous to an instinctive understanding' of the music, this understanding must be based on relationships which, whether or not the listener is consciously aware of them, the music presents as audible phenomena. Although the derivative operations described by Reich may have no value or relevance as abstract precompositional procedures they may, as Perle has said, have relevance if unfolded in such a way that some kind of perceptible relationship is compositionally formed between the resulting derivative material and what has gone before. I have already discussed some examples in *Lulu* of Berg's use of chains of relationships which enable the listener to see the compositional development of one group of material from another.

In fact, in the case of the triads shown in Ex. 146, such a relationship between the triads and the basic set is, as Reiter points out, compositionally unfolded at bars 86–90 of *Lulu*, the passage which precedes the appearance at bar 92 of the chords quoted in the above example. In this passage the four triads, in their original order rather than the permuted order in which they appear at bar 92, are formed by sustaining certain notes of the basic set in the orchestral part (Ex. 148).

Ex. 148

My purpose in quoting Reiter's description of the methods by which the triads of Ex. 146 are derived from the basic set and in showing that these triads can as easily be derived from another set (and, in this case, the series of a work that is technically and stylistically quite different from *Lulu*) is not to question the compositional unfolding of this particular derivation but to show that the derivative methods do not, in themselves, automatically guarantee the existence of any significant relationship between the original and the derivative sets.

If the listener is to hear the subsidiary sets of *Lulu* as being derived from the basic series, rather than as independent sets, then it seems that the process which generates the subsidiary sets must be compositionally unfolded in a way that makes the derivative process capable of being perceived by the listener. As corollaries of this condition, one would expect that this unfolding should take place on the first appearance of the subsidiary set[1] and would expect the passage in which the generative process occurs to be in some way distinguishable from those passages in which two or more sets are employed simultaneously.

Of the derivative sets in *Lulu* – with the exception of Lulu's series and the Marquis's series, which I have discussed above[2] – only the generation of that associated with Schigolch is projected in any significant way. According to Reich, and to Berg's own sketches and set tables, Schigolch's serial trope is derived from the basic set by overlapping the two hexachords of the basic set and then extracting notes 1, 4, 11, and 12 so as to form the three four-note groups shown in Ex. 149.

Ex. 149

The first appearance of Schigolch's serial trope in the body of the opera is at bar 112f. of Act I, sc. 1, following Alwa's reference to Lulu's then husband, the Medical Specialist. The appearance of Schigolch's serial trope at this point is, perhaps, intended to suggest the more basic mythological relationship between Schigolch and Lulu. The overlapping of the two hexachords of the basic set, the first step in the generation of Schigolch's serial trope, is projected as a compositional event at bar 112. In the following two bars the second step in the generative process, the derivation of the four-note chromatic segments, is unfolded, bar 113 showing the derivation of these

---

[1] Both musically and dramatically the parade of characters and themes in the Prologue to *Lulu* is an introductory foretaste of the material to be used later in the work; I shall, therefore, disregard the appearances of the derivative sets in the Prologue for present and consider the first appearance of these sets in the body of the opera as being the point at which one would expect the generative process to be unfolded.

[2] See pp. 85–7 and 109–11 above.

segments from the prime form of the basic set and bar 114 from the inversion (Ex. 150).

Ex. 150

The same generative procedure is also projected in the passage which precedes Schigolch's entrance in Act I, sc. 2 (bar 458f.) and, in a modified form, in the passage which precedes his entrance in Act II, sc. 1. The operations by which Schigolch's serial trope is derived from the basic series are, therefore, whatever the theoretical validity of these operations, clearly presented as compositional events. As I shall show, these operations and the ways in which they are unfolded are very similar to those employed in certain passages of the *Lyric Suite*.[1]

The operations by which the other subsidiary sets of *Lulu* are derived from the basic series are not, however, projected with the same clarity. The first important appearance of Dr. Schön's series in the main body of the opera occurs at bar 534 of Act I, sc. 2, where the series acts as the main theme of the Sonata movement. This passage is shown in Ex. 151. Both Reiter and Carner argue that this passage, placed significantly at the opening of the Sonata

[1] See pp. 126–9 below.

movement, demonstrates the way in which Schön's series is derived from the basic series.[1] There are two major objections to such an interpretation. First, as can be seen from Ex. 151, the passage can only be obtained from the

Ex. 151

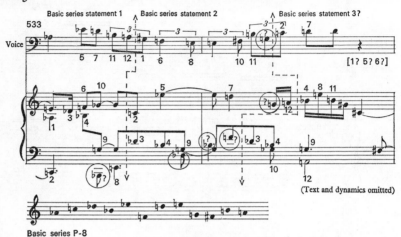

Basic series P-8

basic series by omitting certain notes and by altering the order in which other notes of the set appear. Such a practice is not uncommon in Berg's twelve-note music but seems inadmissible in a passage the supposed function of which is to demonstrate the derivation from the basic series of one of the most important sets in the work. Indeed such omissions and alterations would appear to invalidate the whole procedure. Secondly, as Perle has remarked,[2] there is nothing which distinguishes this from the many other passages in the opera in which notes common to two sets simultaneously function as members of both. There is, for example, no reason why one should regard this passage as more significant than that at bar 523, in which Schön's series is obtained from Schigolch's serial trope (Ex. 152). Since the passage shown

Ex. 152

---

[1] Reiter, *Die Zwölftontechnik in Alban Bergs Oper 'Lulu'*, Regensberg, 1973, pp. 43–4, and Carner, *Alban Berg*, London, 1975, pp. 207 and 218, who claims that 'Schön's series is the only one whose derivation from the BS (basic series) is shown as a compositional process'.

[2] See Perle, *Music Review*, 26, 1965, p. 295.

in Ex. 152 precedes that in which the derivation of Schön's series from the basic series is supposedly unfolded, it could be claimed, with rather more justification, that Schön's series is derived from one version of Schigolch's serial trope.

The serial trope associated with the figure of Countess Geschwitz is particularly interesting since, of all the derivative operations described by Reich, those which produce the Countess's trope are the most complicated. The derivative procedure necessitates five separate operations:

1. Every fifth note is extracted from successive statements of the basic set.
2. This series is then cyclically permuted so as to begin with its tenth note, producing the series shown in Ex. 153a.
3. Two notes are extracted from this cyclically permuted series and are presented as a simultaneity.
4. The remaining notes are partitioned into two five-note segments.
5. The notes within these segments are permuted to form two scale-like patterns.

This sequence of operations is illustrated in Ex. 153b.

Ex. 153

Perle has claimed that the series shown in Ex. 153a (the series resulting from the application of the first two steps in the sequence of operations described above and which I shall refer to as series $X$), cannot be found in the opera itself but only in the manuscript examples which Berg prepared for Reich; series $X$ is therefore, Perle claims, 'an hypothetical intermediary set'.[1] This is incorrect for, although Geschwitz is usually represented by the trope shown as the last example of Ex. 153b, and although the complete sequence of operations by which the trope is derived from the basic set is nowhere unfolded in the opera, the ordered intermediary series $X$ does appear on a number of occasions.

Series $X$ appears three times in Act II; at bars 4–5 and bars 9–11 when the

[1] See Perle, 'Erwiderung auf Willi Reichs Aufsatz: "Drei Notizblätter zu Alban Bergs *Lulu*" ', *Schweizerische Musikzeitung*, May–June, 1967, p. 165.

Countess's opening words in the opera are set to an inversion of this series
(Ex. 154), at bar 673, also in its inverted form, and in the 'Film Music'
interlude between Act II, scenes 1 and 2. The appearances of this series in Act

Ex. 154

Series X (I)

III of the opera are both more extensive and more significant; it may well be
that Berg intended the ordered series *X* to become gradually more prominent
as the figure of Countess Geschwitz develops in dramatic importance during
the final act of the opera. Many of the appearances of series *X* in Act III,
sc. 2, can be found in those portions of the act which Berg brought together
to form the Adagio of the *Lulu* Suite. The melody at bars 28–33 of the Adagio
(which reappears at bar 99f.) presents a horizontal statement of ten of the
notes of the ordered series *X*, the remaining two notes (those which form the
fifth dyad of Segment *A* of the Countess's trope in Ex. 109g) being sustained
in the bass.[1] The same ten-note melodic pattern that appears at bar 28 and
bar 99f. of the Suite, rhythmically altered but with same contour and over
the same sustained two-note chord in the bass, forms the basis of Countess
Geschwitz's 'Nocturno' in the unpublished portion of Act III, sc. 2; in the
opera the Nocturno[2] immediately precedes Lulu's death cry which appears
at bar 78 of the published Suite. A further version of series *X* occurs at bars
1124–64 of Act III, sc. 2 (the passage which precedes Jack's first entry) as
Geschwitz, alone on the stage, contemplates suicide. These bars form the
opening forty bars of the Adagio of the Suite and statements of series *X* can
be found at bars 6–10, 14–17 and 21–3 of the published score. In these pas-

────────

[1] The published score of the *Lulu* Suite has two sets of bar numbers. I shall refer to
bars in the Suite by employing those numbers which indicate the bars in the Suite movements themselves rather than those which appear enclosed in squares which are based on
Berg's own bar numbers and indicate the position of these bars in the body of Act III of
the opera.

[2] In Stein's revised bar numbers the Nocturno appears at bars 1257–71 of III/2.

sages the sustained fifth dyad, which was extracted from the series in the passages at bars 28–33 and 99–100 discussed above, again appears in the bass; the remaining notes of the series are presented as a sequence of two-note chords in the manner shown in Ex. 155.

Ex. 155

The 'intermediary series $X$, which results from the application of the first two steps in the sequence of operations by means of which Countess Geschwitz's trope is derived from the basic set, thus appears at a number of significant points towards the end of the opera. Moreover, since series $X$ is often presented in such a way that the two notes which correspond to Segment $A$ of the serial trope shown in Ex. 109g are isolated from the rest of the series, it is possible to argue that an audible relationship is established between the ordered series $X$ and the serial trope with which Countess Geschwitz is usually associated. At no point in the opera, however, is the relationship between series $X$ and the basic series itself unfolded.

The extent to which the derivation of the subsidiary sets associated with particular characters in *Lulu* is compositionally projected on their first appearance in the opera may be summarized thus:

*Projected Derivations*
1. The series associated with Lulu and the serial trope associated with Schigolch are derived from the basic series: the derivation of Schigolch's trope in particular is projected as a compositional event.
2. The series associated with the Marquis in Act III, the Manservant in Act II, and the Prince in Act I is derived from three sets – the basic series, the series associated with Dr. Schön and that associated with Alwa. This derivation is also projected as a compositional event.

*Unprojected Derivations*
1. The series associated with Dr. Schön is used together with the basic set at the beginning of the Sonata Exposition in Act I; the two sets are not, however, employed in a way that demonstrates the derivation of Schön's series from the basic set.

2. The procedures by means of which Alwa's series, the series associated with the Athlete and the serial trope associated with the Schoolboy are derived from the basic set are not projected at any point in the opera.

3. The relationship between the Countess's serial trope and the ordered series $X$ is revealed and exploited to a certain extent (mainly in Act III, sc. 2) but at no point is the sequence of operations by means of which the basic set gives rise to the serial trope unfolded.

That the supposed derivation of the majority of these subsidiary sets from the basic series is not shown in the opera does not mean that the relationships described by Reich may not be exploited as compositional events. The relationship between Schön's series and the basic series, for example, is – as Perle has observed[1] – impressively exploited at the moment of Dr. Schön's death in Act II, sc. 1, when his series is absorbed into the basic series. The exploitation of the relationship at this point does not, however, make the music previously associated with Schön more 'valid' in any way; nor does it suggest that Schön's series is derived from the basic series, any more than the passage at bar 523 of Act I, sc. 2[2] suggests that his series is derived from Schigolch's serial trope.

Obviously Berg could have unfolded all the subsidiary sets in the opera in a way that made clear their origins in the basic series had he wished to do so. Had the unity of the opera rested on the fact that 'a single twelve-note series determines the whole musical action',[3] the projection of some such perceptible relationship would have been necessary. In fact, the unity of the opera rests on those harmonic and thematic relationships between the different sets which were discussed at the beginning of this chapter. It is significant that Schigolch's serial trope, which lies outside the network of harmonic and tonal relationships described earlier, is one of the few subsidiary sets the derivation of which from the basic set is compositionally projected.

George Perle has remarked that 'obvious and, in principle, equally valid variations' of the procedures described by Reich 'will generate other, quite different, twelve-tone sets'.[4] Berg's sketches show that he did, in fact, investigate and reject many of the other sets which can be produced by derivative operations similar to those which produce the subsidiary sets employed in the opera. Thus, besides investigating the sets produced by extracting every second, every third, every fifth and every seventh note of the basic set (the procedures which produce the sets which appear in the opera, as the Athlete's series, the Schoolboy's serial trope, Countess Geschwitz's ordered series $X$ and Alwa's series respectively) he investigated and rejected the sets

[1] Perle, *Music Review*, 26, 1965, p. 295.
[2] See p. 92 above.
[3] Reich, *Alban Berg*, London, 1965, p. 161.
[4] Perle, *Music Review*, 26, 1965, p. 294.

produced by extracting every fourth, every sixth, eighth, ninth, tenth, and eleventh note of the basic set. He also investigated the potential of the different sets produced by applying to the basic series variants of the method which produces Schön's series. There is amongst Berg's sketches, for example, one for the set shown in Ex. 156, which is derived from the basic set by successively omitting notes according to the pattern 0, 1, 2, 3, 3, 2, 1, 0 and stating the remaining three notes as a simultaneity. Berg's use of the

Ex. 156

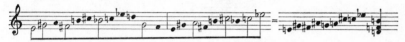

derivative sets employed in the opera, in preference to these other sets investigated in his sketches, is due to 'musically significant properties . . . rather than to generative procedures whose connection with these properties is entirely coincidental'.[1]

A curious feature of the Reich–Perle controversy discussed above is that it has been entirely concerned with Berg's use of derivative sets in *Lulu* – Berg's use of similar techniques in his other twelve-note works has gone unmentioned and unquestioned. Yet the use of such derivative sets is an important feature of Berg's twelve-note practice. None of Berg's twelve-note works employs a single set; most employ a basic series and a number of subsidiary sets which are derived from the basic series in a variety of ways. A survey of this aspect of his techniques will show that Berg's handling of the derivative sets in *Lulu* is entirely consistent with his handling of the derivative sets in his other twelve-note works.

Of the six movements of the *Lyric Suite,* only two complete movements (the first and the sixth) and certain parts of two other movements (the outer sections of the third movement and the 'Tenebroso' sections of the fifth) employ the twelve-note method of composition. The twelve-note movements and twelve-note sections of the *Lyric Suite* employ a number of sets, each set being related in some way to the set which has appeared immediately before. The original set of the first movement is, thus, gradually modified as the work progresses, the different sets forming a chain of relationships similar to the chains of melodic and harmonic relationships found in *Lulu* and *Der Wein* which have been already discussed. Berg seems to have regarded the process of alteration and modification by which the basic set of the opening 'Allegretto giovale', with its clear tonal implications, becomes the chromatic and tortuous series of the final 'Largo desolato' as having a programmatic significance and, in his writings on the piece, described these modifications

[1] Ibid., p. 294.

as being important 'not for the line but for the "character" of the row – "suffering a fate"'.[1]

Series *A* (Ex. 157a), the basic series of the first movement, and the two subsidiary sets to which it gives rise have been discussed above.[2] Series *B* is the basic series of the 'Allegro misterioso' sections of the third movement (Ex. 157b). Series *C* and *D* (Exx. 157c and d) are employed throughout the

Ex. 157

finale. Series *B* is obtained by interchanging notes 4 and 10 of the first movement series, series *A*; series *C* is obtained from series *B* by interchanging notes 5 and 10 and interchanging note 6 and note 8. The procedure by which series *B* is derived from series *A*, and by which series *C* is derived from series *B* – that is, the actual process of interchange – is never compositionally unfolded; in each case Berg assumes that the motivic similarities are sufficient to form perceptible relationships between the different series. The motivic similarities between the first movement series (*A*) and the series of the third movement (*B*) are, however, emphasized in the passage from bars 16–32 of the second movement (and in the fragmentary restatement of this passage at bars 93–112), where figurations derived from the two series are juxtaposed. Ex. 158 shows the main melodic lines in the section from bars 19–28 of the second movement. In this section, and in the rest of this and later passages from the same movement, the two series are employed at the same or equivalent pitch levels in order to enhance the similarities between them. As I have already observed,[3] this choice of pitch level is determined by the fact that the transposition of series *B* employed during these bars is one of the four levels at which it contains the notes A–B flat–B–F as

[1] Berg, 'Nine Pages on the *Lyric Suite*' reprinted in Rauchhaupt (ed.), *Schoenberg – Berg – Webern: The String Quartets*, Hamburg, 1971, p. 102.
[2] See pp. 82–3 above.
[3] See p. 82 above.

adjacent pitches. The role which this four-note collection plays in the third movement of the *Lyric Suite,* and in the work as a whole, has been discussed earlier.'[1]

Ex. 158

The presence of the four-note group A–B flat–B–F in both series *C* and *D* serves to relate these two series to series *B*. Series *C* at the transpositional level shown in Ex. 159a begins with a version of this collection whilst the two levels of series *D* shown in Exx. 159b and 159c also contain versions of the same collection (indicated by square brackets).

Ex. 159

Series *C* and *D* are used simultaneously throughout the sixth movement; the relationship between the two apparently independent series is revealed at bar 30 of the finale, when series *C* is shared between the first and second violin in such a way that violin 1 plays the notes of the first hexachord and violin 2 the notes of the second hexachord of *D* (Ex. 160). Series *D* is, thus, compositionally related to series *C* in a way similar to that which, in *Lulu,* relates Schön's series to the basic series of the opera at the moment of Schön's death. Although the passage shown in Ex. 160 is the most dramatic

[1] See pp. 27–9 above.

compositional exploitation of the relationship between series *C* and *D*, the connection between the two series has already been revealed in the 'Tene-

Ex. 160

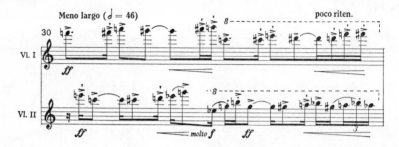

broso' sections of Movement V. The two 'Tenebroso' sections of the otherwise non-twelve-note fifth movement are based on series *C*. The first section (bars 50–120) is built of overlapping chords, obtained by stating adjacent notes of the series simultaneously. During the second 'Tenebroso' section the chords derived from series *C* are arranged in such a way that the resulting horizontal lines gradually form statements of series *D*, the process culminating at bar 281 where the two hexachords of series *D* are stated simultaneously (Ex. 161).

Ex. 161

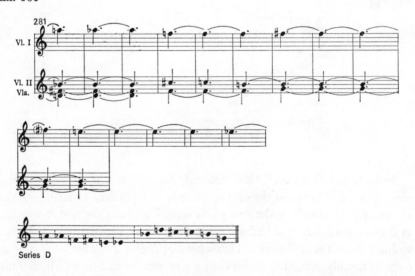

A further complete statement of *D* in the fifth movement, with the two hexachords played consecutively rather than simultaneously, appears at bars 374–83 of the final Presto section. This statement of series *D* is at the transpositional level shown in Ex. 159, at which level it contains the four-note collection B flat–B–A–F which it holds in common with series *B*. Series *A*, the basic series of the first movement of the *Lyric Suite*, gives rise, during the course of the movement, to the two subsidary sets *A1* and *A2* (Exx. 107a and 107b). The relationship between these two sets and the basic series *A* is primarily harmonic and tonal and has been already discussed.[1] Set *A1* is also related to the basic series through its intervallic characteristics, in that the sequence of fourths and fifths which characterize *A1* (and which are suggested in the chords, built of superimposed fifths, which open the first movement) are implicit in the melodic contour which the basic set assumes when it forms the main theme of the first movement. This relationship is emphasized at bars 42–5, where the main theme is divided between viola and cello in such a way that each of the two voices forms a chain of fourths and fifths similar to those of *A1* (Ex. 162).

Ex. 162

Using the same basic series as that shown in Ex. 158a above (series *A*) Berg's 1925 setting of 'Schliesse mir die Augen beide' presents an interesting variant of the technique employed in the first movement of the *Lyric Suite*, a variant which seems to anticipate some of Berg's later methods of set-handling. The piano part at bars 11–13 of 'Schliesse mir die Augen beide' presents the series shown in Ex. 163, which I shall call *A3*. This series, a further derivative of the basic set, does not appear in the *Lyric Suite*.

Ex. 163

Series A3

In 'Schliesse mir die Augen beide' the opening statement of the basic set has the same contour as the theme of the first movement of the *Lyric Suite*. Like series *A1* of the *Lyric Suite*, series *A3* above springs from the sequence of fourths and fifths implicit in this contour. Series *A3* is obtained by arranging ascending and descending sequences of fourths symmetrically around the opening F of the basic set at P–O and extracting notes from each sequence in turn (Ex. 164). The ordering of the notes within this series is

[1] See pp. 82–3 above.

reflected in the vertical ordering of the notes in the twelve-note chord (the all-interval, so-called 'Mother' chord of F. H. Klein)[1] which ends the song.

Ex. 164

Although, like the basic set, this new series has the tritone F–B between its first and last notes and the tritone D–A flat at its centre, $A_3$ destroys the harmonic and tonal identity of the two hexachords of the basic set, a feature that is maintained by the two subsidiary sets which appear in the first movement of the *Lyric Suite*. One can postulate a number of hypothetical methods (similar to those described in connection with the subsidiary sets of *Lulu*) by which $A_3$ is derived from the basic set but no generative process is unfolded during the course of the song. Series $A_1$ of the first movement of the *Lyric Suite*, which, consisting as it does of a sequence of fourths and fifths, would seem to form the most obvious link between $A_3$ and the basic set, does not appear in 'Schliesse mir die Augen beide'. One other method of row-handling in the *Lyric Suite* also anticipates Berg's later techniques. The series employed in the third movement of the work (series $B$) is shown in Ex. 158d. For much of the movement Berg chooses to project this series as two interlocking segments, a five-note and a chromatic seven-note segment. The way in which this is achieved is shown in Ex. 165.

Ex. 165

Although these two segments usually appear in the interlocking form shown in the above example, and are only occasionally used consecutively so as to produce a new series, this method of splitting the series is similar to and anticipates that by which Schigolch's serial trope is derived from the basic set of *Lulu*. In both cases the series is stated as notes of equal duration and the method of splitting the series generates rhythmic patterns which have an important independent structural function.[2] A comparison of Ex. 165 and Ex. 160 will reveal the extent to which this method of row splitting also corresponds to the method by which series $C$ and $D$ are associated at bar 30 of the final movement of the *Lyric Suite*.

[1] See Redlich, *Alban Berg*, London, 1957, pp. 135–6.
[2] The rhythmic aspects of this method of row splitting are discussed in Ch. IV, pp. 156–158 below.

Berg's methods of handling the twelve-note sets in both *Lulu* and the *Lyric Suite* are determined by his desire to create a certain kind of tonally orientated twelve-note language. The necessity of reconciling the apparently conflicting demands of the twelve-note method and the tonal system, which the creation of such a language entails, raises a number of technical problems. Because of the specifically tonal connotations of their respective sets, these problems are posed in their most acute form in *Der Wein* and the Violin Concerto.

The nature of these problems becomes clear when one compares the two systems. In both the twelve-note method and the tonal system the twelve notes of the tempered chromatic scale represent the total available material. In the tonal system a key consists of seven notes, selected from the possible twelve according to a conventional arrangement of tones and semitones. Every key is characterized by and differs from every other key by the fact that, of the total available material, the selection of notes which it includes and excludes is unique. The order in which this unique selection of notes is presented in the course of a composition can be varied at will, the selection itself defines the key. The two most typical key-defining patterns in tonal music (the scale and the triads built on the tonic, dominant and subdominant) have in common only the fact that both patterns include all seven of the notes selected from the total available material and exclude all the remaining notes. The two patterns are united by their common unique content, the scale defining this content as a horizontal melodic phenomenon, the primary triads defining the content as a vertical harmonic phenomenon. The tonal system is, therefore, an 'exclusive' system.

The twelve-note system, on the other hand, is an 'inclusive' system. Each set includes all twelve notes of the chromatic scale, that is to say it includes all of the total available material. One twelve-note set differs from another set not by the fact that it has a unique selection of notes but by the fact that it presents the available material in a unique order.

In tonal music there is no conflict between the scalic and triadic formations since they respectively represent the horizontal and vertical aspects of the same unique collection from the chromatic scale. The way in which vertical and harmonic formations relate to one another is, on the other hand, one of the more problematic areas of twelve-note theory. Traditional twelve-note theory, as expounded by Rufer and many other commentators[1], defines only one method of deriving chords from a series – that of playing adjacent notes of a series simultaneously. From a purely theoretical point of view this method (which is usually termed 'simultaneity') inevitably destroys certain aspects of the interval succession upon which the identity of the series is supposedly based. If one considers the extreme case of a twelve-note chord,

[1] See Rufer, *Composition with Twelve-notes*, London, 1955, p. 85.

for example, it is clear that such a chord, in theory, represents any twelve-note set.[1] Moreover, simultaneity also creates new 'non-row' intervals. The decision to present notes 2, 3, 4, notes 6, 7, 8 and notes 10, 11 and 12 of a series as three three-note chords in the manner shown in the following diagram, for example, creates new 'non-row' intervals between notes 2 and 5, 6 and 9, and 9 and 12. These non-row intervals are marked by asterisks in the following diagram:[2]

```
              *              *     *
        ┌─────────┐   ┌─────────┬─────────┐
   1    2         5   6         9        12
        3             7                  10
        4             8                  11
```

Another method of obtaining twelve-note harmony, although one not discussed by Rufer, is the simultaneous use of two or more set forms. This method does not create new intervals horizontally, as does simultaneity, but the vertical relationships between the parts – the intervals formed between the different set forms – are not automatically controlled by the series.[3] Many of the chains of relationships which generate new material in Berg's music come about through a deliberate exploitation of the ambiguous association between the vertical and horizontal aspects of twelve-note music.

The methods of row-handling employed in *Der Wein* and the Violin Concerto are an attempt to reconcile the different ways in which the horizontal and vertical aspects relate to one another in tonal and twelve-note music. The necessity for such methods springs from the fact that the set of each of these works resembles one of the two most characteristic key-defining patterns of tonal music – that of *Der Wein* beginning with the first seven notes of the minor scale, that of the Violin Concerto consisting of a sequence of major and minor triads based on the circle of fifths. Thus, whilst the scale-like fragment of the series of *Der Wein* naturally gives rise to scale-like melodic formations, reminiscent of those of tonal music, it cannot, at least by the methods laid down by twelve-note theory, produce triads and other obviously tonally-orientated formations of a kind that would comple-

[1] In practice a composer may, however, imply a horizontal order in a number of ways – by the way in which he chooses to space a chord, by emphasizing certain notes through the orchestration or through their position in the chord and so on. Thus, though the twelve-note chord which accompanies Lulu's death cry in Act III, sc. 2 of *Lulu* could in theory be a vertical statement of any twelve-note series, the chord itself is so arranged as to emphasize its derivation from trope *I*. (The chord appears at bar 80 of the Adagio of the *Lulu* Suite.)

[2] I am here concerned only with the series as an abstract entity. In practice the extent to which the listener might be aware of these intervals as being 'non-row' intervals depends on many other factors such as articulation, phrasing, whether the intervals formed in this way are already a feature of the series, etc.

[3] See P. Westergaard, 'Toward a Twelve-Tone Polyphony' in *Perspectives on Contemporary Music Theory*, ed. B. Boretz and E. Cone, W. W. Norton and Co. Inc., New York, 1972, p. 243.

ment and provide a harmonic structure consistent with these melodic figurations.

Many of the thematic figurations in *Der Wein*, and the most important of the work's harmonic characteristics, spring, not from the basic series, but from subsidiary sets that are themselves derived from the basic row. These subsidiary sets are usually stated initially as chord sequences which then give rise to new melodic figurations. Four such subsidiary sets are employed during the course of the work.

1. At bars 8–10 the clarinets present two sequences of three-note chords derived from the basic row by extracting alternate notes from a cyclically permuted version of I–5 (bars 8–9: Ex. 166). In effect, the passage presents

Ex. 166

a new twelve-note set consisting of notes 1–3–5–7–9–11–2–4–6–8–10–12 of the original note-row; I shall call this new set 'trope *A*'. The method by which this trope is derived from the basic series is identical with that by which the Athlete's series is derived from the basic set of *Lulu*. At only one point in the work (the passage at bars 8–10, shown in Ex. 166) is this set presented as four three-note chords; harmonic statements of this set elsewhere in the work usually present it as a sequence of three four-note chords (Ex. 167).

Ex. 167

Although the order of the chords which make up these harmonic statements of trope *A* usually follows that implied by the set, the horizontal ordering of the notes within the chord sequence often varies from one statement to another and I shall therefore term this characteristic harmonic form of the set 'harmonic trope *A*'. Statements of harmonic trope *A* play an important role in the orchestral introduction and coda and in the transitional passage that leads to the second subject group.[1]

2. Another subsidiary set, which I shall call 'trope *B*' consists of three four-note chords produced by partitioning the basic row into four three-note segments and stating these segments simultaneously in the manner shown in Ex. 168. Ex. 168 shows this operation applied to the inverted form of the

Ex. 168

I-3                                                                      Harmonic trope B

basic row since, with the exception of a single statement which accompanies the voice part at the opening of the first song (bar 17) and the reprise of this passage at bar 74 and bar 196, it is from this form of the row that statements of harmonic trope *B*, like those of harmonic trope *A*, are always derived. Statements of harmonic trope *B* appear mainly in the orchestral passages which open and close the work, where they are usually arranged in such a way that the last chord of one statement overlaps with the first chord of another. Bars 11–13 of the orchestral introduction show the kind of chord sequences produced by such overlapping statements of the trope.

3. Of the four subsidiary sets employed in *Der Wein*, that which I shall call 'trope *C*' is the most obviously derived from the basic row of the work. The most characteristic harmonic form of trope *C* is shown in Ex. 169; it consists of three triads (I, II and III below) derived from notes 1–3–5, 6–7–8, and 9–10 (or 11) –12 of P and I forms of the basic series (or the equivalent notes of the retrograde forms); the remaining notes of the set are usually stated as grace notes. Trope *C* appears only in the central section

Ex. 169

= Trope C

I          II                  III

of the work, the second song 'Der Wein der Leibenden'. The chords of trope *C* usually, but not always, maintain the order implied by the basic series, from which they derive. The first complete statements of the trope to appear in the piece (on the strings at bars 92–7), for example, are derived from R–11, P–9 and P–1; the statements derived from P–9 and P–1 are both based on cyclically permuted versions of these forms.

[1] The formal design of *Der Wein* is discussed in Ch. V, p. 186 below.

4. The fourth trope (trope *D*) is shown in Ex. 170 and has been discussed earlier in this chapter.[1]

Ex. 170

The triadic and quartal formations which characterize tropes *A*, *B* and *C* are deliberately reminiscent of traditional tonal music. The three tropes, thus, produce a tonally orientated harmonic structure which is consistent with the tonally orientated melodic figurations suggested by the structure of the basic series of *Der Wein*. At points in the work where these tropes are not themselves employed, similar chord formations are obtained by bringing together a number of different set forms according to pre-conceived 'non-dodecaphonic' criteria. It is these non-row criteria which, to a large extent, determine Berg's choice of transpositional levels and the way in which he handles the series.

The process by which the tritones of trope *D* are derived from the basic set is compositionally unfolded at bar 15 of *Der Wein* and has been discussed above. The process by which the remaining tropes are generated is not projected in any way.

Like the harmonic tropes of *Lulu*, these tropes, once stated as chord sequences, give rise to new melodic figurations. As a harmonic phenomenon trope *A* is usually regarded as being composed of three four-note segments; as a source of melodic figurations, on the other hand, it is usually regarded as consisting of two six-note segments, the ordering of which, both internally and in relation to one another, can be changed at will. Ex. 171a shows the first of the melodic figurations derived from trope *A* to appear in the work (bars 41–3). Trope *A*, at the transpositional level shown in Ex. 171a, can be derived

Ex. 171

[1] See pp. 108–9 above.

from four forms of the basic row (I–2, R–8, P–8, RI–2). Ex. 171b shows how it can be derived from one of these forms (RI–2). One hexachord of the trope is stated as a chord; the other (with the exception of the note C) as a melodic figuration on the trumpet. The arpeggio-like ascending thirds in the trumpet part in this example are always associated with melodic statements of trope *A*.

Melodic statements of trope *A* appear only in the two parts of the second subject group,[1] although they are, to some extent, anticipated at bar 19 where the clarinet has an arpeggio-like figuration derived from notes 1–7 of P–3, the remaining notes of the row appearing as a chord on the harp.

There are no melodic statements of trope *B*, although the superimposed fourths and fifths which characterize the chords of this harmonic trope are reflected in many of the melodic patterns that appear during the course of the work. The parallel fourths at bars 42–7, for example, are produced by partitioning the basic row into three-note cells in a manner similar to that which generated trope *B*.

Horizontal statements of trope *C* give rise to the arpeggio-like figurations which appear at bar 97f.

The series of the Violin Concerto is shown in Ex. 172. As in *Der Wein* the main motivic patterns which characterize the series (in the case of the Violin Concerto the chains of thirds and the whole-tone segment) often appear as independent elements. At some points in the work the series is cyclically permuted so as to begin on the second note, the first note appearing at the end of the series as a means of extending the whole-tone sequence formed by notes 9–12; at other points there appear chains of whole-tones not directly derived from the set itself.

Ex. 172

To an even greater extent than in *Der Wein* the methods of set-handling employed in the Violin Concerto are determined by a desire to enhance the tonal implications inherent in the structure of the series – tonal implications that are confirmed by the inclusion, in the work, of non-dodecaphonic material in the form of a Bach chorale and the melody of the Carinthian folk-song, 'Ein Vogel auf'm Zwetschgenbaum'.[2]

The extent to which tonal criteria determined Berg's handling of the set in the Violin Concerto is shown by his working sketches for the piece, on one sheet of which the chords that can be derived from the series are marked with chord symbols indicating their tonal relationship to one another.

---

[1] See p. 186 below.

[2] See Herwig Knaus, 'Berg's Carinthian folk tune', *Musical Times*, June, 1976, p. 487.

Throughout the work reordering of the internal order of segments of the series is frequently adopted as a means of emphasizing tonal connotations; Ex. 173 shows bars 176–7 of the first movement, where the opening notes of the I form of the series are reordered so as to produce an F major root position chord.

Ex. 173

As I have said above, the R and RI forms of the series of the Violin Concerto present cyclically permuted versions of the P and I forms. The passage at bars 38–9 of the first movement of the Concerto, for example, can be considered as being derived from a cyclically permuted version of either R–5 or I–9 (Ex. 174).

Ex. 174

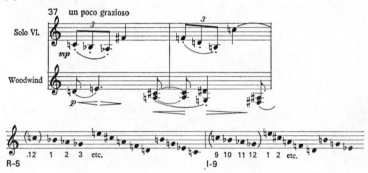

Since, in the Violin Concerto, as in *Der Wein* and Berg's other twelve-note works, cyclic permutation is accepted as a normal method of row handling, the series has, in effect, no distinct retrograde. Because of this, and because reordering of the segments in relation to one another is also common procedure, it is frequently difficult to assign a passage to one specific form of the series with any certainty.

The series of the Violin Concerto poses the opposite problem to that posed by the set of *Der Wein* for, while giving rise to triadic harmonic formations and triadic melodic figurations that are reminiscent of traditional music, the series does not lend itself to the formation of the non-triadic patterns – such as chromatic or scale figures – that characterize tonal music.

Such figures are obtained from the series in a number of ways during the course of the work. The open fifths that appear in the introduction to the first movement, and reappear at various points through the work, are produced by extracting alternate notes from the series in a manner similar to that which generated the Athlete's series in *Lulu* and trope *A* of *Der Wein*. Bars 1, 3, 5 and 9 of the first movement of the Violin Concerto present notes 1–9 of P–3 in this way, alternating with a similar statement of notes 1 to 9 of P–0 at bars 2, 4, 6 and 10. Bar 7 presents notes 10, 11, 12 and 1 of P–3 and bar 8 notes 10, 11, 12 and 1 of P–0 permuted to form a sequence of sevenths and tritones (see Ex. 175).

Ex. 175

Many non-triadic figurations are obtained by partitioning the series into segments and stating these segments as chords in such a way that the horizontal movement of parts produces new melodic patterns. The chromatic figurations of the second Trio (bar 155f.) are obtained by presenting the series as a three-, four- and five-note chord sequence in the manner shown in Ex. 176.

Ex. 176

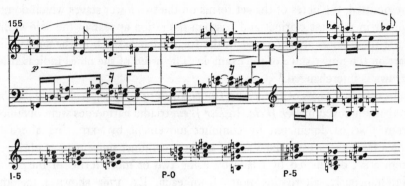

These chromatic figurations are then handled as independent motives in the cadenza of the second part of the work. Elsewhere, non-triadic figurations are obtained by combining different set forms in a variety of ways. One such way is illustrated diagrammatically in Ex. 177, the opening bars of the angular melodic line on the bass clarinet and bassoon which accompanies the solo violin at bar 35f. of the second part of the concerto. The bass clarinet and

Ex. 177

bassoon figuration is derived from the overlapping set forms shown on the lower staves of Ex. 177; the figuration itself is shown on the stave above. During these bars the solo violin unfolds successive statements of I–2, and P–2. With the exception of those notes indicated by square brackets, which are omitted, the notes of the set forms on the two lower staves which do not appear in the bass clarinet and bassoon figuration appear in the solo violin part; these notes are indicated in the fragmentary sketch of the solo violin part on the upper stave of the example. The order of the notes indicated by arrows is interchanged.[1]

In other passages of the Violin Concerto Berg adopts a technique similar to that employed in *Der Wein*. In *Der Wein* triadic harmonies were obtained from a series dominated by conjunct movement by extracting alternate notes from the set; in the Violin Concerto conjunct movement is obtained from a set dominated by triads by using two or more forms of the series simultaneously, alternating notes from each. Ex. 178a shows a melodic figuration from the first movement of the concerto produced by stating the notes of P–1 and P–3 alternately; Ex. 178b shows a passage from the Adagio of the second movement which employs three transpositions of the series simultaneously.

Ex. 178

Although the procedures in *Der Wein* and the Violin Concerto spring from the unusual nature of the basic set of each of these works, the derivative

---

[1] I am indebted to Michael Taylor for his help in unravelling this passage.

operations by which the subsidiary sets of these pieces, and of the *Lyric Suite*, are obtained are very similar to those employed in *Lulu*. Berg's handling of these derivative sets is consistent with his handling of the derivative sets in *Lulu* and with other aspects of his twelve-note technique. I have said earlier that Berg usually regards his twelve-note sets as having characteristics in addition to those of interval succession and that these other characteristics are often assumed to be as important and, on occasions, more important a feature of set-identity as the interval succession. The relationship between the derivative and the basic sets in Berg's twelve-note music depends less on the preservation of interval succession than on the maintenance of these other associated characteristics. Berg may or may not choose to project compositionally the processes by which the basic set gives rise to various derivative sets; the extent to which he chooses to do so varies from work to work. Even when Berg does choose to project this process, however, the significance of the subsidiary sets depends, not on this generative process itself, but on harmonic, motivic, tonal and other properties which they hold in common with the basic set.

Berg's handling of the twelve-note method displays a typically Bergian paradox in that it seems to be based on two contradictory and, indeed, apparently mutually exclusive attitudes. On the one hand Berg's twelve-note techniques are essentially practical, pragmatic and directly concerned with the auditory experience of the listener. Thus, the Bergian series is regarded, not as an abstract interval sequence, but as a thematic phenomenon associated with a specific and easily identifiable melodic and rhythmic shape. Unless, as in *Der Wein* and the Violin Concerto, the nature of the series is such that the most important melodic and thematic features of the original are maintained in the retrograde forms, it is assumed that the retrograde forms destroy many of the identifying characteristics of the set and that the relationships between the retrograde forms and the original and inverted forms of the series are not easily perceptible; such forms are, therefore, usually avoided. Melodic fragments derived from the series are, however, frequently employed as independent figurations. Any easily recognizable characteristic or figuration may acquire its own independent identity, and, as in traditional music, the interval succession originally associated with it may be modified in order to enhance this identity. In many cases the most important characteristic of such a figuration is its tonal connotations; the implied presence of tonal criteria as factors determining Berg's handling of the set and his choice of harmonic and melodic formations itself makes the music more immediately comprehensible to the listener. All such modifications of Schoenberg's twelve-note system seem to be directly concerned with giving a definite concrete shape to the otherwise abstract interval sequence so that the listener may recognize and follow its progress more easily.

On the other hand, alongside this concern with employing the set in such a way that it produces audible and clearly perceptible relationships, there exists in Berg's music evidence of a deep interest in the abstract, intellectual possibilities of the twelve-note method; a fascination with the mechanics of set-handling. In many passages of *Lulu* the exploitation of the relationships between different sets reaches a degree of complexity that suggests a sheer intellectual delight in exploring the technical possibilities which the twelve-note system presents. The combination of seven different sets in the 'Film Music' Ostinato between Act II, scenes 1 and 2, the exploitation of the relationships between Alwa's and Schön's series in Act II, sc. 1, when Schön overhears Alwa declare his love for Lulu,[1] and the rhythmic canon at bars 811–32 of Act I, sc. 2 which combines Schön's, Alwa's and Lulu's series and the basic set are amongst the most obvious examples of such passages. It is noteworthy that these three passages, each of which is a technical *tour de force*, are amongst the most exciting in the work; I shall discuss the significance of this point in Chapter VI.[2] Although Berg's exploitation of the complexities of set-handling in *Lulu* has its origins in the libretto and in the dramatic situation, it is entirely typical of one aspect of Berg's character that the more elaborate and 'abstract' of his technical procedures are such that they are, by their very nature, incapable of being perceived by the listener.

George Perle has pointed out the unusual conceit with which Berg illustrates the confusion of Alwa's words 'In der Redaktion weiss Keiner was er schreiben soll' ('No-one in the editorial office knows what to write'), at bar 808 of Act I, where the vocal line represents two cyclically permuted forms of Alwa's series stated simultaneously. Similarly the curiously and inconsequently dream-like nature of the dialogue between Lulu and Alwa at bars 922–35 of the same scene is symbolized by a sequence of cyclically permuted statements of Alwa's series.[3] When in Act I, sc. 1, Schön tells the Painter that the portrait needs more work done on it, the lack of formal clarity is represented by a vocal line that consists of a number of permutations of a note-collection that could be obtained from a variety of set-forms.[4]

Whatever the psychological and emotional reasons behind Berg's adoption of the twelve-note method and his desire, using this method, to write music which emphasizes its link with traditional music, there can be little doubt that he was fascinated and stimulated by the technical and intellectual problems which his attempt to reconcile the twelve-note method and the tonal

[1] II/1, bars 274, 294, 296f., 313f., 338f., 341f., 344f. The passages are discussed in Perle, *Music Review*, 26, 1965, p. 282.
[2] See p. 224f. below.
[3] See Perle, *Music Review*, 26, 1965, p. 282.
[4] See Reiter, *Die Zwölftontechnik in Alban Bergs Oper 'Lulu'*, Regensberg, 1973, p. 73.

system raised. The bringing together of such apparently conflicting elements is a constant feature of Berg's music.

The confrontation of twelve-note and tonal material in the Violin Concerto (in which Berg employs the Bach chorale 'Es ist genug') and in *Lulu* (in which Wedekind's *Lautenlied* appears in Act III) are the most obvious examples of this bringing together of seemingly contradictory elements. Since in these works the twelve-note music is itself tonally orientated and, in certain passages, seems to work according to traditionally tonal criteria, the conflict between the tonal and twelve-note material is not as great as it might have been. The technical conceit by which Berg reconciles the two groups of material is, however, indicative of the intellectual fascination which the mechanics of twelve-note composition exerted upon him.

In the Violin Concerto the first three phrases of the chorale melody first appear on the solo violin at bar 136, where they form part of a number of

Ex. 179

statements of the basic series, the remaining notes of the series appearing on the bassoons, violas and second violins. The three phrases are then repeated by the wind instruments in Bach's harmonization. The way in which the first three phrases of the chorale melody are derived from the twelve-note series is shown in Ex. 179. The remaining phrases of the chorale are then unfolded in the same way, each phrase appearing first on the solo violin as part of a statement of the series, or of a number of forms of the series, and then on the wind instruments in Bach's tonal harmonization.

The melody of the Wedekind *Lautenlied*, which plays an important role in Act III of *Lulu*, undergoes the same process as the chorale of the Violin Concerto but in reverse, the tune being originally presented as a diatonic melody which is then gradually absorbed into a twelve-note context. The tune first appears on the solo violin as a counter-melody to the 'Procurer's Song'[1] which the Marquis sings in Act III, sc. 1, and reappears in a more chromatic form at two later points in the same scene. The process by means of which the melody is absorbed into the twelve-note context can be seen in the orchestral interlude between Act III, sc. 1, and Act III, sc. 2, which appears as the Variation movement of the *Lulu* Suite. The first of the four variations is in an unambiguous C major and is essentially a repetition of the 'Procurer's Song' of the previous scene; the second variation is polytonal and presents the theme as a two-part canon, one group of instruments playing in C major whilst the other group plays in G flat major; the third variation is 'atonal', the theme being harmonized with chords built of superimposed fourths or of superimposed fourths and tritones; in the fourth variation the theme is finally absorbed into a twelve-note context in the way shown in Ex. 180.[2]

The revelation of the relationship between the melody of the *Lautenlied* and the basic set of the opera does not, of course, make the earlier, non-twelve-note, statements of the melody more significant or more relevant in any way, any more than the relationship between Schön's series and the basic set, which is revealed at the moment of Schön's death in Act II, adds greater significance to Schön's earlier Sonata movement. Indeed, the identity of the Wedekind tune as a self-sufficient melodic entity is so strong that the listener is probably unaware, in the fourth variation, that it forms part of a number of

---

[1] The opening bars of the 'Procurer's Song' are given in Redlich, *Versuch einer Würdigung*, Vienna, 1957, p. 249, Ex. 315. The saxophone part in this example doubles the voice part which is not given.

[2] In the *Lulu* Suite the fourth variation is followed by the first two phrases of the theme itself before being interrupted by the chords of the Marquis's Chorale which close the movement as they began it; in the opera the curtain rises at the end of the fourth variation and the original theme, now in E flat major, is heard in its entirety (played on an off-stage barrel organ) against a tremolando A major chord sustained by the orchestra, as an accompaniment to the spoken conversation between Alwa and Schigolch which opens Act III, sc. 2.

Ex. 180

statements of the basic series. In both the Violin Concerto and *Lulu*, the growth of the tonal melody out of, or its absorption into, the twelve-note set is a conceit that comes about because of Berg's fascination with the mechanics of row-handling and his desire to reconcile, technically and intellectually, the two conflicting groups of material. On certain occasions Berg's methods of handling the twelve-note set are so elaborate and 'abstract' that, while they affect the audible features of the music, the methods themselves are incapable of being perceived. The relationship between the original set and the material produced by such methods depends upon factors other than the elaborate twelve-note procedures which, like Berg's use of ciphers and his use of mathematical and numerological formulae,[1] are essentially inaudible and private pre-compositional devices.

George Perle has opined that the methods by which the derivative sets in *Lulu* are obtained from the basic set of the opera indicate that Berg simply desired to supply some verbal evidence of his adherence to Schoenberg's principle that one should not 'use more than one series'[2]. Berg himself claimed that the use of derivative sets in *Lulu* was necessitated by the dramatic structure of the work, which required that the many different characters in the opera be individualized in some way.[3] The use of subsidiary sets, obtained from the basic set by methods similar to those employed in *Lulu*, is however a feature of all Berg's twelve-note works.

Rather than being the result either of a desire to demonstrate his conforming to Schoenbergian practice or of dramatic necessity when writing *Lulu*, Berg's use of subsidiary sets offers an interesting insight into his musical psychology. That he should feel it necessary to derive these subsidiary rows from the basic set by means of the extraordinary operations shown in his sketches is symptomatic of Berg's love of technical problems and his tendency to impose intellectual constraints upon himself. The operations themselves may have little bearing on the musical experience; the setting up of technical and intellectual problems, such as these derivative operations represent, was, as I shall try to show in the concluding chapter, an essential part of Berg's creative process.

[1] See pp. 225–30 below.
[2] Perle, *Serial Composition and Atonality*, 2nd edn., London, 1968, p. 74.
[3] See Reich, *Alban Berg*, London, 1965, p. 161.

# IV

# Rhythmic Techniques

Writing, in his dedicatory 'Open Letter' to Schoenberg, about the use of a 'constructive rhythm' in the 'Rondo Ritmico' of the Chamber Concerto Berg says:

> It was in a scene in my opera, *Wozzeck*, that I showed for the first time the possibility of this method of allotting such an important *constructive* role to a rhythm. But that such a degree of thematic transformation on the basis of a rhythm, such as I have attempted in the Rondo under discussion, is admissible, was proved to me by a passage from your 'Serenade', where in the last movement (admittedly for quite different motives) you place a number of motives and themes from preceding movements on rhythms that did not originally belong to them. And I have just read an article by Felix Greissle (*Anbruch*, February 1925) about the formal foundations of your Wind Quintet in which he writes, among other things, in the last sentence, 'The theme always has the same rhythm but in each case is made up of notes from a different series', and this seems to me to be further proof of the rightness of such a method of rhythmic construction.[1]

A study of the rhythmic techniques employed in Berg's music, however, suggests that this modest disavowal of originality is not to be taken seriously. Berg's experiments in rhythmic and metric organization are not confined to the use of such 'constructive rhythms', although such rhythms have a structural importance and are handled with an ingenuity and an inventiveness in his music that far surpass those of the works he cites as models.

I shall here use the term 'constructive rhythm' to denote any recurrent rhythmic pattern which operates independently of harmonic or melodic material. The ways in which Berg uses such rhythmic patterns vary from work to work and I shall later attempt to distinguish between different types of constructive rhythm.

While the 'Invention on a Rhythm' of *Wozzeck* (Act III, sc. 3) is the earliest example of Berg's use of a rhythmic pattern as the main structural element in an extended passage of music, rhythmic patterns which function

[1] In Reich, *Alban Berg*, London, 1965, pp. 146–7.

independently of melodic and harmonic material can be found in works as
early as the Four Songs, op. 2 of 1909–10. Here a syncopated rhythm, on a
repeated low E flat, at the end of the second song of the set reappears as the
rhythm of a repeated chord in bars 2–4 and bars 9–12 of the third song and
appears again as the rhythm of a melodic figuration at bars 4–6 of the fourth
song (Ex. 181).

Ex. 181

A similar rhythmic motive (Ex. 182) is employed in the first of the Three
Orchestral Pieces, op. 6 as a means of marking important structural points.

Ex. 182

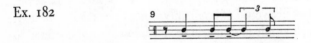

This rhythm, which gradually evolves during the opening bars of the
piece, is first stated by the trombone on a repeated E flat (bar 9). It later
appears on the whole orchestra as the rhythm of the cadential chord
which ends the introductory section (bars 14–15) and as the rhythm of
a repeated horn chord (bar 36) at the climax of the piece (heralding the
appearance of a new fanfare-like motive, itself based on this rhythmic
pattern, which is to become one of the main motives of the second piece).
The final appearance of this rhythm in the 'Präludium' on a repeated E flat
in the flute and bassoon parts at bar 42 marks the beginning of the closing
section of the piece – a harmonic retrograde of the opening. The final bars
(bars 119–20) of the second piece, 'Reigen', state the rhythm in its original

form. Rhythmic patterns similar to, but not identical with, this constructive rhythm appear at a number of points elsewhere in the Three Orchestral Pieces. Both the repeated bassoon chords at bar 25 of the 'Präludium' and the drum rhythm at bars 142–3 of the 'Marsch', for example, are reminiscent of this constructive rhythm, as is the rhythmic structure of the main theme of the 'Präludium' (bar 28). The rhythmic pattern of this main theme, with its characteristic triplet figure on the fourth beat, appears in a variety of melodic guises throughout the Orchestral Pieces.

A more extensive and more complicated use of rhythmic motives is to be found in the *Altenberg Lieder*. Mark DeVoto has drawn attention to the prominent role which the rhythm of the oboe figuration at bars 9–10 of the third song plays in the fifth song of the cycle.[1] In fact, this rhythm is but one variant of a rhythmic motive that appears throughout the cycle. The source of this rhythmic motive can be found in bars 26–8 of the first song[2] where it is announced in canon by the double basses and (in a modified form) by the cellos as part of a complex of superimposed string ostinati (Ex. 183).

Ex. 183

The rhythm of this modified cello figuration (which I shall call *x*) reappears on the strings in the second song (bars 5–6), where it overlaps with another variant of the same rhythm on the harp (Ex. 184).

Ex. 184

At both these appearances the rhythm is announced on a repeated single note. The rhythm of the oboe figuration at bars 9–10 of the third song, subsequently referred to as 'variant *y*', is closely related to rhythm *x* (Ex. 185).

Variant *y*, which has already appeared fleetingly as the rhythm of a series of clarinet chords in bars 24–5 of the first song, is usually associated with the

[1] See DeVoto, 'Some notes on the unknown Altenberg Lieder', *Perspectives of New Music*, 5, Fall/Winter, 1966, pp. 37–74.
[2] An almost inaudible version of the rhythm appears on the piano at bar 13 of the first song as part of the complicated web of sound with which the cycle opens.

melodic figuration shown in Ex. 185. This variant reappears, with similar melodic material, as the rhythm of a figuration shared between the flute,

Ex. 185

clarinet and oboe in bars 10–11 and later, in imitation, on the first violin, horn and cello in bars 35–8 of the fifth song of the cycle. In all these figurations the rhythm of variant *y* – the unbracketed part of Ex. 185 – appears on a repeated single note. The two rhythmic patterns – rhythm *x* and variant *y* – are superimposed at the climax of the final song (bars 30–35). The following diagram shows the rhythmic structure of bars 32–3 of the final song. Here rhythm *x* appears as repeated chords on the cello and clarinet, in canon with a modified form of *x* as repeated chords on the horns and violas. Against these, the main passacaglia theme of the song is stated, in the rhythm of a modified version of variant *y*, as repeated notes on the bassoon (Ex. 186).

Ex. 186

Variant *y* also appears as the rhythm of the final cadential chord of the cycle (Ex. 187).

Ex. 187

In the early works such recurrent rhythmic patterns function only as motivic elements and, unlike those of the later pieces, exert little effect on the overall structure of the work. The recurring thematic motives in the *Altenberg Lieder* have been discussed in Chapter 2.[1] Mark DeVoto has described the 'motivicity' of the *Altenberg Lieder* as being the cycle's 'most powerfully cohesive structural force';[2] the rhythmic figuration discussed

[1] See pp. 34–7 above.
[2] DeVoto, *Perspectives of New Music*, 5, Fall/Winter, 1966, p. 72.

above is simply one of a complicated web of motives which runs through the cycle and which binds the different songs into a single unit.

The rhythmic motives in the early works, and the way in which they are handled, already exhibit three features which are to characterize many of the constructive rhythms which appear in Berg's later works:

(i) The recurrent rhythmic patterns are highly syncopated, tending to cut across the established metrical pulse and to stress those parts of the bar that would normally be unaccented.

(ii) Although such rhythmic patterns are often applied to different thematic and harmonic material they are frequently stated by the percussion or as a repeated single note in such a way as to emphasize their purely rhythmic characteristics. Such rhythms are almost always stated initially in this 'non-melodic' form and are, thus, established as independent rhythmic motives before being applied to thematic material.[1]

(iii) The rhythmic patterns are often subjected to different kinds of modification, transformation or permutation. They may appear in augmented or diminished forms and may be extended, abbreviated or varied in a number of ways.

The rhythmic procedure to which Berg himself drew attention was the use of a 'Hauptrhythmus', which he describes, in his 'Open Letters' on the Chamber Concerto, as 'a rhythm that can be considered as a sort of a motive'.[2] In the scores of the Chamber Concerto, the Violin Concerto and *Lulu* such constructive rhythms are indicated by the symbol 'RH', a symbol which I shall adopt here. The angular and strongly syncopated nature of these patterns and Berg's practice of establishing them as self-sufficient rhythmic patterns before using them in association with thematic material (characteristics which have already been observed in the constructive rhythms employed in the early works) are usually amongst the distinguishing features of such Hauptrhythmen.

Occasionally a Hauptrhythmus first appears as the rhythm of a thematic figuration before being stated non-melodically – by the percussion or on a repeated note or chord – as a purely rhythmic motive. The Hauptrhythmen of the Violin Concerto, the Chamber Concerto and one of the variants of the RH of *Lulu* (that which is particularly associated with the Medical Specialist)[3] all evolve from melodic figurations in this way. It is significant, however, that the first appearance of the symbol 'RH' in the published scores of both the Violin Concerto and the Chamber Concerto coincides with the first non-melodic statement of their respective Hauptrhythmen.

Hans Redlich has described Berg's use of a Hauptrythmus as having its

---

[1] See W. M. Stroh, 'Alban Berg's "Constructive Rhythm"', *Perspectives of New Music*, Fall/Winter, 1968, pp. 18–31.
[2] Reich, *Alban Berg*, London, 1965, p. 145.
[3] See pp. 165–7 below.

roots in the fateful 'death rhythms' of Mahler's Sixth and Ninth Symphonies.[1] Emotional connotations similar to those of Mahler's 'death rhythms' seem to be an essential characteristic of Berg's Hauptrhythmen. It is known that Berg considered the RH of the second movement of the Violin Concerto as having a fateful programmatic significance[2] and the Hauptrhythmen of both *Wozzeck* and *Lulu* also acquire specific associations of this kind. The Hauptrhythmen of the op. 6 Orchestral Pieces and the Chamber Concerto inhabit a similar emotional world and, although he did not reveal the programmatic significance of these rhythms, Berg may well have regarded them as having the same kind of emotional and dramatic connotations as those of the Violin Concerto and the two operas.[3]

In certain works Berg uses constructive rhythms that are not projected as independent musical elements and which do not function as self-sufficient rhythmic motives in the way that the Hauptrhythmen do. I shall call such rhythms 'structural rhythms', a term that is not intended to imply that other constructive rhythms, such as Hauptrhythmen, do not affect the structure of the works in which they appear or that all such structural rhythms have a similar function; as I shall show, some structural rhythms may be easily perceived and act as recognizable rhythmic 'themes' whilst others may be employed as procedural devices of which the listener will probably be unaware. There is some evidence to suggest that Berg himself distinguished between Hauptrhythmen and other types of constructive rhythms, for although the structural rhythms of the third and fifth movements of the *Lyric Suite* (which are discussed in detail below) are indicated by 'RH' in the manuscript of the work this symbol does not appear in the published score.

The structural significance of Berg's rhythmic motives – whether Hauptrhythmen or structural rhythms – differs from work to work. The RH of the Violin Concerto is unusual in that it is used throughout as a rhythmic ostinato and produces no polyphonic or contrapuntal statements.[4] The finale of the Chamber Concerto, on the other hand, is one of Berg's most radical experiments in the possibility of using rhythm as a self-sufficient structural element.

The finale of the Chamber Concerto – which Berg entitles 'Rondo Ritmico' – is a simultaneous recapitulation of the two earlier movements. All the thematic and harmonic material of the finale has already appeared earlier in the work. The movement has, therefore, no independent thematic identity and the role of defining the formal structure – usually borne by the thematic, harmonic and tonal elements in a traditional Rondo or Sonata movement – is

---

[1] See Redlich, *Alban Berg*, London, 1957, p. 70.

[2] As is indicated in Reich's essay on the work which, Reich says, was suggested and authorized by Berg himself. (Reich, *Alban Berg*, London, 1965, pp. 178–9.)

[3] Berg does say in his 'Open Letter', however, that the Chamber Concerto hides 'a world of spiritual and human references' that would make 'the adherents of programme music go mad with joy'. (Reich, op. cit., p. 148.)

[4] See Stroh, *Perspective of New Music*, Fall/Winter, 1968, pp. 18–31.

here borne by the rhythmic elements. In his 'Open Letter' on the Chamber Concerto Berg summarizes the rhythmic structure of the movement as follows:

> Three rhythmic forms: a main rhythm, a subsidiary rhythm and a rhythm that can be considered as a sort of motive, are laid under the melody notes of the main and subsidiary voices. The rhythms occur with manifold variations – extended and abbreviated, augmented and diminished, in stretto and in reverse and in all imaginable metrical shifts and trans-positions, etc.[1]

The 'rhythm that can be considered as a sort of motive' is the Haupt-rhythmus which first appears in the second movement of the work, where it develops from a melodic figuration on the solo violin in bar 294. It is stated non-melodically, as a purely rhythmic motive, on a repeated A at bar 297 and appears in this and its retrograde form at a number of points in the second movement. Like all such Hauptrhythmen it has a strongly syncopated, angular rhythmic shape.

Although applied to various types of thematic material, the RH is fre-quently presented as a repeated single note or chord during the course of the finale itself. The Hauptrhythmus is shown in Ex. 188 below.

Berg does not identify the other two rhythms which he mentions in the 'Open Letter'. The 'main rhythm' (which I shall call RT) is the dotted rhythm which appears on the solo violin at the beginning of the 'Rondo Ritmico' (Ex. 188b); the 'subsidiary rhythm' (which I shall call RS) is probably the demi-semiquaver figuration which first appears at bar 550 (Ex. 188c).

Ex. 188

The following chart details the points at which these rhythms appear, and the way in which the RH itself is handled, during the course of the finale. The RH appears in various guises throughout the movement whilst the RT

[1] Reich, *Alban Berg*, London, 1965, p. 145.

and the RS recur in the way that a theme and an episode might in a traditional thematic Rondo movement:

### RONDO RITMICO

| Bar Numbers | Rhythmic Treatment | Formal Function |
|---|---|---|
| 481–534 | (Two appearances of RH at opening as a repeated single note and as a repeated chord) | Introduction (entitled 'Introduzione' in the score) |
| 534–9 | RT | Theme |
| 540–49 | RH (+fragmentary version of RS) | Transition |
| 550–70 | RS (+RH) | Episode |
| 571–90 | RT (+RH) | Return of Theme |
| 591–601 | (Modified RT) | Transition |
| 602–29 | RS (+modified RH and RT) | Return of Episode |
| 631–62 | RH (Retrograde and varied) | |
| 663–84 | (Fragments of RH retrograde and RT in modified versions) | |
| 685–96 | RH (Original and retrograde forms). One appearance of RS | Development Section |
| 696–709 | Unaltered passages from earlier movements juxtaposed | |
| 710b–37 | RT | Final return of Theme (entitled 'Coda' in the score) |
| 737–85 | RH and RT | (entitled 'Stretta' in the score) |

In a letter to Webern, dated 1 September 1923 – at which time the first movement of the Chamber Concerto was already written and the overall shape of the work must have been clear in his mind – Berg described the final movement of the work, the 'Rondo Ritmico', as a 'Sonata movement'.[1] As the above chart shows, the overall rhythmic plan of the movement defines a formal structure that has both Rondo and Sonata characteristics; the two rhythmic themes (RT and RS) can be regarded as the first and second subjects of a Sonata movement, the immediate return of these themes in bars 570–90 (RT) and bars 602–29 (RS) corresponding to the traditional repetition of a Sonata exposition.

The central part of the movement (bars 631–709) functions as a development section and is separated from what has gone before by a bar's silence. Certain methods of handling the rhythms are reserved for this section of the movement in the same way that certain thematic procedures are usually reserved for the development section of a traditional Sonata movement; the retrograde version of the RH, for example, appears for the first time in the finale at the beginning of this central development section, where a lengthy passage is devoted to various contrapuntal statements of this form.

The final section of the movement, which Berg entitles 'Coda' in the

[1] Redlich, *Alban Berg*, London, 1957, p. 116.

published score, is preceded by a double bar line. If Berg's directions are observed the final section is also preceded by a repetition of the whole 'Rondo Ritmico' up to that point. Beginning with the return of the main rhythm (RT) at bar 710b – and with the return of melodic material similar to that with which it was associated on its earlier appearances – the closing section acts as a Sonata recapitulation or a final reprise of the Rondo theme. Although the three most important appearances of the main rhythm (RT) are all associated with similar melodic material, the Sonata Rondo form of this finale is primarily defined by rhythmic elements.

Like the rhythmic motive of the *Altenberg Lieder,* the three rhythmic patterns of the Chamber Concerto are subjected to various forms of modification. The rhythmic configurations of much – though not all[1] – of the thematic material presented during the course of the movement spring directly from the RH, RT and RS or their variants. The RT and RS are extended or abbreviated and appear in various augmented or diminished forms; the Hauptrhythmus itself gives rise to a number of more complicated variants, some of which are shown in Ex. 189.

Ex. 189

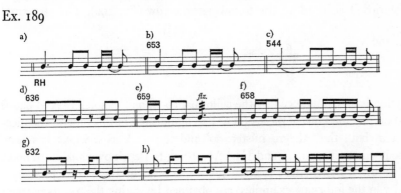

Ex. 189a shows the RH in its original form; 189b shows an inexact diminution; 189c an inexact augmentation; 189d an abbreviated version in which one quaver of the original is omitted and rests are substituted for part of the original note values; 189e and 189f both show retrograde versions of the RH in which added notes fill out the original note values; 189g a modified form in which the position of one note value is altered. This permuted version is marked 'RH' by Berg himself in the published score. Ex. 189h shows a rhythmic pattern which plays an important role in the passage from bar 676 to 684. The pattern is a compounded version of the original and the retrograde forms of the RH, although it bears a marked resemblance and has a similar consequent to the dotted rhythm of RT. This pattern is also marked 'RH' in the published score of the work.

[1] The development section, in particular, gradually moves towards a point at which unaltered passages from the earlier movements are juxtaposed.

Many appearances of the RH in the Chamber Concerto and other works are not indicated in the published score; a number of obvious statements of the Hauptrhythmen of the Chamber Concerto and *Lulu* are not marked with the symbol 'RH'. That Berg here indicates the rhythms shown in Exx. 189f and 189g by the symbol 'RH' demonstrates the extent to which he intentionally and quite consciously employed such apparently abstract, pre-compositional techniques as a means of determining the rhythmic structure of much of his music.

The *Lyric Suite* has no rhythmic motive which can be considered a true Hauptrhythmus. The third and fifth movements of the work, however, employ structural rhythms which, though never stated as independent motives, play an important role in determining the rhythmic structure of certain passages. The structural rhythm of the third movement is easily perceived; that of the fifth movement is applied in a more abstract way and, although it sometimes appears as the rhythm of a melodic figuration, is less easily apprehended.

The main body of the third movement of the *Lyric Suite* (the 'Allegro misterioso') is based on the following note row (Ex. 190). The structural

Ex. 190

rhythm is first announced by the cello (bars 6–9) on the notes F–A–B flat–B and on permutations of these notes. The significance of this four-note collection in both the 'Allegro misterioso' and the work as a whole has been discussed in Chapters II and III.[1] According to Berg's own analytical notes on the *Lyric Suite*,[2] the two segments which make up the pattern (marked *x* and *y* in the following examples) are obtained by stating the row as notes of equal value and dividing it into a seven- and a five-note group in the manner

Ex. 191

shown in Ex. 191 below. This method of dividing the note row appears in bar 10 of the movement. At the pitch shown in the above example, this method of derivation produces a chromatic scale covering the tritone F–B, the rhythmic segment *x* in the upper voice, and the rhythmic segment *y* in

---

[1] See pp. 27–9 and 82 above.
[2] See Berg's 'Nine Pages on the *Lyric Suite*', in Rauchhaupt (ed.), *Schoenberg – Berg – Webern: the String Quartets*, Hamburg, 1971, pp. 106 and 110.

the lower.[1] During the course of the movement these two rhythmic segments are employed simultaneously, to produce the interlocking figuration shown in Ex. 191 and in Ex. 192a, a figuration which I shall call the vertical form and shall indicate by the symbol $\frac{x}{y}$; they are also juxtaposed to produce the composite pattern shown in Ex. 192b (an augmented version of which is stated by the cello at bars 6–9) and which I shall call the horizontal form, indicating it by the symbol $x+y$.

Ex. 192

As with the Chamber Concerto, the formal structure of the 'Allegro misterioso' can be defined purely in terms of the way in which these rhythmic patterns are handled. The following chart shows how canonic passages based on these two segments alternate with passages based upon the semiquaver ostinato figuration with which the movement begins. Each canonic passage exploits a different method of handling the rhythmic segments which make up the structural rhythm. The first main section (bar 10–17) presents two statements of the vertical form $\frac{x}{y}$ as a rhythmic and melodic canon; bars 22–5 present the horizontal form $x+y$ on all four instruments as a series of rhythmic canons; bars 30–8 present a series of rhythmic canons based on a modified version of $\frac{x}{y}$ in which the two segments no longer interlock, as in Ex. 192a, but continually change position in relation to one another. The two methods of employing the segments, $x+y$ and $\frac{x}{y}$, are then superimposed in bars 42–4; this leads to a series of melodic canons based on the rhythm of the semiquaver ostinato figuration. The chart summarizes the formal design of the 'Allegro misterioso' from the beginning of the movement to the beginning of the central Trio (bar 70). The Trio is followed by a retrograde version of the 'Allegro misterioso'. The semiquaver ostinato figure is represented by the symbol $O$.

*ALLEGRO MISTERIOSO*

| Bar Numbers | Rhythmic Treatment | Formal Design |
|---|---|---|
| 1–10 | Horizontal form against $O$ | Introduction |
| 10–17 | Canonic statements of Vertical form | $\frac{x}{y}$ Canons |

[1] This method of dividing the row into two groups of notes, and the rhythmic segments which it produces, reappears in the final movement of the *Lyric Suite*, at the point at which the relationship between the two, apparently independent, series employed in the movement is revealed. (See pp. 127–8 above.)

| 17–19 | O | Episode |
|-------|---|---------|
| 19–21 | Horizontal form as chords | Transition |
| 22–5 | Canonic statements of Horizontal form | $x+y$ Canons |
| 25–8 | Horizontal form against O | Episode (cf. Introduction) |
| 30–8 | Canonic statements of Vertical form modified | $\frac{z^1}{y}$ Canons |
| 39–42 | O | Episode |
| 42–4 | Vertical and Horizontal forms superimposed | Transition |
| 45–69 | O | O Canons |

The rhythmic material of the 'Allegro misterioso' of the *Lyric Suite* thus results from operations which are applied to the pitch material of the movement. Other examples of rhythmic patterns similarly derived from the twelve-note set can be found elsewhere in Berg's music. The rhythmic motive associated with the figure of the Medical Specialist in *Lulu* (Ex. 193a) is compositionally derived from a twelve-note set in a way that is closely related to that which generates the rhythmic patterns of the 'Allegro misterioso' of the *Lyric Suite*. Ex. 193b below shows bars 113–4 of Act I, sc. 1 of *Lulu*, the passage in which Schigolch's series is derived from the basic series of the opera.[1] In these bars a modified version of the basic series is presented in notes of equal value, and divided between the upper and lower voices in the manner shown in the following example. The rhythm of the lower voice is that of the Medical Specialist's rhythmic motive, the significance of which will be discussed later in the chapter.

Ex. 193

The rhythmic patterns of the statements of basic cell I[2] in the 'Film Music' interlude, between Act II, scenes 1 and 2, of *Lulu* result from a similar procedure. Bars 670–74 of the 'Film Music' superimpose repeated statements of the basic series and the series associated with Schön, Alwa, the Schoolboy, Countess Geschwitz and the Athlete. Each series is presented as notes of equal value and at a pitch level at which it includes the notes of the basic cell in the order: E–A–B flat–E flat. The notes of the basic cell are extracted from each series and prolonged by the piano and the strings in the

---

[1] The methods by which Schigolch's serial trope is derived from the basic series are discussed on pp. 118–19 above.

[2] See p. 92 above.

manner illustrated in Ex. 194, the rhythm of each statement of the cell being determined by the position of its constituent notes in the relevant series.

Ex. 194

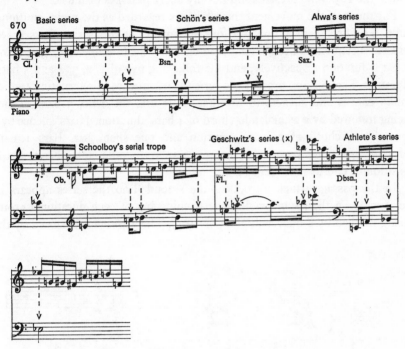

Berg's practice, when generating such rhythmic patterns, of removing other rhythmic features of the pitch material by presenting the series as notes of equal value (as in the above examples) has interesting parallels to his practice, when first establishing a Hauptrhythmus, of presenting it either on percussion or as a repeated note or chord and thus drawing attention to the rhythmic features of the music by removing thematic elements.[1]

The structural rhythm of the fifth movement of the *Lyric Suite* consists of a decreasing series of durational units in the ratio 5 : 4 : 3 : 2 : 1. This series is used in both its original and retrograde forms. Although the listener will be aware of the effects of this durational series, in that he will be aware of the complex polyrhythmic effects and the gradually increasing (or – in the retrograde form – decreasing) speed of events which its application produces, the series functions less as a perceptible rhythmic pattern than as a private compositional device. The series is neither as exclusively nor as consistently employed as are the constructive rhythms found in Berg's other works.

---

[1] It is significant that the relationship between the two rows employed in the finale of the *Lyric Suite* is also revealed in a passage in which the two interlock to produce a sequence of equal durations.

Apart from the first of the two Tenebroso Trio sections in the movement
(the rhythmic structures of which are almost completely based upon statements of this series) the series is employed as an incidental feature and determines the rhythmic presentation of only short passages of music.

For much of the movement the 3/8 bar is regarded as the basic durational
unit. The first Trio is built on four statements of this series: bars 51–80
present a sequence of ten overlapping chords – the first five of 5, 4, 3, 2 and
1 bar's duration respectively, and the following five of 1, 2, 3, 4 and 5 bars'
duration. Bars 86–100 present the series as a sequence of alternating tremolando chords and silences in the first violin and the cello, 5 bars' silence
being followed by a tremolando chord of 4 bars' duration, 3 bars' silence by a
tremolando chord of 2 bars' duration and one silent bar. Bars 101–15
present this same version of the series in retrograde, interchanging the
position of chords and silent bars.

In the passage which introduces the second Trio the series appears in
retrograde on the second violin, the opening bar of each durational group
being marked by a quaver duplet (Ex. 195). This passage is balanced by the

Ex. 195

passage which leads from the second Trio back into the main Presto movement, where the series appears in its original form with the opening bar of
each durational group being marked by a similar quaver duplet.

Chordal statements of the series, in which the 3/8 bar is regarded as the
main durational unit, also appear at bars 133–47 of the Presto section, where
the opening of the first Trio is superimposed upon the material of the Presto,
and at the end of the movement where two overlapping statements of the
series on the cello determine the rhythm of the final cadence. The following
diagram (Ex. 196) shows the rhythmic structure of the two voices in the cello
part in these final bars of the movement.

Elsewhere, the series determines the rhythmic presentation of incidental
thematic and harmonic elements; in such cases the quaver is regarded as the
basic durational unit and the series is presented as notes of 5, 4, 3, 2 and 1

quaver's duration respectively. A rhythmic canon based on this form of the rhythmic series, applied to a repeated rising seventh figuration which appears

Ex. 196

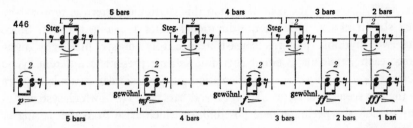

in all four instrumental parts, appears at bars 20–35. In the passage which follows (bar 36f.) a melodic figuration of four quavers' duration is presented in such a way that successive groups of entries are respectively 4, 3, 2, and finally 1 quaver apart (Ex. 197).

Ex. 197

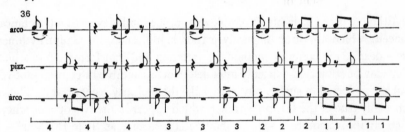

Another rhythmic canon appears at bars 421–30, where the main theme of the Presto is partitioned to produce four three-note chords which are then presented as a four-part canon (the duration of each repeated chord being determined by the rhythmic series). Further statements of the rhythmic series, associated with melodic material, appear in the first and second violin parts in bars 345–55 and on the first violin and viola in the important passage at bars 375–9, the point at which series *C* of the movement is arranged in such a way as to present simultaneous statements of the two hexachords of series *D*.[1] Durational series of this kind, which are never projected as rhythmic motives in their own right, play a smaller, but nonetheless important, role in Berg's music than do the more characteristic Hauptrhythmen. The isorhythmic organization of the accompaniment of Dr. Schön's Ballade[2] 'Das mein Lebensabend' in Act II, sc. 1 of *Lulu* is based on two such durational series. The thematic material of the accompaniment consists entirely

[1] See p. 128 above.
[2] See p. 202 below.

of the seven-note figure shown in Ex. 198a below, the last seven notes of Schön's series at I–O. In the opening and closing sections of the Ballade the rhythmic material consists of repeated statements of the durational series 3–1–1–1–4–2, the unit being the semiquaver. This rhythm is shown in Ex. 198b below. In the central section this rhythmic pattern is replaced by that shown in Ex. 198c on the durational series 1–1–1–3–4–1–1–3. Since the two rhythmic patterns consist ,respectively, of six and eight durations, each statement of either rhythmic scheme presents a different cyclic permutation of the seven-note thematic figure.[1] A similar example appears in the Inn scene (Act II, sc. 4) of *Wozzeck*, bars 692–736 of which systematically exploit the permutational possibilities which arise from the pairing of rhythmic and melodic patterns of different lengths.[2]

Ex. 198

Although Berg delights in employing procedural devices and technical conceits which are often of purely private significance, his Hauptrhythmen are – despite the complex methods of variation and transformation to which they may be subjected – usually intended to act as audible referential motives and are projected in such a way as to make them clearly recognizable. This is especially true of the Hauptrhythmen which appear in the two operas, where such rhythms acquire a specific motivic significance as 'Fate rhythms' – a connotation which, as I have said, seems to be inherent in Berg's use of Hauptrhythmen, even in his chamber and orchestral works – through their association with certain dramatic and textual events.

Of the two Hauptrhythmen in *Wozzeck*, one – that which appears in the opening scene of Act I – functions only as a rhythmic motive and has little effect on the large-scale musical structure of the scene. The rhythm is first announced in bar 25 on a repeated C sharp/D flat (the note on which it appears throughout and which acts as the tone centre[3] of the scene), where it accompanies Wozzeck's opening words, 'Jawohl, Herr Hauptmann'. Berg's usual practice of first presenting a Hauptrhythmus on a repeated single note or chord here acquires dramatic significance as a symbol of Wozzeck's

[1] The opening bars of Schön's Ballade reappear, at their original pitch and with their original contour, but without the rhythmic pattern which characterized their first appearance, when Jack re-enters having murdered Lulu in Act III, sc. 2 (bar 91f. of the Adagio of the published *Lulu* Suite). The association between the characters of Jack and Dr. Schön is discussed on pp. 198–200 below.
[2] See Hilmar, *Wozzeck von Alban Berg*, Vienna, 1975, p. 41.
[3] See Perle, *Music Forum*, I, New York, 1967, pp. 204–7.

impassive acceptance of the humilitation which he is forced to bear. The dramatic significance of the rhythm is further emphasized by its appearance in the orchestra at the beginning of Wozzeck's monologue (bar 136), where it accompanies the first statement of the words 'Wir arme Leut' ('We poor folk') and the musical motive associated with these words, and at the end of the monologue (bar 151) to the words, 'Folk like us are always unfortunate . . . I think that if we went to heaven we should have to make the thunder.' The rhythm appears in the orchestra as the Captain taunts Wozzeck (bars 76–9) and in the Captain's part as he laughs at Wozzeck's stupidity. Although this Hauptrhythmus dominates the opening scenes of the opera it appears at only two other points in the work, and in both instances in a modified form: a variant of the rhythm appears in the orchestra in Act II, sc. 1 (bar 114), as an accompaniment to the 'Wir arme Leut' motive, and reappears in Act III (bar 361) where the passage from Act II, sc. 1 is incorporated into the final orchestral interlude.

The other Hauptrhythmus in *Wozzeck* is that which appears in the interlude between Act III, scenes 2 and 3 and which forms the basis of the following scene, the 'Invention on a rhythm'. Appearing immediately after the murder scene, between the two crescendos on the note B natural (the note which dominates the murder scene itself), the rhythm becomes a symbol of the murder of Marie. The Hauptrhythmus is repeated in various forms throughout the tavern scene (Act III, sc. 3) and determines the rhythmic presentation of all the important musical elements in that scene, the obsessive repetition of the RH representing Wozzeck's memory of the crime. The increasing tension of this scene and the mounting sense of guilt and fear which culminates in Wozzeck's panic-stricken exit at the end of the scene, is reflected in the increasing complexity of the polyphonic statements of this rhythm. The rhythm appears fleetingly in the following scene (Act III, sc. 4, bars 252–4) as Wozzeck searches for the knife which can incriminate him.

During the course of the tavern scene the RH appears in augmentation, diminution, in various overlapping canonic statements and in a number of modified forms such as the inexact augmentation shown in Ex. 199b and the

Ex. 199   a) RH   [musical notation]

b)   [musical notation]

c)   [musical notation]

form shown in Ex. 199c in which additional notes fill in the original note values.

The rhythm does not appear in its retrograde form and is not subjected to
the more complex methods of variation and permutation employed in the
Chamber Concerto. These more complex methods are, however, an important feature of Berg's handling of the Hauptrhythmus of *Lulu*.

Unlike the Hauptrhythmen of *Wozzeck*, each of which plays an important
role in only one scene of the work, the Hauptrhythmus of *Lulu* permeates
the whole opera, appearing at every important point in the development of
the dramatic action and having a far-reaching musical and dramatic function.[1]

The RH of *Lulu* is shown in Ex. 200. Statements of this RH not only open

Ex. 200

and close all three acts of the opera and mark every turning point in Lulu's
career but also subtly underline every significant word and phrase. Thus, for
example, a statement of the RH as a repeated chord accompanies Dr. Schön's
prophetic words, 'One cannot even be sure of one's own life' in his Ballade
'Das mein Lebensabend' in Act II, sc. 1; the significance of these words
becomes clear when the same passage of music reappears as the introduction
to the 'Five-strophe Aria' which culminates in Schön's death. The same
version of the RH appears elsewhere in Act II, sc. 1, when Lulu accuses
Schön of suffering from a persecution complex – Schön himself has told the
police in Act I that the Painter's death was caused by his suffering from a
persecution complex. Particularly significant are the overlapping statements
of the RH which accompany the shouts and cheers of the off-stage audience
watching Lulu's theatrical performance in Act II, sc. 3, cheers which lead
Alwa to comment that the crowds sound like 'beasts in a menagerie at feeding
time' – a comment that is crucial to our understanding of the work.[2]

Extended passages of music based on canonic statements of the RH or its
variants accompany the deaths of the Medical Specialist (Act I, sc. 1), the
Painter (Act I, sc. 2), Dr. Schön (Act II, sc. 1) and Alwa (Act III, sc. 2).[3]
The coda theme of the Sonata movement of Act I, which represents Schön's
inability to free himself of Lulu, is based upon repeated statements of the
RH.[4] Similar repeated statements appear in the orchestral bass at the opening
of, and at various points during, the three ensemble numbers of Act III, sc. 1,
where the presence of the RH underlines the superficiality and falseness of

[1] The following discussion of the rhythmic procedures employed in *Lulu* is adapted
from my article: 'Some rhythmic and metric techniques in Alban Berg's *Lulu*', *Musical
Quarterly*, 56: 3, July, 1970.
[2] See p. 234 below.
[3] See Perle, *Music Review*, 26, 1965, p. 273.
[4] The significance of this coda theme is examined in Perle, *Music Review*, 25, 1964,
pp. 311–19.

the apparently brilliant stage action.[1] Act III, sc. 2, is completely dominated by statements of the opera's Hauptrhythmus.[2]

Two important variants of the RH of *Lulu* are shown in Ex. 201. A further variant, which is particularly associated with the Countess Geschwitz, will be discussed later. The variant shown in Ex. 201a is associated with the Medical

Ex. 201

a)

b)

Specialist in Act I, sc. 1, of the opera and reappears in Act III, sc. 2, when Lulu enters with the Professor.[3] That shown in Ex. 201b accompanies the Canon between Lulu and the Painter in Act I, sc. 1. Both of these variants evolve gradually from the music of Act I, sc. 1, and appear in a number of fragmentary versions before being stated in their complete form. Fragmentary or modified statements of the Medical Specialist's RH appear in bar 91 and bar 103; that in bar 91, on a repeated F sharp, is marked 'RH' in the published score of the opera. The variant which accompanies the Canon (Act I, sc. 1, bar 156f.) evolves from the piano figuration at bars 125–31, although the symbol RH does not appear until it returns in a purely rhythmic form on the triangle at bar 167.

The most obvious statements of the variant shown in Ex. 201a appear in the Melodrama which accompanies the death of the Medical Specialist in the first scene of the opera; here it appears for the first time as purely rhythmic motive. The first half of the Melodrama is built upon canonic statements of this RH variant on the percussion; the second half upon statements of the variant as a repeated two-note chord on harp or as overlapping vocal and instrumental statements. However, the rhythmic structure of much of the passage from bar 107 to bar 225 of this first scene is affected by the characteristics of the Medical Specialist's RH variant. The first complete statement of this variant appears as a melodic figuration at bars 108–10, where it accompanies Alwa's words, 'But where is your husband?' Two statements of the Medical Specialist's RH are here followed by a further variant which incorporates a number of extra notes into the original rhythmic pattern; this

[1] The opening bars of the first of these ensembles (which are also the opening bars of the Third Act) can be seen at bars 9–17 of the Prologue to Act I, where they appear with a different time signature and at a different speed.

[2] Much of the music of Act III, sc. 2, consists of a reprise of those sections of music from the earlier Acts which are themselves based on the RH. The formal structure of Act III is shown in Ch. V, p. 206 below.

[3] The role of the Professor in Act III, sc. 2, is played by the same actor as played the Medical Specialist in Act I. The doubling of certain roles in *Lulu* is discussed in Ch. V, pp. 198–200 below.

further variant is marked *z* in Ex. 202. The rhythmic shape of the Medical
Specialist's RH and of the variant *z* in the Ex. 202 are used with considerable

Ex. 202

freedom and are subjected to a number of methods of rhythmic transformation during the course of the scene. Many of the resulting transformations
are far removed from the RH from which they derive. The Medical Specialist's
RH thus affects, and is absorbed into, the musical texture of the whole scene.

   The following example shows two of the many variations of the Medical
Specialist's RH employed in the introduction and the coda to the Canon in
this scene. In the first bar of Ex. 203a the cello presents an augmented version
of the Medical Specialist's RH in which the first note (B flat) is extended
from three to five demi-semiquavers' duration; in the second bar the original
version of the Medical Specialist's RH is combined with a version of the
variant *z* in the vocal part. The three-note pattern *x* which ends the vocal
phrase appears throughout the scene. This pattern can be seen in the two
subsidiary instrumental parts of Ex. 203a – both of which are themselves
variants of the Medical Specialist's RH – the bass and the bassoon line using
this three-note figure to point the RH rhythm of the cello part in the first bar
of the example, the flute and viola line using it in the second bar. The second
bar of Ex. 203b combines an augmented version of variant *z* with a statement

Ex. 203

a)
147 LULU

Ja, mir wär'es auch lie - ber,   er wä-re endlich da.

Fl., Vla.

Vlc.

Cb., Bsn.

b)

137 LULU

Mein Mann——wird gleich hier    sein    mir scheint    da    ist er

Bsn.

of the original version of the Medical Specialist's RH in the voice part. Similar examples can be seen in bar 141, where the durations of the original version of the Medical Specialist's RH on the woodwind are partly filled with the three-note figure *x*, and in bar 136, where a version of variant *z* is shared between the double bassoon and voice parts. The three-note figure *x* which dominates the introduction and the coda to the Canon in Act I, sc. 1, is particularly associated with the Painter and reappears at the beginning of the next scene where it introduces the Duettino between the Painter and Lulu.

The variant shown in Ex. 199c above represents the RH in skeletal form and appears at the climax of the Monoritmica. The Monoritmica, which leads up to the suicide of the Painter in Act I, sc. 2, is an extended passage of over three hundred bars, the rhythmic structure of which is based throughout on repeated or superimposed statements of the RH.

The handling of the RH in the Monoritmica can be understood as an extension and an intensification of the techniques employed in the Rondo Ritmico of the Chamber Concerto. Whereas in the last movement of the Chamber Concerto the rhythmic transformation of themes from the earlier movements served a purely musical purpose, in *Lulu* the same techniques serve both a musical and a complex dramatic purpose.[1]

The Monoritmica is the only section of *Lulu* which makes extensive use of the retrograde form of the RH. The retrograde first begins to appear at bars 675–6 (it has appeared only once before in the opera, at bar 85, where it led 'backwards' from the Prologue into Act I, sc. 1). Even in the Monoritmica, however, the retrograde RH is used far less frequently than is the original form, its appearance being usually reserved for particular effects. The typically Bergian conceit of setting Schön's remarks 'I didn't come here to make a scandal, I came to save you from one' (bars 680–1) and 'With an upbringing such as Mignon's had you can't expect her to abide by the standards of bourgeois society' (bars 708–9) as melodic and rhythmic palindromes, which I have already mentioned,[2] are examples of such 'effects'.

The Monoritmica is also subjected to a highly organized method of tempo

[1] The musico-dramatic design of the Monoritmica is discussed on pp. 212–15 below.
[2] See pp. 104–5 above.

control which determines the overall shape of the passage. Starting with a metronome marking of ♪ = 76 at bar 666 (the tempo of the Sonata coda which leads into the Monoritmica), the tempo progresses through a sequence of mathematically related metronomic speeds until it reaches 𝅗𝅥 = 132 at bar 748; it then decreases to the original ♪ = 76, at which point (bar 957) it resumes the interrupted recapitulation of the Sonata coda. Of the eighteen sections which make up the first half of the passage, seven have metronome markings moving from ♪ = 76 to ♪ = 132 (marked ♪ = 76, 84, 92, 100 108, 120 and 132 respectively), six from 𝅗𝅥 = 76 to 𝅗𝅥 = 132 (𝅗𝅥 = 76, 86, 96, 106, 118 and 132) and five from 𝅗𝅥 = 76 to 𝅗𝅥 = 132 (𝅗𝅥 = 76, 86, 96, 112 and 132). The eighteen sections of the second half of the Monoritmica have the same metronome markings but in the reverse order. The central climax coincides with the discovery of the Painter's corpse.

Although the dramatic effect of this composed accelerando–ritardando is unusual,[1] this method of controlling and interrelating tempi through the use of mathematically related metronome markings is a common feature of Berg's music.

In many sections of *Lulu* Berg exploits the sense of formal cohesion that such a sequence of interrelated tempi can give as a means of binding the separate numbers into larger musical and dramatic units. Act II, sc. 1, of *Lulu*, for example, consists of three main dramatic units – a scene between Lulu and Dr. Schön (which is preceded by a short introductory scene with the Countess Geschwitz), an ensemble scene between Lulu and her admirers (which includes the exposition of Alwa's Rondo movement) and a final scene between Lulu and Dr. Schön which culminates in Schön's death. The first of these three units consists of an opening recitative, a solo Ballade for Schön and a Cavatina for Schön and Lulu. The opening recitative moves between three interrelated tempi marked ♩ = 52, ♩ = 65 and ♩ = 78 (inter-related in that these tempi are 13 × 4, 13 × 5 and 13 × 6 respectively). The Ballade has a metronome marking of ♩ = 52. Beginning with a metronome marking of ♩ = 65, the Cavatina moves to ♩ = 78 and ends ♩ = 52, the tempo at which the whole section began. The central section of the Ballade has a metronome marking of ♩ = 66 rather than ♩ = 65; this tempo is related to that of Dr. Schön's Aria in the final section of the scene, which begins with a repetition of a passage from the earlier Ballade in note values that are twice as long as those of the original and which has a metronome marking of 𝅗𝅥 = 132 (i.e. ♩ = 66). The Grave passage which accompanies Schön's

---

[1] Though not employing mathematically related metronome markings, Act III, sc. 2, of *Lulu* is, however, based on an overall tempo plan similar to that of the Monoritmica. The scene is designed as a composed ritardando, its ten sections moving from the opening Presto (𝅗𝅥 = 184) through Allegro (𝅗𝅥 = 136), Allegretto (𝅗𝅥 = 100), Moderato (𝅗𝅥 = 88), Sostenuto (𝅗𝅥 = 76), Andante (𝅗𝅥 = 67), Adagio (𝅗𝅥 = 58), Lento (𝅗𝅥 = 52) and Largo (𝅗𝅥 = 46) to the final Grave (𝅗𝅥 = 42).

death at the end of the scene has a metronome marking of 𝅗𝅥 = 44, at which tempo the duration of a minim is equal to that of a dotted minim at the 𝅗𝅥 = 66 of the Aria which precedes it. Not only is each of the three units which make up the scene thus defined as a separate musical and dramatic structure, but the first and the last units are also linked in a way that reflects their dramatic similarities and separates them from the central ensemble section.

One of the most extended and most interesting examples of this technique occurs in the second and third scenes of Act I of *Lulu*, where a series of interrelated tempi bind together nearly a thousand bars of music. The following diagram shows the metronome markings of the whole of this section, from the opening of Dr. Schön's Sonata movement at bar 533 of Act I, sc. 2 to the end of Act I, sc. 3:

| Bar Numbers | Formal Function | Metronome Marking |
|---|---|---|
| *Act I, sc. 2* | *Sonata Exposition* | |
| 533 | First subject | 𝅗𝅥 = 80 |
| 554 | Bridge passage: Section A | 𝅗𝅥. = 46  (𝅗𝅥 = 69) |
| 563 | Section B | 𝅗𝅥. = 46 |
| 579 | Section C | 𝅗𝅥 = 52 |
| 587 | Second subject (Gavotte) | 𝅗𝅥 = 69 |
| 615 | Coda | 𝅗𝅥 = 58 |
| | *First Sonata Reprise* | |
| 625 | First subject | 𝅗𝅥 = 80 |
| 633 | Bridge passage | 𝅗𝅥. = 46 |
| 650 | Second subject | No metronome marking (See footnote, p. 170) |
| 666 | Coda | 𝅗𝅥 = 76 |
| 669 | *Monoritmica* | 𝅗𝅥 = 76 accelerating to 𝅗𝅥 = 132 and returning to ♪ = 76 |
| 957 | *Interlude* | 𝅗𝅥 = 38 (𝅗𝅥 = approx. 40 at end) |
| | | |
| *Act I, sc. 3* | | |
| 992 | Jazz band | ♪ = 120 ( ♪♪♪ = ³♪♪♪ of previous tempo) |
| 1020 | Orchestra | 𝅗𝅥 = 60 |
| 1113 | Chorale | 𝅗𝅥 = 80  (𝅗𝅥. = 𝅗𝅥 of previous tempo) |
| 1150 | Orchestra ('Animato') | 𝅗𝅥 = 120 (♪. = 𝅗𝅥 of previous tempo) |
| 1155 | Jazz band | 𝅗𝅥 = 120 (as at bar 992 but note lengths doubled) |
| | *Sonata Development* | |
| 1209 | | 𝅗𝅥 = 80  (𝅗𝅥 = 𝅗𝅥. of previous tempo) |
| 1236 | | 𝅗𝅥 = 52  (𝅗𝅥 = 𝅗𝅥. of previous tempo) |
| 1248 | | 𝅗𝅥 = 80 |
| 1275 | | 𝅗𝅥 = 120 (𝅗𝅥 = ♪. of previous tempo) |
| 1284 | | 𝅗𝅥 = 80 |
| | *Final Sonata Reprise* | |
| 1289 | First subject | 𝅗𝅥 = 80 |
| 1299 | Bridge passage | 𝅗𝅥 = 138 (𝅗𝅥 = 69 as at bar 554) |
| 1309 | Second subject | No metronome marking but indication 'Quasi tempo di Gavotte' (i.e. 𝅗𝅥 = 69) |
| 1356 | Coda | 𝅗𝅥 = 46  (𝅗𝅥 = 𝅗𝅥. of previous tempo) |

The relationships between the tempi of the different sections are shown in brackets in the above diagram;[1] those of the Sonata exposition, however, demand a more detailed discussion.

In the bars immediately preceding the bridge passage (bars 552–3) quaver and semiquaver triplets are introduced into the 4/4 metre. The exposition of the first subject ends with a ritardando which slows the music down to a speed at which the quaver triplets of the first subject group are equal to three quavers in the 6/8 metre of the bridge passage. The bridge passage is in three sections, the first two of which have a metronome marking of ♩. = 46 (i.e. ♩ = 69). In the first of these sections the metre is 6/8 and the quaver is the basic note value; in the second, the metre is 3/4 and the crotchet is the basic note value. To the listener the second section seems to be moving at half the speed of the first – that is, the dotted crotchet seems to equal 23 and the crotchet 34½. In the third section the material of the first and second sections is superimposed. The third section has a metronome marking of ♩ = 52, a tempo which is half-way between the ♩ = 69 of the first and the apparent ♩ = 34½ of the second section of the bridge passage; Berg writes 'slower than the first and faster than the second time' in the score at this point. The value of a crotchet in this third section is equal to that of the dotted crotchet in the first subject group (♩ = 80, ♩. therefore = 52). The tempo of the second subject (Gavotte) is the same as that of the first section of the bridge passage.

Not only are the different tempi of the two scenes covered by the Sonata movement related to one another mathematically. In many cases (and particularly in the Sonata development of Act I, sc. 3) the relationships between the tempi are shown in the music itself, a new speed evolving from the preceding speed so that the listener feels the gradual progression from one tempo to the next. Thus the transition from ♩ = 120 to ♩ = 180 at the beginning of the development (bar 1209) is effected by introducing the first subject as quaver quadruplets into the 6/4 metre of the previous section; at the transition from ♩ = 80 to ♩ = 120 (bars 1274–5) a triplet quaver at ♩ = 80 becomes a quaver at ♩ = 120; at the return from ♩ = 120 to ♩ = 80 (bars 1283–4) the coda theme in crotchet duplets is introduced into a 6/4 bar of the ♩ = 120 tempo; the transition from ♩ = 69 to ♩ = 46 (bars 1355–6) is effected by the introduction of a syncopated dotted quaver rhythm which becomes the quaver pulse of the following section. Ex. 204 below shows

---

[1] There are a number of inconsistencies in the metronome markings and the tempo indications of the published score. The reprise of the Gavotte (bar 650), for example, has no metronome mark but has the indication 'Quasi Tempo di Gavotte' (i.e. ♩ = 69); the following Coda reprise, however, has the mm. ♩ = 76 and the indication, 'Twice as slowly'. Similarly the indication ♫ = ♫ appears at bar 1299 of the Final Reprise (when the tempo changes from ♩ = 80 to ♪ = 138) but is not preceded by the necessary ritardando marking. Had Berg lived to supervise the publication of the score he would, perhaps, have removed these and similar inconsistencies.

a passage from the final Sonata reprise (bars 1336–40) in which two tempi are superimposed; in this passage the music of the Gavotte (♩ = 69) is under-pinned by a 'syncopated' statement of the coda theme moving at the speed at which it appears in the final bars of the act (Ex. 204).

Ex. 204

In a letter to Reich, Berg pointed out that the dramatic construction of *Lulu* necessitated a different approach from that adopted in *Wozzeck*: 'Lulu called for a musical orientation more along the lines of the human personali-ties that run through the work . . . and practically a leitmotif treatment of both melodic and harmonic elements.'[1] In fact, this leading-motive-treat-ment of the musical elements is much more radical than Berg suggests for, as well as being associated with characteristic harmonic and melodic figura-tions, several of the figures in *Lulu* are also associated with specific rhythmic and metric patterns.[2] The characters most clearly associated with such rhythmic and metric patterns are Schigolch, the Athlete and the Schoolboy (the three characters who appear in the big ensemble scene at the end of Act II, sc. 1) and the Countess Geschwitz.

The figure of Schigolch is associated with quadruplets in simple metre. In the ensemble scene of Act II, sc. 1 and the central section of the Chamber Music of Act I, sc. 2, the figuration appears as quaver quadruplets in 4/4 (Alla breve); in the slower moving tempi of the outer sections of the Act I Chamber Music and the Prologue, where the Animal Trainer identifies Schigolch as the 'worm', the figuration appears as semiquaver quadruplets in 4/4 or 3/4 metre, in Act III, sc. 1, as semiquaver quadruplets in 2/4.

The Athlete is associated with compound metre. Quaver triplets are introduced into the 3/4 metre of the Prologue and lead to a short section in 9/8 when the Animal Trainer, accompanied by the Athlete's note row, refers to the 'bear'; triplets are also introduced into the 2/4 recitative metre of

[1] Reich, *Musical Quarterly*, 22, 1936, pp. 383–401.
[2] Some of the characters in the opera are also associated with certain instrumental colours. (See p. 215f. below.)

Act II, sc. 2 for the Athlete's short arioso at bar 751f. In the ensemble scene of Act II, sc. 1, the Athlete's part is notated either in 6/4 ($\downarrow$. = 56) against the 4/4 ($\downarrow$ = 56) of Schigolch's part, or as crotchet triplets in 4/4. Throughout the duet between the Athlete and Lulu in Act III, sc. 1 (bars 272–330) Lulu's part is written in 3/4 and the Athlete's in 6/8. The Schoolboy is usually associated with quaver triplets in 9/8, the metre of the Chamber Music in Act II, sc. 2, which starts as the Schoolboy enters and which includes his short arietta, 'Mein Lebens ist so wenig mehr wert'. The Schoolboy is less important a figure than either Schigolch or the Athlete and his musical characteristics are less clearly defined. He is occasionally allotted quaver duplets instead of triplets and his part often seems to fluctuate between 9/8 and 6/8.

One of Berg's sketches for the opera suggests that he was, at one point, during the composition of the work, considering organizing the rhythmic structure of the ensembles of Act III, sc. 1 by allotting different durational patterns to each of the main characters involved.[1]

The Countess Geschwitz is associated not with a particular metre but with a rhythmic pattern consisting of a group of notes of increasing or decreasing durations (Exx. 205a and 205b). The two figures are often juxtaposed to form a rhythmic unit with an accelerando–ritardando pattern (Ex. 205c); in such cases the rhythmic retrograde is usually a melodic retrograde as well.

Ex. 205

a)                              b)                              c)

The accelerando–ritardando pattern first appears in the Prologue (bars 39–41) when the Countess is identified as the 'crocodile' in the Animal Trainer's menagerie (Ex. 206) and, thereafter, permeates all the music associated with her. The figuration appears, for example, when the Countess

Ex. 206

1 The Marquis was to have been associated with the durational pattern ♫♫ , Lulu with ♫ , Schigolch with ♫♫♫ , the Athlete with ♫♫ , the Banker with ♪♪♪ and the rest of the Ensemble with ♪♩.

enters and hides behind the firescreen in Act II, sc. 1 (bars 89–92), and when she enters at the moment of Schön's death (bars 606–7). The same pattern dominates the recitative which opens Act II and also appears at bars 748–51 of the second scene of the act, where it accompanies a recitative by the Countess, and at bars 818–33 as the Countess prepares to leave for the hospital where she will change places with Lulu. The most important and extensive statements of the Countess's rhythm appear in Act III, sc. 2.[1] The vocal and bass lines of the Nocturno[2] in Act III, sc. 2 consist entirely of repeated statements of this rhythmic pattern. Similarly, bars 1–45 of the Adagio of the *Lulu* Suite, which Berg intended to accompany a passage in Act III, sc. 2 when the Countess is alone on the stage, are almost completely built of variants of this rhythmic pattern. The same pattern appears later in the *Lulu* Suite at bars 80–89.

An important variant of the RH, built of a group of notes of decreasing duration, is specifically associated with the Countess Geschwitz. This variant first appears in bar 779 and in bar 808 of Act II, sc. 2 (Exx. 207a and 207b) and reappears in Act III, sc. 1 when the Countess agrees to a rendez-vous with the Athlete (Ex. 207c). In all three examples the RH and its retro-grade are juxtaposed to form the accelerando–ritardando pattern associated with the Countess. Canonic statements of this RH lead up to the point in Act III, sc. 2 when the Countess reveals the portrait of Lulu. This RH variant also appears at the end of Act III at the moment when Jack the Ripper stabs the Countess (bars 90–91 of the *Lulu* Suite: Ex. 207d). The four statements of this RH variant shown in Ex. 207 are all marked 'RH' by Berg and all four present the RH 'non-melodically' as a repeated single note or chord or on the percussion. Reiterated statements of the Countess's RH also determine the

Ex. 207

---

[1] The increasing prominence of the role played by the Countess's rhythmic pattern is mirrored by the extent to which her ordered series gradually emerges during the course of the opera. (See p. 122 above.)

[2] See p. 206 below.

rhythm of the figuration that appears in bars 25–8 of the Adagio of the *Lulu* Suite.

Berg's use of mathematical durational schemes, as a means of determining the large-scale structure of his music, and his conception of rhythmic patterns as self-sufficient elements – elements which could be subjected to various methods of transformation and permutation and to which could be applied many of the procedures traditionally applied to thematic elements – has no precedent in eighteenth- and nineteenth-century music. Indeed, such was the nature of the tonal system and so close the interdependence of rhythm, metre, melody and harmony within that system that such a concept would have been quite alien to the musical thought of Berg's more immediate forerunners. Eric Gräbner has pointed out[1] that although Berlioz (in his 1837 article on 'The Future of Rhythm') had lamented that no composer had treated rhythm as anything but 'an adjunct of melody and harmony', to have opposed the interdependence of harmony and rhythm would, given the nature of the tonal system, have produced only incoherence. Even Berlioz's own ingenious handling of rhythm and metre takes into account, and ultimately depends on, the interdependence of these musical elements. To find rhythmic and durational techniques comparable to those used in Berg's music one must go back to the Renaissance composers – composers with whom, in this and other respects, Berg has much in common.[2]

[1] See Gräbner, 'Some aspects of rhythm in Berlioz', *Soundings*, 2, 1971–72.
[2] See footnote 1, p. 239 below.

# V

# Formal Structures

Nowhere is that fusion of conservative and progressive elements which characterizes Berg's music more apparent than in his handling of large-scale formal structures. Unlike either Schoenberg or Webern, Berg was never really attracted to the shorter musical forms as a means of expression. His sense of emotional and spiritual kinship with the Mahlerian symphonic tradition, his overtly traditional conception of thematic structure and development, his natural lyricism and his innate feeling for the large-scale theatrical and dramatic gesture all demanded more room in which to expand than was afforded by the inhibiting confines of the miniature forms.

All Berg's music, with the exception of the op. 5 Clarinet Pieces and the settings of individual songs, is conceived on a large scale. Even the *Altenberg Lieder*, although consisting of a sequence of miniatures, reveals a large-scale architectural plan when the cycle is considered as a whole.

Berg's adherence to formal designs of a kind traditionally employed in tonal music has been frequently noted. Indeed, he himself drew attention to his use of these traditional formal archetypes in his 1929 lecture on *Wozzeck* and elsewhere.[1] *Wozzeck* is, to a large extent, based on form-types, such as passacaglia, fugue and the eighteenth-century dance suite, that are not only traditional but are, as Berg himself observed, 'more or less archaic'.[2] *Lulu* reverts to the vocal forms of the traditional eighteenth-century 'number' opera. I shall discuss the formal organization of the two operas in detail later.

No archaic forms are employed in Berg's instrumental music, and far fewer specific traditional forms than in the two operas. It is a characteristically Bergian paradox that while those specific forms that are traditionally associated with 'absolute' music appear, and are handled quite strictly, in the vocal works (and, with the exception of the Passacaglia which forms the last of the *Altenberg Lieder*, only in the operas) the instrumental music tends to employ forms, such as ternary form, rondo or scherzo and trio, which,

[1] See Redlich, *Alban Berg*, London, 1957, p. 268 and Berg, 'Die Musikalische Formen in meiner Oper *Wozzeck*' in Reich, *Alban Berg*, Vienna, 1937, pp. 178–80.
[2] Redlich, *Alban Berg*, London, 1957, p. 269.

although traditional, are freer or more simple in outline than the specific form-types employed in the two operas.

Of the more specific formal patterns associated with tonal music only sonata form is regularly employed in Berg's instrumental music and even this is subjected to radical modification. Amongst the instrumental works only the op. 1 Piano Sonata and the first movement of the op. 3 Quartet employ the thematic plan and the three-section division of the traditional sonata form. Even in these works, however, the usual distinctions between the different subject groups are obliterated by their common motivic content. Thematic relationships between the different subject groups are not uncommon in eighteenth-century sonata movements; they are, for example, a feature of many of Haydn's sonata structures. When there are no thematic contrasts in an eighteenth-century sonata movement the formal design is still clearly articulated by the tonal structure. In the tonally more ambiguous musical idiom of Berg's op. 1, however, key relationships can no longer define the precise role played by a thematic element and the whole structure becomes more fluid and more ambiguous as a result of these motivic associations.

I have already shown[1] how in the Piano Sonata the articulative function of traditional key relationships is taken over by the different tempi associated with each theme. In the first movement of the String Quartet op. 3 the different subject groups, although motivically linked, have distinct thematic identities and the movement presents a relatively regular and clear sonata structure. The formal ambiguity of the Quartet lies not within this first movement itself, but in the way in which the two movements relate to one another,[2] the second movement, in many respects, representing a reworking of the first movement material. Redlich has suggested that the relationship between the two movements is that of exposition and development section,[3] the sonata structure of the first movement thus forming a part of the larger sonata structure of the work as a whole. Such a relationship between the smaller and larger formal designs of a work is a frequent feature of Berg's music. On the other hand, the String Quartet may also be regarded as the first example of Berg's using the same thematic material to produce two or more quite different movements, a procedure later employed in, amongst other works, the *Altenberg Lieder* (where the first and last songs of the cycle, though very different, are built of the same basic motivic material) and, in a different form, in the Chamber Concerto (where 'a variation movement of c.9 minutes duration and a broadly sung, extended Adagio' are combined to make a new movement of 'a quite independent tone'.)[4]

---

[1] See pp. 31–2 above.
[2] See pp. 32–4 above.
[3] See Redlich, *Alban Berg,* London, 1957, p. 50.
[4] Berg, 'Open letter on the Chamber Concerto' in Reich, *Alban Berg,* London, 1965, p. 145.

That Berg used anything approaching a traditional sonata form in op. 1 and op. 3 may, perhaps, be due to the influence of Schoenberg, under whom Berg was studying when the works were written. It is significant that not only do those peculiar formal designs which characterize all Berg's mature music first begin to appear in the *Altenberg Lieder* (that is, in the first of the works written after his period of study with Schoenberg) but also that, although sonata form is often felt as a background presence in many of the later works, Berg never, except in the two operas, used a traditional sonata structure in any of the works written after the op. 3 Quartet. Thus, the opening movement of the *Lyric Suite* has the general plan of a sonata structure, in that the first half of the movement follows the usual thematic lay-out of an exposition section and this exposition is then recapitulated in the second half, but the movement has no development section and, as in the Piano Sonata, thematic distinctions between the different subject groups are undermined by the presence of many common melodic and rhythmic elements. The concert aria *Der Wein* also resembles a sonata movement in the thematic plan of its opening section and in having a final section which functions as a recapitulation. Like the first movement of the *Lyric Suite,* however, the aria has no formal development section, the usual sonata development being replaced by a broad lyrical section and the overall shape of the work thus suggesting a song-like ternary form. In the 'Marsch' of the Three Orchestral Pieces the three-sectioned sonata design, distinguishable in the background plan of the piece, is exploded by the constant motivic development and the unrelenting presentation of apparently new material; sonata form is here destroyed from within by its own developmental tendencies.

Elsewhere in Berg's instrumental music sonata form is often combined with some other form to produce a complex synthesis of the two. The second movement of the String Quartet fuses sonata and rondo forms to produce, not a traditional sonata-rondo form, but a movement that can, with equal justification, be analysed as either a 'pure' sonata or a 'pure' rondo structure.[1] The first movement of the Chamber Concerto is a set of variations but, as is shown by Berg's own diagrammatic representation of the movement reproduced below,[2] a set of variations arranged in such a way that the overall shape of the movement suggests a sonata design. The central variations, variations 2, 3 and 4, constitute the development section of the sonata and are concerned with the theme in its retrograde, inverted, and inverted retrograde forms. The theme and first variation present the theme in its original form and constitute the exposition and the first reprise of the sonata, the

---

[1] Compare, for example, Schweizer, *Die Sonatensatzform im Schaffen Alban Bergs,* Stuttgart, 1970, p. 79, where the movement is analysed in terms of Rondo form, and Archibald, 'Harmony in the Early Works of Alban Berg', unpublished Harvard Univ. thesis, 1965, where it is analysed in terms of Sonata form.
[2] See Redlich, *Alban Berg,* London, 1957, pp. 124–5.

theme being announced first by the wind and then being repeated by the solo piano as the first variation. The fifth variation, a canonic restatement of the theme in its original form by both wind and piano, constitutes the recapitulation.

---

*Movement I – Theme with Variations*

| Theme in the basic shape | Var. I | II retrograde | III inversion | IV retrograde inversion | V basic shape |
|---|---|---|---|---|---|
| (Exposition) | (First Reprise) | (Development) | | | (Second Reprise) |
| bars: 30 | 30 | 60 | 30 | 30 | 60 |

---

The combination of sonata and rondo forms in the third movement of the Chamber Concerto, and the way in which the structure of the movement is articulated by rhythmic rather than thematic elements, has been discussed in Chapter IV.[1]

The term 'sonata form', as it is generally employed when referring to eighteenth- and nineteenth-century music, usually indicates both a tonal and a thematic plan. In an eighteenth-century movement the tonal and thematic aspects of the form are, of course, closely linked; it will, however, be useful to attempt to distinguish between the two. The eighteenth-century sonata form is essentially concerned with the tension created by tonal contrasts. It is from this tension that the movement derives its long-term feeling of directed forward motion and overall architectural balance. The traditional three sections of a sonata movement – exposition, development and recapitulation – correspond respectively to the creation, the maintenance or heightening and the final resolution of this tonal tension. A common, but less important, feature of the traditional sonata movement is the way in which the tonal contrasts set up in the exposition are emphasized by thematic contrasts, the different keys being associated with different themes, and the way in which the resolution of tonal tension by the return to the tonic at the beginning of the recapitulation is underlined by the return of the original thematic material.

Hans Redlich describes Berg's use of traditional forms as an 'endeavour to compensate for the weakened feeling of tonality by establishing associations with historical musical forms and techniques', and considers this endeavour to be one of the elements of Berg's musical idiom which remained 'constant and immutable'.[2] While it is, of course, possible to write a non-tonal movement which follows the general thematic plan of one of these historical forms, such a procedure cannot, in itself, compensate for any weakened

---

[1] See pp. 152–4 above.
[2] Redlich, *Alban Berg*, London, 1957, pp. 23–4.

feeling of tonality. I have already described some of the ways in which Berg – through his use of primary tonal centres in the later twelve-note works, his use of contrasting 'black-note' and 'white-note' harmonic areas in the first movement of the *Lyric Suite* and *Lulu,* his habitual practice of associating specific themes with specific pitch levels – established certain harmonic collections and tone centres as referential areas which acquire some of the functions associated with a traditional tonic key. I have also discussed the extent to which the balance of tonal and atonal elements in Berg's music creates tensions and relaxations which are employed as a means of articulating the large-scale formal design.

Although Berg's handling of sonata form in the instrumental works is far from being a simple adoption of the thematic plan and the developmental techniques of the music of an earlier period, the very fact that he employs sonata form at all, let alone his use of 'more or less archaic form-types' in the operas, suggests a certain conservative and backward-looking attitude. There can be no doubt that Berg was deeply aware of his position as part of that long line of composers who together form the great eighteenth- and nineteenth-century tradition of Austro–German music and that the formal structures of tonal music were an essential part of that tradition.

The traditional forms in Berg's music have a double function, however, for they not only, through their very presence, assert the relationship between his music and that of composers before him but also act as a clear and generally recognizable framework alongside or within which a less orthodox and peculiarly Bergian sense of formal organization and balance operates.

Although Berg himself sanctioned the performance of individual movements of the op. 6 Orchestral Pieces, the Chamber Concerto and the *Lyric Suite* there is no work by Berg the individual movements of which can truly stand as separate entities.

It is clear from the letter, written to Webern on 1 September 1923, quoted above,[1] that, although in three distinct movements, Berg regarded the Chamber Concerto as being a 'single movement work'; to a certain extent all Berg's works are 'single movement works'. That this is so is due to Berg's characteristic approach to the total work as a single structural whole in which the individual movements, while having on one level an independent self-contained musical structure, are not only linked to one another through recurring motivic material of the kind discussed in earlier chapters (and in some cases not merely by recurring motives but by the recurrence of large sections of music from one movement to the next) but are also components of a larger formal scheme of the most systematic and disciplined kind which embraces the structure of the whole work and the role of the individual elements within it.

[1] See p. 154 above.

Each of the different movements of the *Lyric Suite,* for example, presents a self-contained formal structure, usually one based on a specific traditional form or on traditionally simple formal proportions. The first movement is a sonata form without the traditional development section, the second a rondo with an ABACABA pattern, the third a scherzo and trio, the fifth a similar scherzo and trio, the trio appearing twice to produce an ABABA shape. These independent movements, however, together form a complex and highly original overall design. The order of the movements is arranged in such a way that fast and slow movements alternate, the fast ones increasing, the slow ones decreasing in speed as the work progresses:

| I | II | III |
|---|---|---|
| Allegretto giovale | Andante amoroso | Allegro misterioso |
| IV | V | VI |
| Adagio appassionato | Presto delirando | Largo desolato |

Three types of thematic relationships link the six movements of the work to one another: (i) the recurrence and gradual transformation of the twelve-note set;[1] (ii) the recurring four-note collection discussed in Chapter II;[2] (iii) the reappearance of a section of music from one movement in that which immediately follows it and, occasionally, in other movements as well. Since the first and last movements have material in common the whole work pursues a circular course, its end linking with its beginning and thus defining a single closed form. Although the *Lyric Suite* is one of the few works in which it features in so overt a way, circular motion of this kind is an important characteristic of Berg's formal designs and I shall discuss it in greater detail in the concluding chapter.[3] The following diagram illustrates the overall plan of the *Lyric Suite* but does not take into account appearances of the four-note collection which were discussed in detail in Chapter II. The designation of the different twelve-note sets as *A, B, C* and *D* follows that adopted when discussing these sets in Chapter III.[4]

The most characteristic and the most striking manifestation of Berg's highly individual sense of formal balance and unity is his preoccupation with rigorously organized, symmetrical designs which span the whole work, welding it into a single closed structural unit, and which affect the smallest of the individual elements within it. The use of such symmetrical structural designs, which are evident in all Berg's major works from the *Altenberg Lieder* onwards, is not, in itself, peculiarly Bergian. In the absence of clear and unambiguous tonal relationships such symmetrical designs are a means of defining the boundaries of a piece and of creating the feeling of returning

[1] See pp. 126–9 above.
[2] See pp. 27–9 above.
[3] See p. 237f. below.
[4] See pp. 126–9 above.

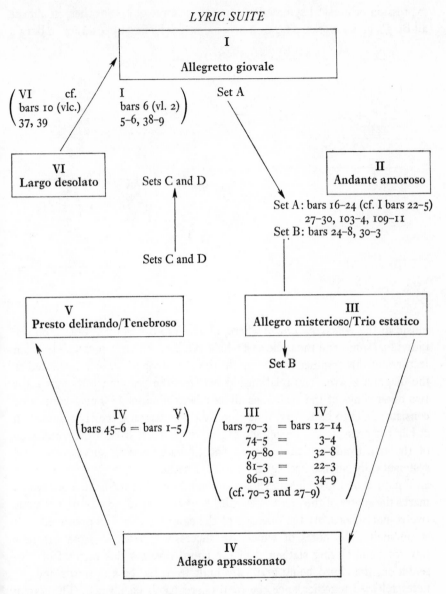

LYRIC SUITE

at the end of a work to an original starting point; as such they are employed in a number of twentieth-century works.[1] Peculiarly Bergian, however, is the frequency with which such symmetrical designs appear in his music, the strictness and complexity of the designs themselves and the extent to which they predetermine the course of large sections of music.

The arch-shape or 'bogen' structure, which is the usual and most obvious

[1] The first movement of Bartok's *Music for Strings, Percussion and Celesta* is a well-known example of a piece built on such a symmetrical design.

expression of musical symmetry, appears, in some guise or other, in almost
all Berg's major works. The arch-scheme makes its first appearance in Berg's

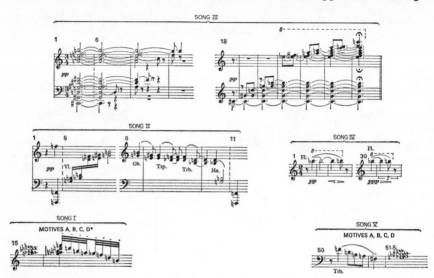

music in the *Altenberg Lieder* where, as DeVoto has pointed out[1] both the
individual songs and the cycle as a whole exhibit such a symmetry. The main
features of this symmetrical design in the *Altenberg Lieder* are illustrated in
the diagram above. The relationship between the first and fifth songs, the
two outer songs of the cycle, has already been discussed.[2] The second song
consists of eleven bars. As can be seen from the diagram, the viola figuration
at bar 5 is presented in retrograde during the last five bars of the song, each
of the five dyads which make up the figuration being successively and
systematically augmented by a quaver. The song opens and closes with
an F natural on the orchestra; F is also the bass note of the held chord which
marks the centre of the piece. The third song opens and closes with the same
twelve-note chord. At the opening of the song the chord is presented as a
simultaneity, the notes of which are successively released from the bass
upwards; the closing statement of the chord reverses this method of presentation, the chord being gradually built from the bass upwards and the
notes released together once the total chord has been formed. The fourth
song begins and ends with the same figuration on solo flute.

The Violin Concerto consists of two parts, each part consisting of two
movements – the first of an Andante and an Allegretto, the second of an
Allegro and an Adagio. In terms of tempi, the plan of the Concerto suggests
an arch-shape design balancing thus:

[1] DeVoto, 'Some notes on the unknown *Altenberg Lieder*', *Perspectives of New Music*,
5, Fall/Winter, 1966, p. 39.
[2] See pp. 34–7 above.

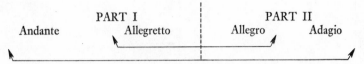

PART I | PART II
Andante     Allegretto     Allegro     Adagio

As in the *Altenberg Lieder* the arch-shape of the whole work is enhanced by the arch-shape of the individual movements. The formal plan of the individual movements is shown in the diagram overleaf. The two movements of Part I and those of Part II are played without a break and the end of each movement is closely linked with the beginning of the movement which follows. In the first Part the open fifths of the introduction return at the end of the Andante and become the accompaniment of the scherzando melody which opens the Allegretto, the 2/4 of the first movement being gradually converted into the 6/8 of the second. At the end of the Allegro which opens Part II, the climactic nine-note chord is progressively dismantled while, at the same time, the opening phrase of the chorale melody which forms the basis of the final Adagio is gradually assembled, note by note, on the solo violin. The Allegretto which ends Part I closes with a chord formed of the first four notes of the set at P-O (a G minor chord with an added major seventh); the Allegretto which opens Part II begins with a cyclically permuted version of the same set form beginning on the fifth note, the opening of the Allegro thus completing the set statement begun with the final chord of Part I. These links are indicated by the curved lines on the diagram below. In the Violin Concerto, as in *Der Wein*, the overall symmetry of the structure is emphasized by means which, to some extent, resemble those of traditional tonality. The B flat major–G minor primary tonal centre, with which the concerto opens and closes, and the various ramifications of this tonal centre during the course of the work, have been discussed in Chapter III.[1] The arch-shape of the piece is also enhanced by thematic relationships, in addition to the chains of whole tones and ascending or descending thirds derived from the most characteristic form of the series, between the different movements. These thematic relationships are indicated by dotted lines on the diagram below. As can be seen from the diagram, the Allegro of Part II is a ternary ABA structure, the central B section of which is itself in ternary form; the thematic material of the two outer parts of this B section are derived from the second Trio, the equivalent section at the centre of the Allegretto of Part I. A closed arch-shape is also imposed by the return, in the final bars of the work, of the opening bars in retrograde. The last section of the Adagio which ends Part II corresponds not only to the opening section of Part I but also to the last section of the Allegretto which ends Part I, the same Carinthian folksong appearing in the coda of each movement. The cadenza of the Allegro of

[1] See footnote 1, p. 103 above.

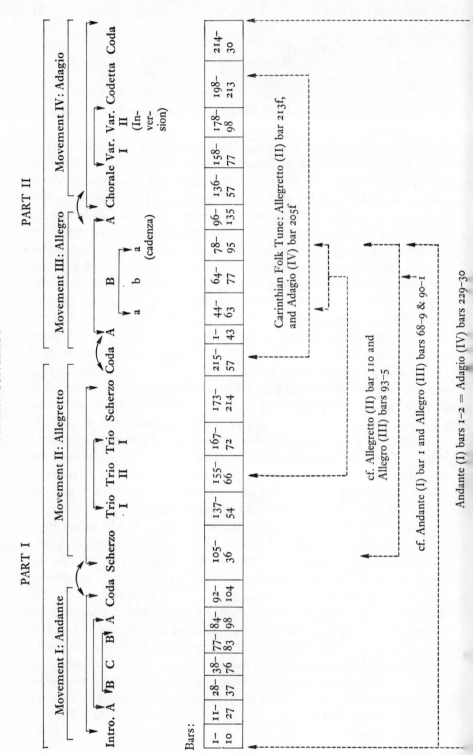

*VIOLIN CONCERTO*

PART I

Movement I: Andante

Movement II: Allegretto

PART II

Movement III: Allegro

Movement IV: Adagio

Intro. A ↗B C B↘ A Coda    Scherzo Trio Trio Trio Scherzo Coda    A    B    A Chorale Var. Var. Codetta Coda
                    I    II    I                                    Var. I    II
                                                              a    b    a         (In-
                                                              ⌐       ⌐  (cadenza)  ver-
                                                                                   sion)

Bars:

| 1–10 | 11–27 | 28–37 | 38–76 | 77–83 | 84–98 | 92–104 | 105–36 | 137–54 | 155–66 | 167–72 | 173–214 | 215–57 | 1–43 | 44–63 | 64–77 | 78–95 | 96–135 | 136–57 | 158–77 | 178–98 | 198–213 | 214–30 |

Carinthian Folk Tune: Allegretto (II) bar 213f,
and Adagio (IV) bar 205f

cf. Allegretto (II) bar 110 and
Allegro (III) bars 93–5

cf. Andante (I) bar 1 and Allegro (III) bars 68–9 & 90–1

Andante (I) bars 1–2 = Adagio (IV) bars 229–30

Part II not only employs material from the second Trio but also makes brief references to many other themes from Part I.

*     *     *     *

In most of Berg's music the symmetry of the arch structure is defined not simply through relationships of tempi and thematic material between corresponding sections, as in the Violin Concerto and the *Altenberg Lieder*, or through reversing the order in which the material of the first half appears in the second half of the arch-shape, but through the strict reversal of a total musical unit so that the second half of the movement or work presents a whole section from the first half in retrograde motion. So important a feature of Berg's structural designs are such large-scale retrogrades that, with the exception of the Violin Concerto, there is not a single major work written after the op. 5 Clarinet Pieces that does not include one.[1] Sections related as original and retrograde in this way always appear at either the centre or at the two ends of the structure; that is, at the most important points of the arch.

The Orchestral Pieces op. 6 and the *Lyric Suite* provide examples of movements which close with retrograde statements of their opening material. The final section of the 'Präludium' of the Orchestral Pieces opens with a reprise of the last three bars of the orchestral introduction and concludes with eight bars which present the harmonic structure of the first eight bars of the piece in retrograde. The final section of the ternary form Allegro misterioso third movement of the *Lyric Suite* is a curtailed, but otherwise exact, retrograde reprise of the opening section. The opening scene of *Wozzeck* has a similar structure which will be discussed later.

In *Der Wein* and the Chamber Concerto the original section and its retrograde are juxtaposed to form a palindrome at the centre of each work. The general plan of the two outer sections of *Der Wein*, with their resemblance to the exposition and recapitulation of a sonata form, has already been discussed.[2] The overall plan of the work is a fusion of sonata form and an arch-shaped structure balanced around the palindromic central section. As can be seen from the following plan of *Der Wein* the symmetry of the whole is emphasized by the reprise of the opening bars of the work in the orchestral coda, and by the superimposition, at the beginning of the third song (bar 173f.), of the vocal line from bars 164–5 on to bars 1–5 of the orchestral introduction. This superimposition is determined by the text; the music which originally appeared to the words, 'Ich mache deines Weibes Augen

---

[1] The qualification 'major' work is made so as to exclude the song 'Schliesse Mir die Augen beide' and the Canon for the Frankfurt Opera.

[2] See p. 177 above.

heiter' ('I make your wife's eyes brighter') now appearing to the words, 'Der sonderbare Blick der leichten Frau' ('Strange glance of light women').

*I. Die Seele des Weines*
bars  1–14  Orchestral Introduction ♩ = 36/44
     14–23  First Subject Group    = 46/52
     24–30  Transition
     31–63  Second Subject, Group 1 ('Tempo di Tango')
     64–72  Second Subject, Group B
     73–87  Closing Group (bars 73–7 = bars 17–21)

*II. Der Wein der Liebenden*
bars  88–111  Group 1 ('Leicht bewegt' ♩. = c. 60)
    112–41  Group 2a
    141–72  Group 2b (= Group 2a in retrograde)

*III. Der Wein des Einsamen*
bars 173–7  Reprise of bars 1–5 with added voice part  = 36/44
    178  Transition (Reprise of bars 29–30)
    179–95  Second Subject, Group A (bars 179–80 = bars 31–2; bars 181–95 = bars 39–52)
    196–208  Closing Group (bars 196–7 = bars 73–4; bar 201 = bars 33–4) ♩ = 46/52
    209–16  Orchestral Coda (Reprise of bars 8–14 of Orchestral Introduction) ♩ = 36/44.

The second, and central, movement of the Chamber Concerto is in two halves, the second of which is a retrograde of the first. The first half is an ABA ternary structure in which the second A section is the inversion of the first. The formal design of the whole movement may, therefore, be represented diagrammatically thus:

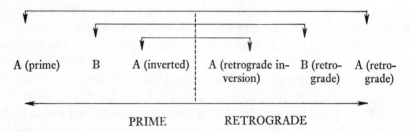

A (prime)    B    A (inverted)    A (retrograde inversion)    B (retrograde)    A (retrograde)

PRIME          RETROGRADE

The extraordinary large-scale formal symmetries of the Chamber Concerto as a whole are well-known from Berg's own description and tabular survey of the work in his dedicatory 'Open Letter' to Schoenberg.[1] The formal designs of the first two movements are based on the presentation of large

[1] Berg's 'Open Letter on the Chamber Concerto' is reprinted in Reich, *Alban Berg*, London, 1965, pp. 143–8. I have been unable to check Berg's original but all reproductions of Berg's tabular survey (see Reich, Redlich and Carner) show a second movement structure which does not correspond to the music itself. The third and fourth sections of the first half of the second movement (and their corresponding retrogrades in the second half) consist, respectively, of 39 and 9 bars, not of 36 and 12 bars.

units of music in prime, inverted, retrograde and the inverted retrograde forms. Both movements have identical proportions, both consisting of the same number of bars and reaching important structural points at bar 30, bar 120 and bar 150. The reason for the structural similarities of the first two movements is made clear in the third, and final, movement which consists of a simultaneous reprise of both the previous movements. The main formal divisions of the third movement correspond to, and are determined by, those of the first and second movements. Thus the introduction to the third movement consists of the first thirty bars (the exposition of the variation theme) of the first movement and the opening section of the second movement; the coda of the third movement consists of the last variation of the first movement and the final section (the retrograde of the opening section) of the second. The silent bar at the centre of the third movement corresponds to both the central point (the end of the second and the beginning of the third variation) of the first movement and the turning point of the palindromic second movement. With the repeat which Berg specifies the third movement has precisely the same number of bars as the first two movements together.

*Lulu* includes two large-scale palindromes. The first is the Sextet in Act I, sc. 3 (bars 1177–1203), which begins as Lulu, followed by the wardrobe mistress, the theatre director and Dr. Schön, returns to her dressing room refusing to perform; it ends as Schön ushers the others out of the room and prepares to confront Lulu alone. The second, and more extended, example is the orchestral Ostinato 'Film Music' interlude at the centre of Act II and at the centre of the whole opera. The palindromic shape of the Sextet is a simple reflection of the stage action. The Ostinato I shall consider later.

Berg's fondness for arch shapes and palindromes affects other musical elements in addition to pitch. The 'Präludium' of the op. 6 Orchestral Pieces defines an arch shape of timbre by its progression from the 'noise' of unpitched percussion instruments, with which it opens, through tuned percussion to the 'music' of pitched instrumental sounds and then back to noise. The precisely balanced arch structure of the Prologue to *Lulu* is defined by every one of its constituent musical and dramatic elements. As can be seen from the following diagram, the different styles of vocal delivery employed during the course of the Prologue define a palindromic progression from spoken text to cantabile singing and back to spoken text. The closing sections of the Prologue present the material of the opening in retrograde (even to the extent of reversing the opening metronome mark of $\downarrow = 80$–90 so that it becomes $\downarrow = 90$–80) while the remaining musical material of the first half is presented in the second half, in reverse order. The following diagram also indicates the textual and dramatic correspondences between the first and second halves, from which the musical symmetries derive. As I shall show

*LULU: PROLOGUE*

| BAR | M.M. & TEMPI | MUSICAL MATERIAL | TEXT | DRAMATIC ACTION | VOCAL STYLE |
|---|---|---|---|---|---|
| 1–4 | ♩ = 80–90 | Basic cells I & II[1] ascending | | | |
| 5 | | Basic cell III (arpeggiated) descending | | Animal Trainer's entry | |
| 6 | | Cymbal and Bass Drum stroke | | | |
| 7–8 | | Drum roll | Hereinspatziert ... | | Spoken |
| 9–15 | Comodo ♩ = 70 | 'Circus Music'[2] | Was seht Ihr ...? Haustiere ... | | Sprechstimme |
| 16 | | Piano: Athlete's chord clusters | | | |
| 17–20 | Tempo rubato | Basic Series | Das wahre Tier | | Halb gesungen |
| 20–41 | (varies) | Exposition of sets associated with main characters | [Animals] | | Parlando gesungen |
| 42–3 | Subito ritmico | Ascending and descending Basic cell IV chords in Hauptrhythmus. Cymbal and Drum | He, Aujust! Bring mir uns're Schlange | | Parlando |
| 44–65 | ♩ = 50 | Lulu's 'Entrance music'[3] and related material | Sie ward geschaffen | Stagehand enters carrying Lulu | Cantabile |
| 66–7 | Subito ritmico | Ascending and descending Basic cell IV chords in Hauptrhythmus. Cymbal and Drum | Hopp, Aujust! Marsch! Trag sie an ihren Platz | | Parlando |
| 68–72 | A tempo ♩ = 60 | Lulu's 'Entrance music' and related material | Die süsse Unschuld ... | Stagehand exits carrying Lulu | Halb gesprochen |
| 73–8 | Comodo ♩ = 70 | 'Circus Music' | Und nun bleibt doch das Beste | | Sprechstimme |
| 79 | | Piano: Athlete's chord clusters | | | |
| 79–80 | | Cymbal and Bass Drum stroke | Verehrtes Publikum | | Spoken |
| 80–82 | | Basic cell III (arpeggiated) ascending | ... Hereinspatziert! | | Spoken |
| 83–5 | ♩ = 90–80 | Basic cell I & II descending | | Animal Trainer's exit | |

[1] See p. 86 above.
[2] See footnote 1, p. 90 above.
[3] The term 'Entrance music' is adopted from Perle, *Journal of the American Musicological Society*, 17, 1964.

later, the symmetrical arch shape of the Prologue to *Lulu* reflects the musical and dramatic shape of the opera as a whole.

The two operas demonstrate Berg's unique sense of formal balance and organization operating over the largest possible scale. Both operas are designed in such a way that a formal framework of the most rigorous kind governs the largest and smallest musical elements and, at the same time, mirrors both the total and the smallest details of the dramatic structure.

The formal design of *Wozzeck* combines a variety of organizational principles operating on different levels. As with the instrumental works discussed above, the opera as a whole is conceived as a single, closed formal entity with each act and each scene within each act forming a self-contained structural unit within the whole. Within this overall design, and within the self-contained musical structure of the individual scenes, are repetitions of large sections of music and of both musical and non-musical motives. There are also certain recurring note-collections and pitch levels which link different groups of material and different scenes and which function as referential elements. The most important of these integrative pitch collections, tone centres and musical leading motives have been discussed in Chapter II.[1] In addition, there are also certain thematic, harmonic, rhythmic and other musical characteristics which are employed as the structural basis of, and whose significance may be limited to, the individual scenes.

The overall formal design of *Wozzeck* is well known from Berg's own tabular survey which has been published in a number of books and articles.[2] Each of the three acts of the opera contains five scenes, and runs without a break, the different scenes within each act being linked by orchestral interludes.

Act I, which is the exposition of the drama, consists of five character pieces – a Suite, a Rhapsody, a Military March and Lullaby, a Passacaglia and a Rondo – each of which introduces one of the main characters in the drama and delineates his or her relationship with Wozzeck. Act III, the climax of the drama, consists of five inventions, each of which is based on one musical characteristic (on a theme, on a single pitch, a rhythmic pattern, a six-note chord and a single note value) which is employed as an ostinato throughout. The final orchestral interlude between Act III, scenes 4 and 5, forms a sixth invention, an 'invention on a key'. The interlude both sums up the main motivic material[3] and, as the only orchestral interlude in the work to have its own distinctive thematic material, also stands as a self-sufficient musical structure in its own right. The central second act is designed as a five

---

[1] See pp. 46–70 above.
[2] See Redlich, *Alban Berg*, London, 1957, p. 95, Reich, *Alban Berg*, London, 1965, p. 121 and Carner, *Alban Berg*, London, 1975, p. 157.
[3] See p. 196 below.

movement symphony and consists of a Sonata movement, a Fantasia and Fugue, a Largo, a Scherzo and a Rondo.

The overall plan of the opera is therefore that of an extended arch structure, the three acts together forming what Berg described as 'the venerable tripartite pattern A–B–A' with the two more loosely structured acts 'embracing the much larger and weightier middle act symmetrically'.[1] The correspondence between the two most striking visual effects in the opera, the setting of the red sun in Act I, sc. 2, and its 'mirror image', the rising of the red moon in Act III, sc. 2, underlines the relationship between the two outer acts.

In *Wozzeck*, as in the *Altenberg Lieder* and elsewhere, the symmetrical arch-shape design of the whole is reflected in the design of its constituent parts; many scenes or sections of scenes, especially in Acts I and II, present symmetrically balanced structures.

The symmetrical design of the opening scene of the opera will be discussed later in this and in the following chapter. The framing of Act I, sc. 3 by two statements of cadential chord *A* has already been discussed in Chapter II.[2] Within Act I, sc. 3, Wozzeck's exit (bar 454) presents the two figures which accompanied his entrance (bar 427) in inversion and in reverse order. Act I, sc. 4 is framed symmetrically by statements of a figuration derived from the final notes of the Doctor's Passacaglia theme, the curtain rising on the scene to descending statements of the figuration and closing at the end of the scene to ascending statements of the figuration. The relationship between the material which opens the orchestral interlude to the final scene of Act I (the 'seduction' scene, Act I, sc. 5) and the cadential chords which close the scene has been discussed in Chapter II.[3] A horizontal statement of the last of these chords, and of the same tremolo figuration which ended Act I, opens Act II of the opera. Within Act II the orchestral interlude which links scenes 1 and 2 is framed by two C major glissandi, the curtain falling on scene 1 to a descending glissando and rising on scene 2 to an ascending glissando. Act II, sc. 3, the central scene and the dramatic turning point of the opera, itself an arch-shape ternary form, closes (bars 406–11) with a retrograde statement of its opening material (bars 363–7). The penultimate section of the fourth scene of Act II, the epilogue to the Trio (bars 641–69), presents a retrograde statement of the introduction to the Trio which forms the second section of the scene (bars 448–55). A final, and particularly curious, symmetrical relationship is that between the end of Act II and the beginning of Act III. Act II ends with four silent 2/4 bars, in the last two of which the curtain falls; Act III opens with two silent 4/4 bars, during the first of which the

---

[1] Berg's lecture on *Wozzeck* in Redlich, *Alban Berg*, London, 1957, p. 266.
[2] See pp. 60–1 above.
[3] See pp. 47–8 above.

curtain rises. Berg specifies in the score that the first 4/4 bar of Act III corresponds to the last two bars of Act II and the second 4/4 bar of Act III (which is marked by a pause) corresponds to the previous two 2/4 bars of Act II (also marked by a pause). That Berg should choose to impose such rigorous musical symmetries and so tightly disciplined a musical structure upon the opera accords with his formal preoccupations as exhibited by the structural designs of his other works. I shall discuss the reasons for his choosing this method of organizing the overall plan of *Wozzeck*, and its relation to the drama as a whole in the following chapter.[1]

\*    \*    \*    \*

The choice of formal design for each of the individual scenes of *Wozzeck* is primarily determined by dramatic considerations. In both of his operas the musical form of each scene is determined by the form of the verbal text, the different subjects of conversation in the libretto of a scene being arranged in such a way that their recurrence, or the change from one to another, defines a precise musical structure. Thus in Act I, sc. 1 of *Wozzeck*, the musical structure of which has been discussed above,[2] the shape of the verbal text and the nature of the topics discussed during the scene determine the kinds of musical forms employed, the points at which musical material recurs and also affects the choice of instrumentation. Each of the different dance forms which make up the Suite of Act I, sc. 1, corresponds to a different topic of conversation, the reappearance of the music of the first Cadenza, in the second and of the music of the opening Präludium in the Postludium which ends the scene, being determined by the return of the topics of conversation with which each is associated. In the two Cadenzas the Captain extols the qualities of the 'guter Mensch'; in the Postludium he returns to his opening exhortations to Wozzeck to go more slowly. The Postludium repeats the opening Präludium in retrograde,[3] the Captain's final word, 'Langsam' at bar 170, corresponding to the setting of the same word at the beginning of the scene.[4] The retrograde reprise of this opening Präludium at the end of the scene, symbolizing the circular nature of both the conversation and the dramatic structure of Act I, sc. 1 (in which, as Berg himself said, 'nothing really happens'),[5] imposes a closed symmetrical formal design, similar to those of the other scenes discussed above and to that of the opera as a whole, upon the scene. Repetitions of smaller melodic fragments from the vocal line, cor-

[1] See pp. 230–1 and 237f. below.
[2] See pp. 59–60 above.
[3] Bars 157–69 of the Postludium are the retrograde of bars 6–14 of the Präludium.
[4] The word 'Langsam' is set to the tritone dyad B–F, the 'fate' dyad of the opera. The significance of this association is discussed on p. 238 below.
[5] See Redlich, *Alban Berg*, London, 1957, p. 268.

responding to individual words or phrases in the libretto, also appear during this opening scene. The setting of the Captain's 'Ein guter Mensch' at bar 154, for example, repeats the setting of these words, at bars 54–5 and bar 111, in the two Cadenzas. Similarly the setting of the phrase 'Er sieht immer so verhetzt aus' at bar 160 corresponds to that at bar 52. The different dance forms of the scene are defined by instrumentation, the accompaniment to each dance being dominated by a different group of obbligato instruments chosen as a reflection of or a comment upon the dialogue which it accompanies. The Captain's panegyric on the qualities of 'Ein guter Mensch' in the two Cadenzas is accompanied by two solo instruments, the viola in the first and the double bassoon in the second. His moralizing in the Gavotte is accompanied by the brass, his remarks about the windy weather by the deliberately banal and conventional accompaniment of scale passages on three flutes.

The Passacaglia theme of Act I, sc. 4, of *Wozzeck* symbolizes the Doctor's obsession with achieving immortality through the fame which he hopes his dietary experiments will bring him. The treatment of the theme has been discussed in Chapter II.[1] As in Act I, sc. 1, each different conversational topic in Act I, sc. 4 is the basis of a separate musical unit, in this case a separate Passacaglia variation. The scene as a whole is designed as an ABA ternary structure. The central B section (Variations 5 to 12) is devoted to Wozzeck's attempts to describe to the Doctor the mysterious messages conveyed by the natural phenomena of Act I, sc. 2, and consists of reminiscences of material from the earlier scene. The outer A sections are devoted to the Doctor. The symmetry of the scene is emphasized by the relationship between the music which precedes the opening and accompanies the closing curtain of the scene.[2] Within the scene itself the relationship between the outer sections of the ternary form depends on the reappearance, in the final section of the scene, of certain conversational topics and the music associated with them from the first section of the scene. Thus, Variation 17 ('Isst seine Bohnen?') begins with a repetition of the opening of Variation 2 ('Hat er schon seine Bohnen gegessen?') and Variation 19 (Bohnen essen, dann Schöpsenfleisch essen') repeats the music of Variation 3 ('Fangen wir dann mit Schöpsenfleisch an').

With the exception of their brief appearance at the end of Act III, sc. 4, the only other scene in *Wozzeck* in which the Captain and the Doctor appear is the street scene of Act II, sc. 2. The scene is designed as an Fantasia and Fugue. In the first part of the scene the Doctor taunts the Captain about his precarious state of health; in the Fugue both the Doctor and the Captain taunt Wozzeck with hints of Marie's infidelity. The decision to set the second

[1] See p. 72 above.
[2] See p. 190 above.

half of the scene as a Fugue was determined, according to Berg, by the need to contrast the three disparate characters of Act II, sc. 2 with the three characters of Act II, sc. 1, who are 'linked by the ties of blood relationship'.[1] The Fugue is based on three themes, each of which is specifically associated with one of the three characters involved in the scene. The Doctor is represented by the theme which appeared at bars 171–4 of the Passacaglia of Act I, sc. 4, the Captain by the theme which appeared at the beginning of Act I, sc. 1 (bar 4), and Wozzeck by a theme derived from the whole-tone figuration which accompanied his entry at bar 93 of the previous scene. The treatment of the three themes as counterpoints to one another stresses the incompatability of the three characters involved, while the artificiality and calculated nature of the form invests the whole fugal section of the scene with a suitably grotesque and bizarre quality. The Captain's theme forms the first fugue subject. The exposition of this subject (bars 286–92) is followed by an exposition of the Doctor's theme, the second fugue subject (bars 292–7). A passage which combines the two subjects leads to an exposition of the third subject (Wozzeck's theme, bars 313–6), a contrapuntal combination of all three subjects and a final coda. The exposition, and many subsequent statements of the three themes, is at a pitch level at which they have in common the fateful B–F dyad. The plan of the Fugue – the three expositions and the two sections in which the three subjects are contrapuntally combined – is determined by the arrangement of the verbal text. Throughout, each of the three themes is strictly confined to the character with which it is associated, appearing only when that character speaks or when the stage directions indicate a movement of some kind.[2] Even the smallest details of the stage action are drawn into the musical structure of the scene, as at bars 296–7, for example, when the Captain, recognizing the Doctor's allusion to the Drum Major, taps his forehead twice – once to the accompaniment of the prime form of his theme, the second time to the accompaniment of its inversion.

As in Act I, sc. 1, the formal plan of Act II, sc. 2 influences the instrumentation of the scene. The exposition of the Captain's subject is given to woodwind (a reminiscence of the wind quintet with which the scene with the Captain in Act I opened and closed), the exposition of the Doctor's subject begins on the cello (the instrument which first announced the Passacaglia theme of Act I, sc. 4) and that of Wozzeck's subject is given, as was the corresponding theme in Act II, sc. 1, to muted trombones.

The Fantasia which opens Act II, sc. 2, is primarily concerned with the themes associated with the Doctor and the Captain. The Fantasia is in ternary form, with a middle section which is itself a ternary structure. The

[1] See Redlich, *Alban Berg,* London, 1957, p. 275.
[2] See Chittum, 'The triple fugue in Berg's *Wozzeck*', *Music Review,* 28, 1967, pp. 52–62.

relationships between the corresponding sections of the formal structure are
determined by the textual repetitions indicated in the following diagram:

*WOZZECK: Act II, Sc. 2*

*A bars 171–203*
176 & 185    Captain: 'Herr Sargnagel!'
196              Doctor: 'In vier Wochen'
197–8          Captain: 'Es sind schon Leute am Schreck gestorben'

*B¹ bars 203–20*
(204–8        Orchestral Harmonies)
208–14        Doctor: 'Fett, dicker Hals, apoplektische Konstitution'
219              Orchestra

*B² bars 221–34*
221–2          Doctor: 'cerebri kriegen'

*B¹ bars 238–48*
238–44        Doctor: 'Übrigens, . . . Sie einen von den interessanten Fällen
                     abgeben werden'
247              Doctor: 'Experimente . . .'

*A bars 248–65*
248              Captain: 'Herr Sargnagel'
253–4          Captain: 'In vier Wochen?'
255–7          Captain: 'Es sind schon Leute am puren Schreck'
259–62        Captain: (Coughing fit)
262–5          (Orchestral funeral march)

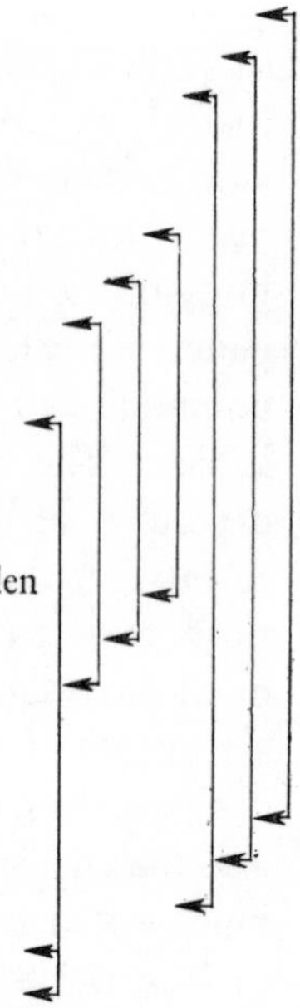

   Berg's use of closed, 'absolute' musical forms in an operatic work, the
feature of *Wozzeck* which has elicited most attention, is not in itself new; the
use of such forms in opera has a long history stretching back to Mozart and
baroque opera. Indeed, the way in which Berg arranges the libretto of each
scene, so that repetitions of the verbal text and of dramatic situations define
a form which is precisely paralleled by the musical design, is very similar to
that in which Mozart structured the text for numbers such as 'Ah, taci
ingiusto core' of Act II of *Don Giovanni* or the Sextet in Act III of *Figaro*,
so as to define a dramatic shape that would find its musical reflection in the
classical sonata form.
   The novelty of *Wozzeck* lies in its use of such specifically 'instrumental'
forms in a work that adheres to the aesthetic and employs the continuous
musical flow and the leading-motive techniques of the Wagnerian music
drama. In many ways Berg's handling of leading motives in the two operas
can be regarded as a development of the motivic and thematic techniques
employed in his instrumental music where the different, and, on one level,
structurally independent, movements of a work are linked by recurrent
themes, motives and sometimes, as in the *Lyric Suite*, sections. Although in

*Wozzeck* the recurrent motives and musical units have dramatic significance, they are, as in the instrumental works, integrated into self-contained musical structures.

The tightly controlled formal plan enables Berg to handle the leading motives with a considerable degree of freedom, allowing innumerable references to previous material or anticipations of future events to be absorbed into the music without them affecting the overall structure of the scene. The central section of Act I, sc. 4, in which many quotations from the music of Act I, sc. 2 are integrated into the Passacaglia structure of the scene, demonstrates how this can be achieved.[1] Since in Act I, sc. 4, and elsewhere in the opera, such reminiscences consist not only of themes, but also of other elements such as note collections, characteristic contours, specific pitch levels and fragments of verbal text which have acquired significance during the course of the work, Berg is able to call into play many different levels and degrees of association.

Act II, sc. 2 incorporates a variety of descriptive effects, such as the irregular violin and drum rhythm that appears when the Doctor feels Wozzeck's pulse at bars 337–8 and the gradual withdrawal of the number of strings playing the repeated G sharp at bars 227–30, illustrating the approaching paralysis of which the Doctor speaks, as well as references to both earlier and later material. The Captain's 'Ein guter Mensch' from Act I, sc. 1, which reappears in the Fantasia and Fugue of Act II, sc. 2, is one example of a verbal motive which, though often set to the same contour and rhythm, is not associated with any distinctive pitch figuration.[2] The word 'Langsam' in the Doctor's opening sentence of Act II, sc. 2 (bar 177), on the other hand, is set to the same F–B dyad as on its appearance at the beginning and end of Act I, sc. 1; in Act II, sc. 2 the word is preceded (bar 174) by a quotation of the opening chords of the opera. The harmonies at bar 190 of Act II, sc. 2 are also a quotation from the opening scene of the opera and are a transposed version of the two chords at bar 11. Particularly ironic is the setting of the Doctor's 'Pressiert, pressiert', at bars 181 and 184–5 of Act II, sc. 2, to the same melodic figure as appeared earlier in Variation 14 of Act I, sc. 4 (bars 569/72) to the words 'aberatio mentalis partialis'. The Doctor's preoccupation with the need for haste has its counterpart in the Captain's preoccupation with the need to do everything slowly; both are symptoms of mental aberrations as deep as those which the Doctor diagnoses in Wozzeck.[3] The Doctor's diagnosis of the Captain's apoplexy, at bars 203–17 of Act II, sc. 2, is set to the slow waltz of Variation 13 of Act I, sc. 4, the music which originally accompanied the Doctor's diagnosis of Wozzeck's *idée fixe*. The

---

[1] The more extended of the quotations from I/2 which appear in I/4 are detailed in the chart on p. 197.

[2] See Perle, *Music Review*, 32: 4, 1971, pp. 281–2.

[3] See pp. 236–7 below.

contour of the opening phrase of the waltz has already been anticipated in the vocal line at bar 200 of Act II, sc. 2. The setting of the word 'Unsterblich' at bar 245 of Act II, sc. 2 is reminiscent of the setting of the same word at bar 630f. of Act I, sc. 4. When, at bar 299 of Act II, sc. 2, the Captain refers to the Drum Major's beard, the contour of the Captain's theme is modified in such a way that it resembles that of the Drum Major's material at bar 709 of Act I, sc. 5; other references to the material of the seduction scene of Act I, sc. 5 appear elsewhere in Act II, sc. 2.[1] An important and bitterly ironic transformation is that which the orchestral material of Act II, sc. 2, bars 221–2, undergoes during the course of the opera. At its original appearance this material accompanies the Doctor's taunts that the Captain might suffer 'cerebral apoplexy' and reappears later in the scene (bars 262–5) as the mock funeral march which accompanies the Captain's vision of the mourners following his coffin. At the end of the opera the Captain's mock funeral march is transformed into the climax of the final orchestral interlude which follows the death of Wozzeck.

The central and closing sections of the final orchestral interlude are a summing up of all the main motivic material of the opera, other than that associated with Marie. The most important of Marie's motives appear in the final scene of the opera which follows the interlude. The following table lists the motives employed in this interlude:

*WOZZECK: INTERLUDE ACT III, Scenes 4–5*

| Bars | Motivic Material |
|---|---|
| 337–8 | Harmonic structure = Act I sc. 2 chords (cf. I/2 bars 203–5) |
| 339–41 | Andre's Song of Act I, sc. 2 (cf. I/2 bars 212–4) |
| 340–2 | Close of Act I, sc. 2 (cf. I/2 bars 302–4) |
| 342–5 | Wozzeck's exit of Act I, sc. 3 (cf. I/3 bar 454) |
| 346f. | Doctor's motives (cf. I/4 bar 562) (See p. 57 above) |
| 347f. | Captain's motives (cf. I/1 bar 4) |
| 347 | Rondo Marziale theme of Act II, sc. 5 (cf. II/5 bar 761) |
| 349 | Passacaglia theme of Act I, sc. 4 (cf. I/4 bars 486–7) |
| 352–6 | Orchestral Introduction to Act I, sc. 5 (cf. I/5 bars 656–60) |
| 357 | Drum Major's motive of Act I, sc. 5 (cf. I/5 bar 666) |
| 358 | Act II, sc. 1, bars 111–3 including 'Wir arme Leut' motive |
| 365f. | Wozzeck's Fugue subject of Act II, sc. 2 (cf. II/2 bars 262–5) |

Not only leading motives and other smaller integrative elements of the kind discussed in Chapter II, but also large sections of music reappear during the course of the opera. The most important of these large-scale reprises are shown in the table below. Shorter quotations of the music of one scene in

[1] Compare, for example, violins bar 308 of II/2, and bar 683 of I/5; viola bars 300–1 of II/2 and horns bar 659 of I/5.

a later scene, such as the appearance of the repeated chord of Act I, sc. 2, bar 270 at bar 550 of Act I, sc. 4 or the reappearance of the three chords which form the harmonic basis of Act I, sc. 2 at bar 553 of Act I, sc. 4, have been omitted from the following table.

### WOZZECK: REPRISE STRUCTURE

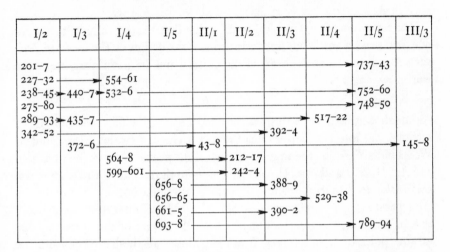

| I/2 | I/3 | I/4 | I/5 | II/1 | II/2 | II/3 | II/4 | II/5 | III/3 |
|---|---|---|---|---|---|---|---|---|---|
| 201–7 | | | | | | | | 737–43 | |
| 227–32 | | 554–61 | | | | | | | |
| 238–45 | 440–7 | 532–6 | | | | | | 752–60 | |
| 275–80 | | | | | | | | 748–50 | |
| 289–93 | 435–7 | | | | | | 517–22 | | |
| 342–52 | | | | | | 392–4 | | | |
| | 372–6 | | | 43–8 | | | | | 145–8 |
| | | 564–8 | | | 212–17 | | | | |
| | | 599–601 | | | 242–4 | | | | |
| | | | 656–8 | | | 388–9 | | | |
| | | | 656–65 | | | | 529–38 | | |
| | | | 661–5 | | | 390–2 | | | |
| | | | 693–8 | | | | | 789–94 | |

As always in Berg's operas, musical reprises are determined by dramatic considerations. The music of Act I, sc. 2 has both general and specific associations. At a general level it represents the natural world and those aspects of the natural world which give rise to the hallucinations which Wozzeck suffers during the course of Act I, sc. 2. The opening bars of Act I, sc. 2 return as the music of the sleeping soldiers at the beginning of Act III, sc. 5 and at a number of points in Act I, scenes 3 and 4, when Wozzeck attempts to describe his visions to Marie and the Doctor. The music of Act I, sc. 2 bars 275–80, which first appears when Wozzeck hears noises below the ground, reappears at bars 748–50 of Act II, sc. 5, along with fragments of the dance music of Act II, sc. 4, when Wozzeck hears voices speaking from the wall. Act I, sc. 2 bars 289–93 are specifically associated with the setting sun and first appear at the moment when the sun touches the horizon. They later reappear when Wozzeck describes the glow in the sky to Marie (Act I, sc. 3 bars 435–7) and when he calls upon God to extinguish the sun in Act II, sc. 4 (bars 517–22). The opening bars of Marie's Lullaby to the child in Act I, sc. 3 (bars 372–6) reappear as the basis of the song which she sings to the child in Act II, sc. 1 and, in a distorted form, as the basis of Wozzeck's song in the tavern scene of Act III, sc. 3; it is the realization of its relationship to the earlier Lullaby, and the memories of Marie which both the text of his song and this realization call forth, that causes Wozzeck to leave the song in Act III, sc. 3 unfinished. The Military March of Act I, sc. 3 and the 'seduction' music of Act I, sc. 5 form the basis of the musical material of the central section of Act II, sc. 3 when Wozzeck first charges Marie with her infidelity. The 'seduction' music also reappears as the waltz music of Act II, sc. 4 as Wozzeck watches Marie and the Drum Major dancing together. The reappearance of the slow waltz from Act I, sc. 4 in Act II, sc.2 has been discussed above (see p. 195).

The repetition of total musical units, rather than the repetition of themes or motives, plays a small but important role in the design of *Wozzeck*; in *Lulu* such repetitions lie at the heart of the musical and dramatic structure of the work.

*     *     *     *

Although designed as a three-act opera, *Lulu* really falls not into three sections, but into two halves, Act I and Act II, sc. 1 (which correspond to Wedekind's *Erdgeist*, the first of his two Lulu plays) forming the first half, and Act II, sc. 2 and Act III (corresponding to the second of the Lulu plays, *Die Büchse der Pandora*) forming the second half of the opera. The two halves are separated by the orchestral Ostinato 'Film Music' interlude. Constructed as a palindrome, the interlude marks both the centre of the opera and the turning point of Lulu's career. Since it includes all the basic cells and the most important of the twelve-note sets, the Ostinato also acts as a summing up of the musical material employed in the work. As Berg himself remarked in a letter to Schoenberg: 'The interlude which bridges the gap between the last act of *Earth Spirit* and the first act of *Pandora* is also the focal point of the whole tragedy. In it begins, after the ascent of the preceding acts and scenes, the descent of the following scenes.'[1] The symmetrical structure of the opera, balanced around this central interlude, is emphasized by the relationships between scene 1 and scene 2 of Act II, the only two scenes in the opera with the same stage set. Much of the musical material of Act II, sc. 2 is a reprise of that of Act II, sc. 1, the change in Lulu's fortunes being suggested by the fact that from the turning point of the interlude the strings and the brass are muted. For much of the following scene the earlier music is repeated 'in slow motion'.

At the same time, the three Acts of *Lulu*, like those of *Wozzeck*, present an overall ABA structure, the final scene of Act III acting as a recapitulation of much of the material of the earlier parts of the opera. The most important of these musical reprises come about as a result of Berg's desire to employ many of the performers in the opera in more than one role and his decision to associate the same musical material with all the roles played by a single performer. Berg seems to have changed his mind a number of times during

[1] See Redlich, *Alban Berg,* London, 1957, p. 176.

the course of his work on *Lulu* about the way in which these dual and triple roles were to be realized. Some of the early sketches for the opera, and a letter written to Schoenberg on 7 August 1930,[1] show that Berg originally intended to follow Wedekind in having Lulu visited by four clients in Act III, sc. 2 and planned to emphasize the palindromic dramatic structure of the opera as a whole by having the roles of these clients played, in reverse order, by the performers who took the parts of Lulu's 'victims' in the earlier part of the opera. Had this plan been realized, the role of the first client in Act III, sc. 2 would have been played by the singer who took the part of the Athlete earlier in the opera, the second client by the singer who took the role of Dr. Schön, the third by the singer who sang the role of the Painter and the fourth client, Jack the Ripper, by the performer who had played the Medical Specialist in Act I. This plan was eventually abandoned. The following Dramatis Personae appears amongst Berg's sketches for the work and shows his later, but not his final, thoughts on the way in which the dual and triple roles were to be realized.

### DRAMATIS PERSONAE

| | |
|---|---|
| Lulu | High Soprano* |
| Countess Geschwitz | Dramatic Mezzosoprano |
| A Wardrobe Mistress in Act I | |
| A Schoolboy (Hugenberg-Hosenrolle) in Act II | Contralto |
| A Groom (Bob) in Act III | |
| Medical Specialist | |
| 1st Visitor in the last scene | Silent role |
| Artist (Schwartz) in Act I | |
| 2nd Visitor in the last scene | Lyric Tenor |
| Dr. Schön, Chief Editor in Acts I and II | Heroic Baritone with touch of |
| 3rd Visitor in the last scene | Lyric |
| Alwa, Dr. Schön's son | Young Heroic Tenor |
| Schigolch | High Character Bass |
| Animal Trainer (singer in Prologue to Act I) | |
| Rodrigo, an athlete | Heroic Bass with touch of Buffo |
| African Traveller (Prince Esczerny) in Act I | |
| Manservant in Act II | Tenor Buffo |
| Procurer (Casti Piani) in Act III | |
| Theatre Director in Act I | |
| Police Commissioner in Act II | Basso Buffo |
| Banker in Act III | |
| Others in ensemble scene of Act III: | |
| A fifteen-year-old (Kadidja) | Soubrette |
| Her mother (Magelone) | Contralto |
| A designer (Bianetta) | Mezzosoprano |
| Journalist (Heilman) | High Baritone |
| A servant | Deeper [Baritone] |

\* Able to reach two or three ledger lines, somewhat coloratura and not without [illegible].

Three Acts: Act I, 3 scenes; Act II, 2 scenes (same set); Act III, 2 scenes. Together: 7 scenes (6 sets).    The director of this opera must be a drama director.

[1] See Redlich, *Alban Berg*, London, 1957, p. 175.

In Berg's final plan of the way in which the double and triple roles were to be effected the part of the Banker in Act III, sc. 1 (given, in the above list, to the performer who played the Theatre Director in Act I, sc. 3, and the Police Commissioner in Act II)[1] is one of three roles played by the performer who takes the part of the Medical Specialist in Act I, sc. 1 and the part of Lulu's first client in Act III, sc. 2; all three figures are associated with the same characteristic twelve-note set. The sketch of the Dramatis Personae reproduced above is undated but must have been made some time between August 1930, when Berg wrote to Schoenberg announcing his original plan of doubling the roles of the clients in Act III, sc. 2, and the end of September 1933, when Berg began work on the first scene of the final act. Having written the provisional Dramatis Personae shown above Berg also decided that all the characters in the opera, other than Lulu, Countess Geschwitz, Schön, Alwa and Schigolch, should remain nameless; the bracketed names in the above list, which are the names of the characters as they appear in the original Wedekind plays, should, therefore, be removed. The name 'Rodrigo', which Berg leaves unbracketed, should also be removed and the character designated simply as 'an Athlete'. The character of Alwa, besides being identified as Schön's son, should be designated 'a composer'. Lulu's first client should be identified as 'a Professor', her second client as 'a Negro' and her third and final client as 'Jack the Ripper'. With these corrections, and with the role of the Banker re-allotted in the way described, the above represents the final and authentic version of the Dramatis Personae in *Lulu* and corresponds to that published by George Perle in his various writings on the opera.[2]

The musical design of *Lulu*, like that of *Wozzeck*, is based upon traditional formal structures. In *Wozzeck* each scene consists of a self-contained, 'absolute' musical form, each act of the opera consisting of five such related forms (a cycle of character pieces in Act I, a cycle of inventions in Act III and a five-movement symphonic structure in Act II); in *Lulu*, on the other hand, each scene consists of a sequence of numbers of a kind traditionally associated

---

[1] Berg's doubling, in the above list, of the roles of the Banker and the 'Police Commissioner in Act II' is clearly a mistake. The Police Commissioner does not appear in Act II but at a point in Act III, sc. 1 of the opera which makes the suggested doubling of this role and that of the Banker an impossibility.

[2] See Perle, *Archiv für Musikwissenschaft* 24, 1967, p. 289; *Journal of the American Musicological Society*, Vol. 17, No. 2, 1964, p. 182; *Music Review*, 26, 1965, pp. 276–7. Although Perle describes the Banker as a baritone, the Particell score of the first Ensemble of Act III, sc. 1 places the vocal lines of the Banker and the Athlete on the two lowest staves and identifies them both as 'bass' (the Ensemble is scored for two sopranos, two mezzos, two contraltos, two tenors, two baritones and two basses). The tessitura of the Banker's vocal line is, however, identical with that of the two designated baritone parts and the layout of the Ensemble seems to be a curious remnant of the plan, shown in the sketch reproduced above, of doubling the role of the Banker with that of the bass Theatre Director. I have, unfortunately, been unable to consult Berg's orchestral score of this section.

with pre-Wagnerian opera (aria, arietta, cavatina, canzonetta and so on), many of the numbers being labelled with their appropriate title in the score of the opera and linked to one another by passages entitled 'Recitative'.[1] This sequence of numbers forms the most immediate structural level, within which smaller integrative elements operate and upon which the larger formal design is superimposed. In some cases the course of the individual numbers is interrupted by interpolations. Dr. Schön's Five-strophe Aria in Act II, sc. 1, for example, is interrupted, first, by the appearance of a 'tumultuoso' Burlesque[2] passage between the second and third strophes and, secondly, by the 'Lied der Lulu' which appears between strophes four and five. Since – as is the case with the 'tumultuoso' Burlesque – these interpolated passages may themselves represent only one segment of a larger musical unit, the juxtaposition of different subsections creates a complex multi-layered structure within the confines of each scene, a stratification of musical areas and characteristics that is reflected in both the larger and smaller musical structures.

On a larger scale than that of the individual numbers, each act of the opera is dominated by one large musical form, the subdivisions of which appear in the different scenes of the act. Thus, Act I is dominated by a Sonata movement, the exposition and first reprise of which appear in Act I, sc. 2, the development section and the recapitulation in Act I, sc. 3. Act II is dominated by a Rondo form, the different sections of which are spread over the two scenes of the act. Act III is dominated by a set of Variations, the theme of which is announced in the 'Procurer's Song', appears briefly in the fourth of the Chorale Variations of scene 1 and is the basis of the set of orchestral Variations which form the interlude between scenes 1 and 2. The theme and individual variations from the orchestral interlude recur at various points during Act III, sc. 2.

The following chart shows the structural plan of the three acts and attempts to indicate the stratification of different musical numbers. The lowest line of each system shows the sequence of individual numbers; the upper line shows the subdivisions of the large-scale form which dominates each act. Where individual numbers are interrupted by interpolations the different subdivisions of each number are linked by dotted lines above or below the lower of the two lines of each system. The published scores of Acts I and II of *Lulu* are inconsistent in their titling of individual numbers, an inconsistency which, presumably, Berg would have removed had he lived to prepare the score for publication. Thus, Dr. Schön's 'Das mein Lebensabend' at the beginning of Act II, sc. 1, though clearly a self-contained musical number, has no title in the published score. George Perle has suggested that the

[1] See Perle, *Journal of the American Musicological Society*, 17: 2, 1964.
[2] See p. 202 below.

number be entitled 'Arietta' as a means of pointing out its musical and dramatic relationship with Lulu's similarly designated number at the end of the same scene.[1] In one of Berg's sketches for the opera 'Das mein Lebensabend' has the title 'Ballade' and I have adopted this title in the following chart. Similarly the 'tumultuoso' sections of Act II, sc. 1 are entitled 'Burleska' in one of Berg's sketches and I have adopted the title 'Burlesque' to identify appearances of these tumultuoso sections throughout the scene. The title 'Rondo' for the musical material which dominates Act II does not appear in the published score of the opera but appears in Berg's sketches and is the title which Berg gave to the movement of the *Lulu Suite* which consists of this material.[2] The titles on those sections of the following chart which show the formal organization of Act III are more problematic. The structure of Act III, sc. 1 is based on the three ensemble numbers, which open, close and form the central section of the scene, and on three numbers between Lulu and the Marquis, Lulu and the Athlete, and Lulu and Schigolch. I have followed Perle in designating these three numbers Duets I, II and III respectively. The three Ensembles are designated as such in the Particell. Apart from the Nocturno none of the numbers in Act III, sc. 2 is given a title in Berg's Particell; I have entitled them in a way that attempts to show the dramatic and musical structure of the scene. In Melodrama I and Melodrama II, Alwa and Schigolch are alone on stage. During the first part of these two Melodramas, the spoken dialogue is accompanied by the theme of the 'Procurer's Song', played in E flat major by an off-stage barrel-organ against a tremolando A major chord on the orchestral strings; during the second part the dialogue is accompanied by three-part tremolando string chords (*am steg*) derived from the sets associated with Alwa and Schigolch.[3] Melodrama III again begins with Alwa and Schigolch alone on stage, but Alwa is now dead, having been killed by Lulu's second client. The three Episodes accompany Lulu's return from the streets with her three clients. In the First Episode, section A, Lulu takes the client across the stage to her room; in the First Episode, section B, she returns to the streets. In the Second Episode Alwa attempts to interrupt and is murdered. In the Third Episode, section A, Lulu enters with Jack the Ripper, her third client, and crosses the stage to her room with him. Section B of the Third Episode[4] begins with Lulu's death cry, continues with Jack's reappearance on stage, his stabbing of Countess Geschwitz and exit, and ends with the Countess's

[1] See Perle, *Journal of the American Musicological Society*, 17, 1964, p. 180.
[2] See Perle, *Journal of the American Musicological Society*, 17, 1964, p. 187.
[3] See Perle, ibid., p. 189.
[4] Third Episode, section B corresponds to the final 33 bars of the Adagio of the published *Lulu* Suite; Jack's four vocal phrases in these bars correspond to (i) the horn part at bars 89–90, (ii) alto saxophone part at bars 91–2, (iii) 1st horn and bassoon parts bars 94–5, (iv) cor anglais part bars 97–8 of the published score.

death. During the section which I have entitled 'Trio', Lulu is preparing to return to the streets when she, Alwa and Schigolch hear someone approaching. Countess Geschwitz enters with Lulu's portrait and the four sing a Quartet. Geschwitz then follows Lulu out onto the streets and Alwa and Schigolch are left alone for the following duet.

In the following chart, the unbracketed titles are those that appear in the published score of the opera, derive from the Particell of Act III or are to be found in Berg's sketches.

The Sonata movement which dominates Act I of the opera is associated with the figure of Dr. Schön, whose attempts, and ultimate failure, to free himself of Lulu form the basis of the main dramatic action. The Sonata movement has two halves which appear in two different scenes of Act I: the exposition and first reprise in sc. 2 and the development and final reprise in sc. 3. The two halves of the Sonata movement emphasize the dramatic similarities between the two scenes in which they appear: in Act I, sc. 2, Dr. Schön, fearing a scandal that could ruin his career, asks Lulu to stop visiting him and gives the fact that he is about to be married to a respectable young lady as his reason for wishing to end their affair. Lulu refuses to take his demands seriously. In a desperate attempt to free himself of Lulu, Schön tells the Painter, Lulu's husband, of their association. Horrified by Schön's revelations the Painter, instead of stopping his wife's affair with Dr. Schön, commits suicide. The coda of the Sonata reprise is interrupted as Schön tells the Painter of Lulu's past and is resumed at the end of the scene, where it forms the orchestral interlude between Act I, sc. 2 and Act I, sc. 3.

In Act I, sc. 3, Schön visits Lulu in her theatre dressing room and repeats his demands that she stop visiting him. A violent argument develops between them. Lulu mocks Schön's attempts to appear respectable, jeers at his fiancée's innocence, and threatens to leave for Africa with one of her suitors. Faced with Lulu's taunts and the prospect of complete separation from her, Schön realizes his inability to sever his ties with Lulu and breaks down in tears. The argument between Dr. Schön and Lulu is set as the development section of the Sonata; the final Sonata reprise begins as Schön breaks down and admits defeat. In the final section of the scene Lulu dictates to Schön the letter he will send to his fiancée to end their engagement.

The musical structure also comments upon the dramatic action in more subtle, and in some cases deeply ironic, ways. Each of the four sections of the Sonata exposition is associated with a particular idea in the conversation between Schön and Lulu. At the beginning of the exposition, Schön's demands that Lulu stop visiting him are accompanied by the Sonata's energetic main theme. Schön's mention of the Painter – 'If Walter weren't such a childish soul he would have known of your escapades long ago' – introduces the bridge passage, in which Lulu complains that she is bored by

## LULU

## ACT I

*Scene 1*

**Recitative**    Introduction   Canon    Coda    Melodrama    Canzonetta   Recitative    Duet    Arioso    *INTERLUDE*

bars 86–131    132–55    156–85    186–95    196–257    258–83    284–304    305–28    329–50    351–413

*Scene 2*

                *SONATA: EXPOSITION*      ------ *FIRST REPRISE*      Monoritmica      ------→ *(FIRST REPRISE contd.)*

Duettino   Chamber Music I    (1st Subject; transition;     (1st Subject; transition;               (Coda)           *INTERLUDE*

                             2nd Subject; Coda)      2nd Subject)

bars 416–62    463–530      533–624       625–68       669–957      958–92

*Scene 3*

------ **Ragtime**   Andante   English Waltz   Recitative   Choral   Ragtime   Sextet    -----→ *DEVELOPMENT* ------→ *RECAPITULATION*

                                                                       (1st Subject; transition;

                                                                       2nd Subject; Coda)

bars 992–1020   1020–40   1040–94   1095–1113   1113–54   1155–76   1177–1208    1209–88               1289–1361

# ACT II

RONDO: EXPOSITION ---→ (EXPOSITION contd.) ---→ (EXPOSITION contd.) ---→ (EXPOSITION contd.) ---→

## Scene 1

| Recitative | Ballade | Cavatina | Langsame | Canon | Ensemble | Burlesque Tumultuoso | Chorale (Main theme: A¹) | (Bridge & Subsid. theme: B) | Burlesque Tumultuoso |
|---|---|---|---|---|---|---|---|---|---|
| bars 1–39 | 40–60 | 61–88 | 94–172 | 173–94 | 195–224 | 225–43 | 243–9 | 250–61 | 262–73 · 274 |

| (Subsid. theme B and Main theme A²) | Chorale | Burlesque Tumultuoso | Chorale | Ensemble (Main theme A² and Coda C¹) | Burlesque Tumultuoso | (Coda themes C¹, C², C³) | Burlesque Tumultuoso | Introduction |
|---|---|---|---|---|---|---|---|---|
| 275–86 | 287–93 | 294 | 295–7 | 298–309 | 310–17 | 318–37 | 338–79 | 380–6 |

| Five Strophe Aria (Strophes 1 and 2) | Burlesque Tumultuoso | Five Strophe Aria (Strophes 3 and 4) | Lied der Lulu | Five Strophe Aria (Strophe 5) | Burlesque Tumultuoso | Grave | Arietta |
|---|---|---|---|---|---|---|---|
| 387–415 | 416–20 | 421–90 | 491–538 | 539–52 | 553–604 | 605–19 | 620–51 |

*INTERLUDE ('OSTINATO')* → 652–721

## Scene 2

(RONDO): MIDDLE SECTION --- RECAPITULATION

| Recitative | Largo | Recitative | Largo and Spoken | Chamber Music [2] | Melodrama | | Musette | | Hymn |
|---|---|---|---|---|---|---|---|---|---|
| bars 722–87 | 788–814 | 815–22 | 823–34 | 834–952 | 953–1000 | 1004–58 | 1059–87 | 1087–96 | 1097–1150 |

ACT III

*Scene 1*

| [Ensemble I] | [Melodrama] | [Duet I]: Concertante Chorale Variations (Variations I and 2) | —— INTERMEZZO I —— (Procurer's Song) | Intermezzo II | Chorale Variations (Variations 3–9) |
|---|---|---|---|---|---|
| bars 1–52 | 53–82 | 83–102 | 103–18 | 119–45 | 146–230 |

*Scene 2*

| Ensemble II | [Duet II] | Pantomime | [Duet III] | Cadenza | [Scena] | Ensemble III | [Recitative] | —— INTERLUDE —— (4 variations on the Procurer's Song of Intermezzo I) |
|---|---|---|---|---|---|---|---|---|
| 231–71 | 272–330 | 331–47 | 348–447 | 448–76 | 477–541 | 542–651 | 652–70 | 671–714 |

*Scene 2*

*Scena 1*

—— THEME —— (of Procurer's Song)*    THEME* ——    VARIATION 4 ——→    VARIATION 2 ——→

| [Melodrama I] [First Episode (A)] | [Melodrama II] [First Episode (B)] | [Trio] | (Reprise) [Quartet] | (Reprise)* [Duet] |
|---|---|---|---|---|
| bars 715–45   746–801 | 802–27   828–47 | 848–65 | 866–1001 | 1002–35 |

*Scena 4*

—— VARIATION 3 —— (Reprise)*

| [Melodrama III] |
|---|
| 1088–1164 |

*Scena 3*

| [Second Episode] | [Third Episode (A)] | Nocturno | [Third Episode (B)] |
|---|---|---|---|
| 1036–87 | 1165–1256 | 1257–71 | 1272–1304 |

* At these points the restatements of the theme and variations of the 'Procurer's Song' are incorporated into and form part of larger musical sections. The precise bars at which the theme and its variations appear in these sections are shown in the chart on p. 211.

her husband – 'He sees nothing . . . He is blind . . . He does not know me at all. What am I to him?' – and Schön complains of the Painter's refusal to take his wife in hand – 'You live in luxury. Your husband owes his position to me. If that isn't good enough for you and he notices nothing . . . leave me out of it!' With typical irony, Berg introduces the theme of the earlier Duettino between Lulu and the Painter, which originally accompanied the Painter's remarks about the happiness of his life with Lulu, as an orchestral countersubject in the final measures of this bridge passage. The second subject group is associated with Schön's wish to marry his fiancée and his hopes of thereby breaking his ties with Lulu: 'I am engaged. I want to bring my bride into a decent house.' Lulu suggests that she and Schön can still meet and is violently rebuffed by Schön: 'We shall not meet anywhere.' This rebuff coincides with the restatement of the first subject theme. 'You yourself don't believe what you are saying,' says Lulu and her reply ushers in the coda theme: 'If I belong to anyone in this world, I belong to you. Without you I should be – I won't say where. You took me by the hand, you fed me, you clothed me . . . do you think that I can forget that?' The coda theme represents not only Lulu's love for Schön and her obligations to him (obligations which she uses as a means of strengthening the ties between them) but also Schön's inability to free himself of Lulu.[1]

The libretto of the rest of the Sonata movement is constructed in a way that will enable Berg to exploit these relationships between music and text.[2] The start of the first reprise coincides with the renewal of Schön's demand that Lulu stop visiting him and the reprise of the bridge passage accompanies Schön's words, 'I had hoped that, with a healthy young man . . . you would finally be content.' Ironically, however, Schön's words are set to the melodic line that Lulu sang in the Sonata exposition when she complained about the Painter's domesticity. The lines which Schön sings to the reprise of the third section of the first subject group (the reprise of which is interpolated between the bridge passage and the second subject group) again renew his demands that Lulu stop seeing him: 'I shall be married,' says Schön with determination to a final statement of the first subject theme. The music moves on to the reprise of the second subject group as the discussion turns to the subject of Schön's marriage. Schon's decision to tell Lulu's husband of their affair – 'I must finally have my hands free!' – is accompanied by the coda theme.

The importance of the associations which have now been established between the music and the text becomes clear in the development section of the Sonata, in which the musical course of events is entirely determined by

[1] The significance of this coda theme is examined in Perle, 'The Character of Lulu: A Sequel', *Music Review*, 25, 1964, pp. 311–9.
[2] A comparison of the libretto with the relevant scenes from Wedekind's *Erdgeist* (II/3 and III/10) shows that Berg has deliberately changed the order of certain passages in the play so as to enable him to exploit the relationships discussed above.

the dramatic action. The development begins with imitative statements of Schön's row, above which are heard fragments of the second subject group as Lulu accuses Schön of trying to humiliate her by making her dance in front of his fiancée. Her references to her indebtedness to Schön – 'I well know what would have happened to me if you had not saved me from it' – are accompanied by fragments of the coda material. As Schön asks why the Prince is in the audience the opening phrase of the Prince's chorale theme (heard earlier in the same scene) introduces a reprise of the bridge passage. Lulu replies that the Prince is taking her to Africa: 'You made me a dancer only so that someone would come who would take me with him.' 'But not to Africa,' replies Schön in horror. The reprise of the bridge passage at this point is bitterly ironic, for the music which had previously been associated with Dr. Schön's attempts to free himself of Lulu by finding her a husband now accompanies Lulu's threats of leaving Schön forever. Faced with the prospect of never seeing her again, it becomes clear that Schön's attempts to find Lulu a husband were a matter of convenience and that he has not the strength to finally free himself of her; the coda theme becomes an integral part of the musical texture after this point.

Lulu's 'No one is keeping you here . . . where is your energy?' brings an ironic return of the main theme of the Sonata (which was originally marked 'Energico'). The final reprise begins as Dr. Schön breaks into tears: 'He is weeping. The man of authority is weeping!', sings Lulu triumphantly to the music which originally accompanied Schön's demands that she stop visiting him. The bridge passage now appears in a modified and purely instrumental form and leads to the 'letter duet', an extended canonic reprise of the second subject group – the music, which was originally associated with Schön's fiancée and his hopes of freeing himself from Lulu by his marriage, now accompanying Lulu's dictation of the letter which Schön will send to his fiancée to end their engagement. This reprise is underpinned by statements of the fateful coda theme, which finally appears in the voice part at the end of the scene as Schön, realizing that he has signed his 'death warrant', sings, 'Now comes the execution!'

Whereas the design of the Sonata movement of Act I is based on contrasting musical and verbal subjects, the various sections of the Rondo which dominates Act II, and is associated with Alwa's declaration of love for Lulu, are less highly differentiated. The only specific associations of musical and textual ideas are those that appear in the coda section and which have been discussed earlier.[1]

The theme of the Variations which dominate Act III first appears on solo violin as the orchestral melody of the Marquis's 'Procurer's Song', which forms the first Intermezzo in the set of Chorale Variations in Act III, sc. 1,

[1] See pp. 99–100 above.

where it accompanies the Marquis's attempts to persuade Lulu to take a job in a Cairo brothel.[1] When Lulu refuses, the Marquis informs the police of her whereabouts and the Variation theme then becomes associated with, and symbolizes, her resulting decline into prostitution. The theme is the melody of Wedekind's *Lautenlied*, 'Konfession'. Although the text of the *Lautenlied* appears in neither the play nor the opera, its relevance to the drama was clearly one of the reasons for Berg's choosing to employ this particular melody. Wedekind's original version of the melody and a translation of the text of the *Lautenlied* appear in Appendix II.

I have already remarked on the extent to which the overall structure of *Lulu* is dependent on the recurrence of large sections of music from one scene in another. The first of the following charts shows the most important of these reappearances in Acts I and II and in Act III, sc. 1. Many of these musical reprises, such as the reappearance of the Prince's chorale theme of Act I, sc. 3 in Act II, sc. 1, when the Manservant appears, and in Act III, sc. 1, as the basis of the Marquis's Chorale Variations, are determined by Berg's use of dual and triple roles. Others, such as the reappearance of the material of the 'Lied der Lulu' of Act II, sc. 1 as the basis of the second Intermezzo of Act III, sc. 1, emphasize the similarities between different events or dramatic situations. The reappearance of a large section of Act II, sc. 1 in Act II, sc. 2 points not only the more obvious dramatic similarities between the two scenes but also their similar structural function in the design of the work as a whole, as the two scenes which flank the central palindromic Ostinato interlude. The recapitulations in Act III, sc. 2 (which is completely dominated by the reappearance of material, both musical and verbal, from the earlier part of the opera) are shown separately on the second of the charts which follow. I shall discuss the dramatic significance of these reprises in Chapter VI.

The following charts indicate those points at which sections of music of some considerable length recur during the course of the opera. In addition to the reappearances of these extended passages a variety of thematic, harmonic, rhythmic and other musical characteristics function as leading motives associated with particular figures or events in the opera and afford a very flexible means of interrelating and commenting upon different aspects of the drama. I have already discussed the different twelve-note sets and rhythmic or metric patterns associated with the different characters in the opera in Chapters III and IV.

A survey of the relation between the text and music of the Monoritmica of Act I, sc. 2 of *Lulu* will give some indication of the way in which Berg's

---

[1] The first ('Grandioso') variation of the published score (minus the statements of basic cell *II* in the harp and piano parts) corresponds to the 'Procurer's Song' in III/1.

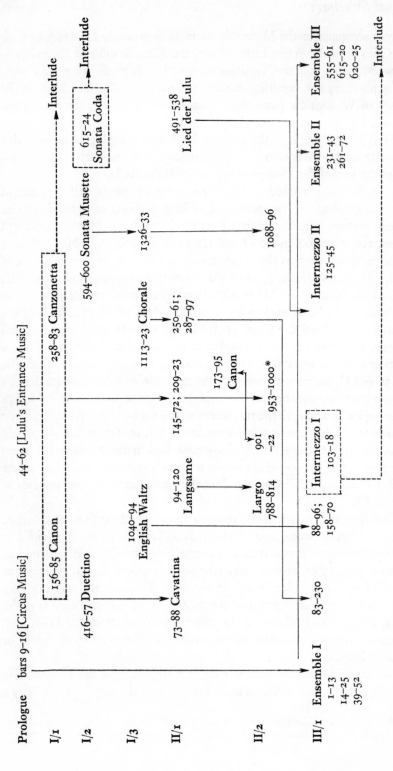

LULU: REPRISE STRUCTURE

* Modified versions of fragments of Lulu's Entrance Music appear at bars 1000–3 and 1010–15 of II/2, are incorporated into the Rondo (bars 1030–1037 and 1080–6) and end III/1 (bars 654–60).

ORCHESTRAL INTERLUDE: [THEME AND] FOUR VARIATIONS bars 671–714

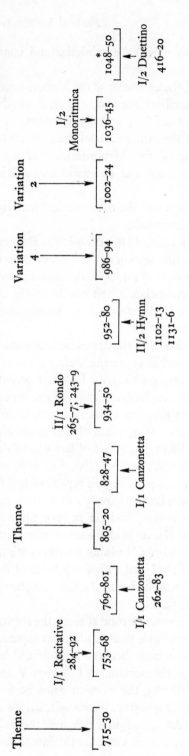

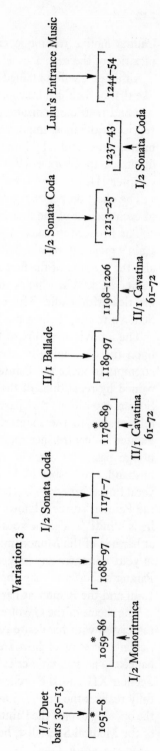

leading-motive technique enables him to reflect the subtleties and complexities of the drama.

Although a self-contained musical unit, the autonomy of the Monoritmica, like that of the third movement of the Chamber Concerto, rests on its rhythmic and metric organization; thematically and harmonically it consists of a reprise of the most important material of the earlier parts of the opera. The metronomic and rhythmic organization of the Monoritmica has been discussed in Chapter IV;[1] the main thematic and harmonic material in Chapter III.

The chart on pages 213–15 shows the text and the main musical material of each section of the first half of the Monoritmica.

The Monoritmica accompanies Schön's attempts to persuade the Painter, Lulu's husband, to take her in hand. The first section of the Monoritmica is also the opening of the first reprise of the coda of Dr. Schön's Sonata movement, the section which comes to represent Schön's fatal inability to break his ties with Lulu. The opening of the coda reprise here accompanies Schön's words, 'I must finally have my hands free'.

The motivic structure of the Monoritmica both illustrates and comments upon the developing course of Schön's verbal argument. Schön's various attempts to make the Painter accept his responsibility for Lulu are accompanied by repetitions of the material from the bridge passage of the earlier Sonata exposition, that part of the Sonata that was concerned with Lulu's relationship to the Painter. Thus, at bars 673–7, when Schön urges the Painter to 'control her more', the vocal line repeats that of bar 579 of the bridge passage (where it appeared to Schön's words, 'I've found you a husband, two husbands!') while the orchestral parts begin a reprise of Lulu's vocal line at bars 579–82, the music to which Lulu originally complained that the Painter 'scarcely knows me – he sees nothing, neither me nor himself, he is blind!' The same vocal line from the Sonata bridge passage reappears, at bar 683 of the Monoritmica, to Schön's words, 'I cannot let you continue in your blindness any longer', where it is combined with a repetition of the Painter's chords as they appeared in the introduction to the Canon between Lulu and the Painter at bar 142 of Act I, sc. 1.

The theme of the Gavotte section of the Sonata second subject, the section associated with his desire to marry a 'respectable young lady', accompanies Schön's account of how Lulu attempted to come between himself and his fiancée. The Painter's cries of 'O God' at the beginning of Section V and Section XII and the orchestral part at bar 703, the moment when he first fully realizes the implications of what Schön is saying, are recapitulations of the opening bars of the Painter's Arioso in Act I, sc. 1, in which, over the body of the Medical Specialist, he first expressed his fears of what the future held

[1] See pp. 167–8 above.

for him. Mention of Lulu's first meeting with the Medical Specialist (bars 694–701) produces a statement of the triads which opened Act I, sc. 1 (bar 92) and of the dyads and the RH variant associated with the Medical Specialist in Act I, sc. 1. The Painter's exit at bars 739–47 of the Monoritmica, ostensibly to speak to Lulu but in reality to commit suicide, is accompanied by an ironic repetition of the music of the final section of the Act I, sc. 1, Arioso, the music to which he originally prayed to be given the strength to deal with whatever lay before him. Equally ironic is the comment on the Painter's capacity for self-deception expressed by the orchestral repetition, at bar 704f., of the Duet of Act I, sc. 1, which originally appeared as he asked Lulu whether she was capable of telling the truth and now accompanies his protestations that Schön's account of Lulu's past life does not agree with what she has told him. The discussion of Lulu's name in Section IX combines a reprise of those parts of the coda to the Canon in Act I, sc. 1 in which she and the Painter discussed the same subject, with statements of Schigolch's serial trope, representing Lulu's mythical origins. The significance of the statement of basic cell I to which is set the Painter's cry of 'All lies' has already been discussed.[1]

## MONORITMICA

*Section I ♪ = 76 bars 666–8*
Text: Schön: 'I must finally have my hands free'

First reprise of Sonata Coda

*Section II ♪ = 84 bars 669–71*
Schön: 'You've married half a million'

Basic series throughout

*Section III ♪ = 92 bars 672–4*
Schön: 'Control her more . . . we aren't children'

Portrait chords
Voice = Schön bar 579

*Section IV ♪ = 100 bars 675–8*

Schön: 'You've married half a million . . . make yourself responsible'

Voice = Sect. II bar 669

Orchestra = bars 579–82 (Sonata Bridge Passage)

*Section V ♪ = 108 bars 679–85*
Painter: 'O God, O God!'
Schön: 'I didn't come here to make a scandal,

Voice and Orchestra = bar 332 (Arioso)
Voice: Schön's series (P); Orchestra: Schön's series (I)

[1] See p. 97 above.

I came to save you from one . . . $\left\{\begin{array}{l}\text{Voice: Schön's series (R); Orchestra:} \\ \text{Schön's series (RI)}\end{array}\right.$

'I cannot let you continue in
your blindness . . .
$\left\{\begin{array}{l}\text{Voice = bars 581-2 (Sonata Bridge} \\ \text{Passage)} \\ \text{Orchestra = bars 143-4 (Introduction to} \\ \text{Canon)}\end{array}\right.$

'She has improved since I knew
her . . .'
$\left\{\begin{array}{l}\text{Voice: Schigolch's trope} \\ \text{Orchestra: Painter's dyads}\end{array}\right.$

Painter: 'Since you knew her . . .?'      Orchestra: Painter's dyads
(cf. bars 385-6 Canzonetta)

---

*Section VI ♪ = 120 bars 687-93*
Schön: 'She sold flowers in front of the      Painter's dyads = Lulu's scale
Alhambra Cafe'

---

*Section VII ♪ = 132 bars 694-701*
Painter: 'How did Dr. Goll come to know      Orchestra: = bar 92 (Recitative)
her?'                                                                  Medical Specialist's RH
                                                                            (Solo cello)

Schön: 'When I met my present fiancée'  $\left\{\begin{array}{l}\text{Voice = Sonata Theme} \\ \text{Orchestra = bars 587-90 (Sonata Gavotte)}\end{array}\right.$

Painter: 'And when her husband died?'      Orchestra: Medical Specialist's dyads and
RH

---

*Section VIII ♩ = 76 bars 702-9*

Schön: 'You married half a million'  $\left\{\begin{array}{l}\text{Voice = Sect. II bar 669} \\ \text{Orchestra: Medical Specialist's dyads}\end{array}\right.$
Orchestra = bar 135 (Introduction to
Canon)

Painter: 'And she told me . . . she had
never loved'
$\left\{\begin{array}{l}\text{Voice = bars 332-3 (Arioso)} \\ \text{Orchestra = bars 305-6 (Duet)} \\ \text{cf. bar 399 (Interlude)}\end{array}\right.$

Schön: 'With a background like Mignon's
you can't judge by the usual      $\left.\begin{array}{l}\\\\\\\end{array}\right\}$ Schigolch's trope
bourgeois standards'

---

*Section IX ♩ = 86 bars 710-16*

Painter: 'Of whom are you speaking?      Orchestra = bars 134-5 (Intro-
. . . Of Eva?'                                              duction to Canon)

Schön: 'I call her Mignon'                                                            Schi-
                                                                                                golch
Painter: 'I thought they called her          = bar 189 (Coda to Canon)      trope
Nelly?'                                                                                      through-
                                                                                                out
Schön: 'That's what Dr. Goll called her'

Painter: 'I call her Eva'                          = bar 190 (Coda to Canon)

---

*Section X* ♩ = *96 bars 717–23*
Schön: 'With a father like Mignon's . . .'    Schigolch's trope

---

*Section XI* ♩ = *106 bars 724–31*
Painter: 'All lies'                    Voice: Basic Cell I
Schön: 'Let her feel your authority'        Sonata Main Theme

---

*Section XII* ♩ = *118 bars 732–8*
Painter: 'O God!'                   Orchestra = bars 332–2 (Arioso)

---

*Section XIII* ♩ = *132 bars 739–47*
Painter: 'You are right, quite right!'    Orchestra = bars 339–45 (Arioso)
                [Painter exits bar 747]

---

*Section XIV* ♪ = *76 bars 748–65*
                    Percussion: Canon on RH
                [Doorbell rings bar 765]

---

*Section XV* ♩ = *86 bars 765–86*        Percussion: Canon on RH
                [Alwa enters bar 787]

---

*Section XVI* ♪ = *96 bars 787–811*        Simultaneous statements of Basic Series,
                    Alwa's Series and Schön's Series

---

*Section XVII* ♪ = *112 bars 812–32*        Simultaneous statements of Basic Series,
                    Alwa's Series, Schön's Series and Lulu's
                    Series
                [Door opens bar 833]

---

*Section XVIII* ♪ = *132 bars 833–42*        Vertical and horizontal statements of
                    Basic Cell III

---

In addition to being associated with particular twelve-note sets and characteristic rhythmic or metric patterns, many of the figures in *Lulu* are also associated with a particular instrument or combination of instruments. The Athlete is associated with the piano and with the brass and percussion, the Schoolboy with the woodwind and horns. The three characters who make up the triple role of the Prince, the Manservant and the Marquis are associated with the solo strings. The Marquis is associated, exclusively, with the solo violin, the Manservant with the solo viola and the Prince mainly with the solo cello. The figure of Schigolch is associated with various chamber com-

binations – a wind nonet in Act I and a small group of strings, consisting of
violas, cellos and double basses, in Act II, sc. 1. Berg did not, when laying
out the score, reach the duet between Schigolch and Lulu in Act III, sc. 1.
Reich refers to this duet as a 'hasty chamber music'[1] and there are indications
at various points in the Particell score of this duet, of parts for horn, bass
clarinet, trumpet, clarinet and pizzicato strings. Since, in Berg's sketches for
*Lulu*, the note 'Chamber symphony-type' appears on a page which consists
of a list of the various possible chamber combinations, he may have intended
to score this duet for an instrumental ensemble similar to that employed in
Schoenberg's First Chamber Symphony.[2]

In the Prologue to *Lulu* the mention of each of the beasts in the Animal
Trainer's menagerie is accompanied by the twelve-note series associated
with one of the figures in the opera. Thus, the tiger is identified as Dr. Schön
through the appearance of Schön's series and the main theme of his Sonata
movement; the camel 'behind the curtain' as the Painter by the appearance of
the opening bars of his Arioso in Act I, sc. 1; the lizard as the Medical
Specialist by the appearance of his characteristic dyads. In those cases where
a figure is associated with other musical characteristics in addition to a
twelve-note set these other characteristics also appear. The Animal Trainer's
reference to the bear, for example, is set to the Athlete's series in the 9/8
rhythm and accompanied by the bass drum associated with him. The monkey
is identified as the Marquis (and the other two figures in the opera who,
together with the Marquis, make up a triple role) through the appearance of
his harmonized chorale theme and a characteristic statement of the series to
which it gives rise on solo double bass, solo cello, solo viola and solo violin in
turn. The worm is identified as Schigolch by the appearance of his serial
trope in its characteristic semiquaver quadruplet figurations. The crocodile
is identified as Countess Geschwitz through the appearance of her trope and
the characteristic accelerando-ritardando rhythmic pattern associated with
her. Mention of the snake, and the subsequent entrance of a stage hand
carrying Lulu, gives rise to a statement of Lulu's entrance music on strings,
flutes, harp and vibraphone. The figure of the Animal Trainer himself is
associated with both the Athlete, through the appearance of the Athlete's
chord clusters on the piano, and Alwa who, as Berg's own representative, is
the composer of the opera which follows.[3] The character of the Schoolboy is
not identified as one of the Animal Trainer's beasts although his serial trope
appears briefly on the horns (the instruments with which he is later associated) as part of the 9/8 section which identifies the bear as the Athlete.

I have already shown how, in Act II, sc. 2, of *Wozzeck*, the three fugue

[1] Reich, *Alban Berg*, London, 1965, p. 173.
[2] There is, however, no trumpet in the ensemble employed in the Schoenberg work.
[3] See Perle, *Music Review*, 26, 1965, pp. 278–9.

subjects are associated with the three characters on stage in such a way that every detail of the design of the Fugue is determined by dramatic considerations. This principle is greatly extended in the ensemble scenes of Act II of *Lulu* where all the musical elements associated with a particular character appear only when that character is singing or when the stage directions in the score indicate that he moves or performs some action. During bars 95–104 of Act II, sc. 1, for example, the asthmatic Schigolch slowly makes his way down the staircase, stopping to rest after every few steps. Schigolch's musical characteristics – chromatic figurations in quadruplets played by a chamber group (in this scene the lower strings) – appear every time he descends a step and disappear whenever he rests, the points at which he rests and moves being meticulously indicated in the stage directions. So close is the association between the music and the stage action that these same chromatic quadruplet patterns on the strings appear at bar 137, when Schigolch is directed simply to stare at the Schoolboy. The ensemble scene of Act II, sc. 1 is a collage of the various musical elements associated with the figures of Schigolch, the Athlete and the Schoolboy. Example 208 illustrates the way in which the different groups of material are superimposed during this scene according to the demands of the stage action. The ensemble scene of Act II, sc. 1, thus, presents a large section of music, the total effect of which results from the interaction of various precompositionally determined melodic, harmonic, rhythmic, metric and timbral details.

Similar passages can be found elsewhere in Berg's music. The outer sections of the third movement, and the 'Tenebroso' sections of the fifth movement of the *Lyric Suite* result from the interaction of predetermined methods of rhythmic and pitch organization. The Rondo Ritmico of the Chamber Concerto provides a similar, though less strictly handled, example of music whose total effect results from the application of an independent rhythmic pattern to pre-existing melodic and harmonic material. Peculiar to *Lulu*, however, is the extent to which such precompositional organizational schemes permeate the whole musical and dramatic structure.

Berg's leading-motive-like handling of the different musical parameters in *Lulu* reaches its climax in the bizarre 'Burlesque' sequences of Act II, sc. 1. Example 209 below shows the opening bars of the Burlesque passage in which – the Manservant having announced the arrival of Alwa – Schigolch, the Athlete and the Schoolboy try to find somewhere to hide. The Manservant announces Alwa to a statement of basic cell V, a cell which is always associated with important entrances. The original form of this cell is shown in Ex. 110; on its appearance at the beginning of the passage shown in the following example, the cell is modified in such a way that its lower notes form a statement of the 'white-note' collection E–A–B–C–F. The structural significance of this collection in the opera as a whole has been discussed

above.[1] The relationship between this modified version of basic cell V and
the other material employed in the scene is exploited in the following two

Ex. 208

bars where the Athlete's 'Der Lumpenkerl', set to an ascending statement of
basic cell II on the five notes of the 'white-note' collection (a setting which
mirrors that of Schön's similar remark, 'Der Kerl hat Mut' at bar 52 of the
same scene), is followed by a statement of the Athlete's series at P–4 (at which
level the first three and last three notes contain the same five 'white' notes)

[1] See pp. 89–90 above.

and a statement of the Athlete's trope. As can be seen from Ex. 209 the actions of each of the characters in this passage, and the period of time within which each action is performed, are indicated by vertical arrows in the score. In the case of Schigolch the timing of each separate step is indicated. The actions of each character are precisely synchronized with the appearance in the orchestra of a fragment of music based upon the pitch, rhythmic and timbral features associated with that character: Schigolch's actions are accompanied by statements of chromatic figurations derived from his serial trope played by a chamber group consisting of the lower strings in what is effectively a 4/4 metre. The Schoolboy is accompanied by statements of his serial trope on woodwind in quaver triplets, the Athlete by statements of his series, his trope or of the five-note 'white-note' collection which it contains on horn or piano in crotchets in 6/4 metre. Lulu is accompanied by her scale figure on the flute. After his initial announcement the Manservant stands motionless in the centre of the room until he eventually leaves accompanied by his chorale theme on solo viola.

George Perle has remarked on the extent to which Berg's handling of the lighting, the curtains and scenic effects such as the setting sun and the rising moon in *Wozzeck* 'play an integral role in the overall design' so that they 'function as themes and leitmotive and are as much part of the total conception as the verbal text and the music'.[1] In *Lulu*, as the Example 209 demonstrates, almost every aspect of the production is determined by the composer and integrated into the musical structure of the opera. Thus, the points at which Alwa strikes the nail, when hanging Lulu's portrait in Act III, sc. 2, are precisely notated in the score, the hammer blows forming a statement of the Hauptrhythmus of the opera. The points at which Lulu fires the revolver at Schön in Act II, sc. 1 are also notated and also determined by structural considerations, the shots marking the climactic notes of a series of figurations (a variant of those shown in Ex. 126) which unfold a statement of the dyads associated with Dr. Schön which were discussed in Chapter III above.[2] Similarly the film which accompanies the Ostinato interlude between Act II, scenes 1 and 2 would, were it ever made in accordance with Berg's intentions, not only mirror the course of the music in its general outlines but itself define a palindrome, every image and every detail in its first half matching a corresponding image in the second half.[3]

\* \* \* \*

Berg's love of 'abstract', precompositionally determined organizational

---

[1] Perle, 'Three Views of *Wozzeck*', *Saturday Review*, 2, Dec. 1967, p. 54.
[2] See pp. 95–9.
[3] See Reich, *Alban Berg*, London, 1965, pp. 229–30, note 19.

Ex. 209

procedures and of complicated and highly artificial symmetries permeates every aspect of the two operas. In the following chapter I shall attempt to show that, in the operas and elsewhere, Berg's constant, almost obsessional, interest in such formal designs and organizational procedures has a symbolic and deeply personal significance.

# VI

## Conclusions

At a time when music was undergoing one of the most profound changes in its history, Berg, more than either Schoenberg or Webern, seems to have felt a need to assert the relationship between the new musical language, which he and his colleagues were evolving, and the great eighteenth- and nineteenth-century tradition of German and Austrian music. However, as I have already said,[1] Berg's attitude to this tradition is more ambivalent and less straightforward than is generally realized. The previous chapters have attempted to show the extent to which certain untraditional organizational and formal preoccupations permeate Berg's music; they have also attempted to give some indication of the ways in which, as Berg's creative career progressed, these preoccupations manifested themselves in structural designs of ever-increasing rigour and organizational procedures which embraced more and more aspects of the music, until, in *Lulu*, almost every musical parameter is affected by some kind of precompositionally determined scheme.

One of the most striking features of Berg's technical procedures is the extent to which they anticipate those of more recent music. In an essay on Elliott Carter, Richard Franko Goldman described Carter's idea of metric modulation as 'a means of going smoothly, but with complete accuracy, from one absolute metronomic speed to another by lengthening or shortening the value of the basic note unit'.[2] Carter himself has described the process in the following words:

> You will find that there is a constant change of pulse. This is caused by an overlapping of speeds. Say, one part in triplets will enter against another part in quintuplets and the quintuplets will fade into the background and the triplets will establish a new speed that will become the springboard for another such operation. The structure of such speeds is correlated throughout the work and gives the impression of varying rates of flux and changes of material and character.[3]

[1] See p. 4 above.
[2] Goldman, 'The Music of Elliott Carter', *Musical Quarterly*, 43, 1957, p. 61.
[3] Carter, 'Shoptalk by an American Composer', *Musical Quarterly*, 46, 1960, p. 193.

Although the changes in the Sonata development of *Lulu* are both less frequent and less complex than those which Carter employs, Carter's description of the process and the effect of 'metric modulation' is as applicable to Berg's music as to his own.

Berg's treatment of the Hauptrhythmen of *Lulu* and the Chamber Concerto as rhythmic cells, which can be subjected to different methods of variation (such as the addition or subtraction of notes, exact and inexact forms of augmentation and diminution, the substitution of rests for notes and various complex forms of permutation), is reminiscent of the methods of varying rhythmic cells which Messiaen describes in his *Technique of my Musical Language* and which Boulez discusses in his analysis of *The Rite of Spring*. Similarly, Berg's use of durational series, such as that employed in the fifth movement of the *Lyric Suite,* looks forward to the durational schemes of works such as Messiaen's *Etudes de Rhythme,* Boulez's *Structures* and Stockhausen's *Kreuzspiel,* a work whose formal plan is also strikingly similar to that of the Berg Chamber Concerto. Perhaps even more noteworthy are rhythmic patterns, such as those employed in the third movement of the *Lyric Suite* or the variant of the Hauptrhythmus of *Lulu,* which appears in Act I, sc. 1, which result from specific methods of handling the pitch material. Such patterns seem to be the result of a reassessment of the traditional relationship between pitch and rhythm (a relationship dependent on tonality) and represent a remarkably forward-looking attempt to establish some kind of new and integral relationship between the different musical parameters. The figure of Countess Geschwitz in *Lulu* is, as I have shown,[1] consistently associated with a rhythmic pattern of regularly increasing or decreasing durations; a passage in Act III, sc. 2 of the opera, in which the Countess's trope is presented as a sequence of chords of systematically decreasing densities, suggests an attempt to establish a similarly integral relationship between density and duration. Elsewhere in *Lulu* the association of particular figures in the opera with characteristic twelve-note sets, rhythms, metres and instrumental colours is so schematic in conception, and so strictly observed in practice, as to bring to mind the total serialism of the music of the early 1950s.

The delight that, in his later works, Berg takes in bringing together and reconciling the conflicting demands of the traditional and the new methods of musical organization undoubtedly springs, in part, from a fascination with the technical problems with which such an attempted synthesis presents him. It has often been argued that Berg's handling of the twelve-note set is so unorthodox that his adoption of this method of composition can only be explained as being either a gesture of solidarity towards, or a manifestation of his psychological dependence on, Schoenberg. Yet, despite his frequent

[1] See pp. 172–4 above.

complaints to Webern that the difficulties of handling the twelve-note system were slowing the pace of work, there is no reason to suppose that Berg's adoption of the system did not result from some creative need. Indeed, Berg's adoption of the system seems a natural extension of the kind of organizational preoccupations revealed by his pre-twelve-note techniques, and a logical outcome of his constant desire to increase the extent to which 'objective' organizational procedures operated in his music. As I have shown, Berg's fascination with the technical possibilities of the twelve-note system and with the opportunities which it provided for complicated conceits led him, on occasions, to abstractions far in excess of anything to be found in the music of Schoenberg or Webern. Berg's addiction to various predetermined organizational schemes, of the kind discussed in the previous chapters, suggests that he, in common with many other composers, found such self-imposed restrictions a necessary stimulus to his creative imagination. It is indicative of the extent to which Berg's imagination was stimulated by such restrictions that the most memorable dramatic or emotional passages in his music are often those in which the apparently abstract methods of handling the different musical elements are most in evidence. The coda theme of Dr. Schön's Sonata movement in Act I, sc. 2 of *Lulu,* for example, is both the most memorable theme in the work and the only theme which is consistently associated with reiterated statements of the Hauptrhythmus; thus, not only are the notes of the coda theme derived from the note row associated with Dr. Schön, but the rhythmic structure of the melody results from the application of a preconceived pattern. Similarly, the emotional climax of the final movement of the *Lyric Suite,* and of the whole work, is the passage at bar 30 in which the relationship between the two apparently independent note rows used in the movement is first openly revealed and the triumphant G major chord (bar 31) to which this passage leads. The move away from this climax to the desolation of the final pages of the *Lyric Suite* is effected by the gradual absorption of the G major chord into the twelve-note series from which it originally sprang. A similar procedure, producing a similar emotional effect, is employed in Act II, sc. 1, of *Lulu* when Schön's death is symbolized by the absorption of his series into the basic series of the opera. And yet, although in his 1929 lecture on *Wozzeck* Berg emphasizes the importance of finding new ways of achieving 'cohesion and structural unification without the use of the hitherto accepted medium of tonality',[1] many of the organizational procedures employed in his music have little to do with formal 'cohesion' and 'unification' but act as purely private compositional restraints which are quite imperceptible to the listener. Berg's habitual use of numerical schemes as a means of determining certain aspects of the music is one such inaudible, self-imposed discipline.

[1] Berg's 'Lecture on *Wozzeck*', in Redlich, *Alban Berg,* London, 1957, p. 262.

The main structural features of the *Lyric Suite*, for example, are determined by the numbers 23 and 50. The first movement has 69 bars (3 × 23) and a tempo marking of ♩ = 100 (2 × 50); the second movement has 150 bars (3 × 50) and a metronome marking of ♪ = 100; the third has 138 bars (6 × 23) and a mm. of ♩ = 150; the fourth has 69 bars and a mm. of ♩ = 69; the fifth has 460 bars (20 × 23) and a mm. of ♩. = 115 (5 × 23) while the sixth has 46 bars (2 × 23) and metronome markings of ♩ = 69 and ♩ = 46. These numbers also determine the length of many of the smaller structural units in the work and the points at which events appear within these units. Thus, the second section of the first movement of the *Lyric Suite* (Più tranquillo, Tempo II) begins at bar 23, the central 'Trio estatico' of the third movement begins at bar 69 and ends at bar 92 and the last quaver of bar 23 of the final movement marks the turning point of an important palindromic figure. The quotation from Zemlinsky's *Lyric Symphony* in the fourth movement of the *Lyric Suite* not only appears at bar 46 but begins on the 184th beat (8 × 23) of the movement. Similarly, as Klaus Schweizer has pointed out, the quotation from *Tristan and Isolde* begins on the 138th beat (6 × 23) of the final Largo.[1]

Although in neither his general writings nor his analytical notes on the *Lyric Suite* did Berg mention the important role played by the number 23, the final pages of the manuscript score of the work are covered with mathematical calculations based on this number and the comment 'followed by a retrograde to end at bar 138 (i.e. 46 bars) N.B. 138 = 6 × 23!' appears in the manuscript at the end of the 'Trio estatico' of the third movement. Almost every aspect of the Chamber Concerto – the length and number of the movements and the subsections within each movement, the types of thematic and harmonic material,[2] the metronome markings – is determined by the number 3. The number 7 plays a similar role in the Passacaglia of Act I, sc. 4 and the Variations of Act III, sc. 1 of *Wozzeck*.[3]

The contrast between these and other such, apparently 'mathematical', 'extra-musical' organizational procedures and the highly charged hyper-emotional atmosphere of the resulting work is one of the most striking features of Berg's music. We are accustomed to thinking of intellectual calculation in art as being the antithesis of spontaneous emotional expression; to find highly schematic procedures giving rise to a work of an intensely emotional and subjective nature may strike us as paradoxical. It is a paradox that lies at the heart of Berg's music.

Highly artificial techniques, rigorous formal symmetries, number symbolism, ciphers, cryptograms and various other conceits are so peculiarly

---

[1] Schweizer, *Die Sonatensatzform im Schaffen Alban Bergs*, Stuttgart, 1970, p. 89.
[2] See pp. 75–8 above.
[3] See Perle, *Music Review*, 32: 4, 1971, p. 307.

Bergian and are so constant and important a feature of Berg's mature music as to suggest that such procedures and devices not only acted as a stimulant to his creative imagination but had a further, and perhaps a deeper and more personal, significance for him.

Much of Berg's music is autobiographical or includes autobiographical elements. Certain aspects of *Wozzeck* reflect Berg's own war-time experiences:[1] 'There is a bit of me in his character', wrote Berg to his wife in 1918, 'since I have been spending these war years just as dependent on people I hate, have been in chains, sick, captive, resigned, in fact humiliated.'[2] In *Lulu* the figure of Alwa, a playwright in Wedekind's original plays, is a composer and represents Berg himself, as is clearly revealed in Act I, sc. 3, when the orchestra accompanies Alwa's words, 'One could write an interesting opera about her' with the opening chords of *Wozzeck*. The Violin Concerto, dedicated 'to the memory of an angel', is a programmatic work – Reich calls it a 'tone poem'[3] – reflecting Berg's sense of loss at the death of Manon Gropius, the 18-year-old daughter of Alma Mahler to whom the Bergs were particularly close. The Chamber Concerto not only begins with musical cryptograms based on the names of Arnold Schoenberg, Anton Webern and Alban Berg but contains, according to Berg's own 'Open Letter', 'a wealth of human and spiritual references that would make the adherents of programme music . . . go mad with joy'.[4] Perhaps the passage at bars 97–102 of the Chamber Concerto, with its prominent rising fourths in the bass line in the manner of Schoenberg's First Chamber Symphony, is one such 'human and spiritual reference'. Such homages to, and quotations from the works of other composers appear throughout Berg's music. The Chamber Concerto itself is written for fifteen instruments, the number of instruments in the Schoenberg Chamber Symphony, while the chamber orchestra of Act II, sc. 3 of *Wozzeck* consists of the same number and the same combination of instruments as the Chamber Symphony. Act I, sc. 4 of *Wozzeck* quotes the 'Klangfarben' chord of the third of Schoenberg's op. 16 pieces;[5] the on-stage band in Act II, sc. 4 of *Wozzeck* acknowledges its Mozartian precedent by quoting from the music of the on-stage band in *Don Giovanni*.[6] The *Lyric Suite* quotes from both Zemlinsky's *Lyric Symphony* and *Tristan und Isolde*. According to Rudolf Kolisch,[7] the *Lyric Suite* had a programme based upon an event in Berg's life. Although Berg never revealed the programme of the

---

[1] See Blaukopf, *Saturday Review*, Sept. 1953 and *Österreichische Musikzeitschrift*, 9, 1954.
[2] Berg, *Letters to his wife*, London, 1971, p. 224.
[3] Reich, *Alban Berg*, London, 1965, p. 179.
[4] Berg, 'Open Letter on the *Chamber Concerto*' in Reich, op. cit., p. 148.
[5] See DeVoto, 'Alban Berg's Picture-postcard Songs' unpublished Princeton Univ. thesis, 1967, p. 100.
[6] Perle, *Music Review*, 32, No. 4, 1971, p. 301.
[7] Personal communication.

228                                                                      *Conclusions*

work some indication is to be found in the tempo indications of the six movements ('Allegretto giovale', 'Andante amoroso', 'Allegro misterioso' and 'Trio estatico', 'Adagio appassionato', 'Presto delirando' and 'Tenebroso', 'Largo desolato'). A further indication of the programmatic nature of the work can be found in the final Largo desolato, many passages of which are accompanied, in the manuscript draft of the work, by a text. At some points (such as bars 22–4, where the text follows the melodic 'cantabile' line passed between the viola and the first violin), the music seems to be a syllabic setting of the text; at other points a few words seem to refer to long passages of music. Most of this text is indecipherable and on occasions consists of only isolated letters. The few words ('ice', 'heart', 'so slowly', 'night') and isolated phrases ('how long can I . . .', 'darkness on the earth . . .', 'I envy you . . .', 'the landscape is dead there, the air is like lead') that are legible, suggest the intensely subjective nature of this text and give some clues to the likely nature of the programme which lies behind the music.[1]

It is well known that the number 23 had a special significance for Berg who regarded it as his fateful number. Reich says that the number first acquired a particular significance because it was on the 23rd day of the month that Berg had his first attack of asthma, an illness which troubled him for most of his life. There is some doubt as to the exact year of this first attack[2] but all authorities agree that it occurred on 23 July. That Berg associated the number 23 with his illness seems to be confirmed by the fact that he mentions his asthma in the manuscript of the *Lyric Suite* where, on the last page of the score, he writes, '30th September, 1926, 1 o'clock a.m. (the morning of a night of asthma)'. Some years after his first attack of asthma Berg was called into

[1] Since the above was written the precise nature of the event in Berg's life on which the *Lyric Suite* is based, and which it records, has become clear due to two important musicological discoveries. In the summer of 1976 Professor Douglass M. Green of the Eastman School of Music, the University of Rochester, unaware that I had previously discovered the text of the last movement of the *Lyric Suite,* examined the draft of the work in the Österreichische Nationalbibliothek and managed both to decipher it and to identify its source as Stefan George's translation of Baudelaire's *De Profundis Clamavi.* In January 1977 George Perle discovered a copy of the published score of the *Lyric Suite* annotated in great detail by Berg himself and presented by him to Hanna Fuchs-Robettin, the woman who inspired the work and to whom it is secretly dedicated. Berg's annotations not only reveal that the omnipresent four-note collection B–F–A–B♭, the musical significance of which I have discussed in earlier chapters, is a cryptogram based on the initials of the names Alban Berg and Hanna Fuchs-Robettin and also show the extra-musical origins of the numerological features described above (although the number 50 should, in fact be regarded as 2+3×10, 10 being the number which Berg regarded as symbolizing Hanna Fuchs-Robettin), but demonstrate too in the most extraordinary detail the programmatic basis of the whole work. Detailed discussions of the programme of the *Lyric Suite* can be found in George Perles 'The Secret Program of the *Lyric Suite*' and Douglass M. Green's 'Berg's De Profundis', *International Alban Berg Society, Newsletter No. 5,* April 1977.

[2] Reich (*Alban Berg*, London, 1965, p. 26) and Grun (the editor of the English version of Berg's *Letters to his wife*, London, 1971, footnote to letter 21) give 1908; Redlich, (*Alban Berg*, London, 1957, p. 294) and Heinsheimer (in Reich, *Bildnis im Wort*, Zurich, 1959) give 1900 as the year of this first attack of asthma.

*Conclusions*          229

the army under regulation 23 and suggested the title '23' for the music periodical which Reich edited.[1]

The number 23 and its multiples, which dominate the *Lyric Suite*, play a fateful, though less all-pervasive, role in many other works. Thus the Hauptrhythmus of the Violin Concerto first appears at bar 23 of the second part of the work; the second part of the concerto has 230 bars in all and an opening metronome mark of ♩ = 69. In *Lulu* the two parts of the bridge passage of Schön's Sonata movement have metronome marks of ♩ = 46 and ♩ = 69, the second subject group a metronome mark of ♪ = 138.[2] When the theme of the coda of the Sonata movement returns, at the end of Act I, to the prophetic words, 'Jetzt kommt die Hinrichtung' ('Now comes the execution'), the phrase has a metronome marking of ♩= 46. Alwa's Rondo in Act II of *Lulu* has a metronome marking of ♩ = 69 while the Medical Specialist dies at the 23rd bar of the Melodrama of Act I. In the Wiener Stadtbibliothek manuscripts, the two early songs 'Im Zimmer' and 'Liebesode' have metronome markings of ♩ = 82 and ♩ = 63 respectively; when Berg published these two works amongst the Seven Early Songs the metronome marks of both were changed to multiples of 23, 'Im Zimmer' now having a metronome mark of ♩ = 69 and 'Liebesode' a metronome mark of ♩ = 46. The number 23 assumed so great a significance for Berg that he frequently arranged to complete a work and to write important letters on the 23rd of the month.[3] Some idea of the extent to which Berg regarded the number 23 as influencing his every daylife can be gathered from the following extract from a letter written to Schoenberg on 10 June 1915:

'. . . that fate of being unable to appear anything but disagreeable to you for years; and even if not through my own fault then certainly in connection with matters which have caused you annoyance. I cannot take responsibility for proving such a fate – I would have to write a book about it; but the interesting thing is that here too a certain number keeps cropping up – a number which has great significance for me. The number 23. I will keep quiet about the many times in my life that I have come up against this number and only give you one or two examples from the recent past:

[1] According to Berg's nephew the composer died not, as is generally thought, on 24 Dec. 1935 but shortly before midnight on the 23rd. (See E. A. Berg, *Alban Berg, Leben und Werk*, Frankfurt, 1976, p. 255.)
[2] Although Berg changed the metronome marking of Dr. Schön's Ballade 'Das mein Lebensabend' to ♩ = 52 the number originally had a metronome marking of ♩ = 69.
[3] See Pernye, 'Alban Berg und die Zahlen', *Studia Musicologica*, 9, 1967, for a detailed discussion of this and other examples of Berg's interest in number symbolism. The reader should, however, note that not all of Pernye's hypotheses fit the facts. Perle has observed (*Music Review*, 32: 4, 1971, p. 308) that Pernye's argument about the role played in *Wozzeck* by the number 1921 is based on the incorrect date of completion given by Reich and Redlich. Pernye's claim that Berg only dates compositions completed on either 23 July or August is equally incorrect – as the manuscripts of the second and last movements of the *Lyric Suite* demonstrate.

I received your first telegram (to go back to the beginning) on 4/6 (46 = 2 × 23). The telegram contained the number Berlin Südende 46 (2 × 23) 12/11 (12 + 11 = 23). The second telegram contained the numbers 24/23 and was sent at 11.50 (11,50 = 50 × 23).'[1]

The number 3 which, in the Chamber Concerto, plays a role similar to that of the number 23 in the *Lyric Suite,* also has a personal significance and symbolizes the three members of the Second Viennese School whose names appear in musical cryptograms at the beginning of the work.

Writing in 1856 to the Princess Carolyne Sayn-Wittgenstein about his work on *The Trojans,* Berlioz said, 'One hurdle in my path is that the feelings to be rendered move me too much. That is bad. One must try to do coolly things that are fiery.'[2] Given the autobiographical nature of much of Berg's music it may well be that he employed the kind of technical procedures discussed in previous chapters because, rather than in spite of, the intense subjectivity of his music, using precompositionally determined organizational schemes as a means of imposing some kind of intellectual objectivity upon the music and thus distancing himself from the 'feelings to be rendered' that 'moved him too much'. At the same time, in the case of the numerological conceits of the *Lyric Suite* and the Chamber Concerto, these objective restrictions have themselves a deeply personal significance. Subjective elements are transformed into objective restraints which, paradoxically, both embody and curb the subjectivity from which they sprang.

Berg's prediliction for symmetrical and palindromic structures also seems to have had both an objective intellectual, and a deeply personal significance. Hans Redlich has remarked on the air of mystery which surrounds those moments at which Berg's palindromic structures begin to move backwards;[3] Misha Donat has said that 'in Berg, retrograde movement represents almost a view of life'.[4] As I shall attempt to show, not only retrograde movement but all Berg's formal preoccupations represent such a 'view of life'. The view symbolized by these preoccupations can be best understood by examining the musico-dramatic structure of the two operas.

*       *       *       *

Many writers have assumed that both *Wozzeck* and *Lulu* are what Redlich has called 'operas of social protest and compassion'.[5] To approach *Lulu* from the viewpoint of the earlier opera, however, inevitably leads to the conclu-

[1] See D. R. Hill, 'Alban Berg. Leben und Wirken in Wien bis zur Uraufführung des *Wozzeck*', unpublished Phil. Diss., University of Vienna, 1974, pp. 162–3. I am grateful to Michael Taylor for drawing my attention to this letter.
[2] Quoted in Barzun, *Berlioz and his Century,* New York, 1956, p. 328.
[3] Redlich, *Alban Berg,* London, 1965, p. 113.
[4] Donat, 'Mathematical Mysticism', *The Listener,* 2 April 1970, p. 458.
[5] Redlich, *Alban Berg,* London, 1965, pp. 74 and 163.

sion that, whatever the purely musical merits of the piece, the plot of the opera is too absurd, too hysterically sensational and too full of ludicrous coincidences for the work to be regarded as making any kind of valid social criticism. As a result, the nature of Berg's aims and achievements in *Lulu* have been consistently misunderstood.

In part this misunderstanding has come about because the continuing unavailability of Act III of *Lulu* has made impossible a full appreciation of the dramatic and musical structure of the opera. To a large extent, however, the misunderstanding has come about because, having wrongly assumed that in *Lulu* Berg was attempting, using similar musical and dramatic techniques, to achieve something similar to that which he had achieved in *Wozzeck*, commentators have judged the opera on the basis of this false assumption.[2] Even on the most cursory acquaintance with the two works it is their differences rather than their similarities that are most striking.

In *Wozzeck* the listener is involved in the fate of the main protagonists in a way that he never is in that of any of the characters in the two published acts of *Lulu*. The libretto of *Wozzeck* ruthlessly excludes everything that is not directly relevant to the unfolding of the tragedy. The three characters who are instrumental in bringing about the final catastrophe are either (as in the case of the Captain and the Doctor) grotesques, obsessed by their own fixations, or (as with the figure of the Drum Major) mere ciphers. The spectator is thus forced, not simply to identify with Wozzeck, but to see events through his eyes and accept the picture of an unfeeling social order in a malicious or, at best, indifferent universe, which the opera presents, as the real world. Being self-contained forms, the musical designs employed in the opera, while reflecting the dramatic structure of the individual scenes, have an independent existence which itself reflects the indifference with which the outside world views Wozzeck and his fate. Only after the tragedy has taken place does the music move from being an objective presentation to become a subjective comment on Wozzeck's situation.

At first glance *Lulu* appears to be more realistic than *Wozzeck*. Its settings range from Germany to Paris and London, its characters eat, drink, smoke and talk of everyday topics in banal colloquial terms; there are constant references to the 'modern' world of newspaper offices, casinos and the stock exchange, of the electric doorbell and the telephone. Set in a precisely defined, and fairly recent, historical period, the settings of *Lulu* seem to have an objective, concrete reality which stands in strong contrast to those of the earlier opera. Despite this superficial realism, *Lulu* is, however, a deeply unrealistic, indeed a surrealistic work. Patrick Waldberg has described surrealist methods of expression as 'recourse to the imaginary, to dreams, to the

---

[2] For a survey of the attitudes of various commentators on *Lulu*, see Neumann, *Music Review*, 35, 1974, pp. 47–57.

unconscious and to chance', and has characterized a certain type of surrealist painting as that in which 'the scene is unreal but the settings, the objects and the figures which comprise it are painted with absolute fidelity'.[1] Both statements are applicable to *Lulu* in which the dream-like unrealities and ludicrous coincidences are set against an apparently realistic background. The Prologue, in which the Animal Trainer comes before the curtain and invites the audience to step inside and see his menagerie, creates an atmosphere of unreality before the work has even begun; the tortuous mechanics of the plot and the absurdities to which they give rise merely extend this unreality into the main body of the work.

The libretto shows a profusion of non-sequiturs and meaningless phrases that are inexplicable on any naturalistic level.[2] The strange conversation between Alwa and Lulu over the corpse of the Painter:

> Lulu: It suddenly dawned on him?
> Alwa: He didn't want to be unworthy of his fate.
> Lulu: He always had a death wish.
> Alwa: He had what a man can only dream of.
> Lulu: He has paid dearly for it.
> Alwa: He had what we do not have.
> Lulu: Ten minutes ago he was lying here.

or the conversation between Lulu and Schigolch in Act I, sc. 3, with its mysterious and unexplained references to Schigolch's concertina and Lulu's learning of French, are typical of the unrealistic nature of much of the dialogue.

The libretto is also full of slight, and apparently unnecessary, inconsistencies. When, for example, the Painter and Dr. Schön are discussing Lulu's name in Act I, sc. 2, the Painter appears not to know her real name, believing that she is called 'Nelly':

> Painter: Of whom are you speaking?
> Schön: Of your wife!
> Painter: Of Eva!
> Schön: I call her Mignon.
> Painter: I thought that she was called Nelly.
> Schön: That's what Dr. Goll called her.
> Painter: I call her Eva.
> Schön: I don't know her real name.
> Painter: Perhaps she knows it . . .

although in the previous scene Lulu denied being called 'Nelly' and told the Painter her real name:

---

[1] Waldberg, *Surrealism*, London, 1965, p. 7.
[2] See Perle, *Musical Quarterly*, 1967, p. 101.

> Painter: I love you, Nelly.
> Lulu: I'm not called Nelly. I am called Lulu.
> Painter: I shall call you Eva.

When, in Act II, sc. 2, Alwa declares his love for Lulu, Lulu murmurs 'I poisoned your mother'. This startling piece of information is ignored by Alwa and is mentioned nowhere else in the opera: earlier in the work Alwa has said that his mother was ill before Dr. Schön adopted Lulu, implying that she died of natural causes. At the beginning of Act I, sc. 2, we are told that Schön's fiancée is called Charlotte Maria Adelaide; this is contradicted at the end of Act I, sc. 3, when we are told that her name is Brigitte. It is unclear whether or not Lulu knows Schön's fiancée; at the beginning of the opera it is suggested that she does not ('And I . . . let me . . . without personally knowing her . . . my regards to your fiancée', says Lulu in Act I, sc. 1) although in the following scene Schön implies that Lulu does know her ('It was after the death of my first wife, when I first made the acquaintance of my present fiancée. She stood between us. She had taken it into her head that she would become my wife.')

It is no accident that, having employed 'abstract' instrumental formal designs in *Wozzeck*, Berg should turn, in *Lulu*, to those forms that are traditionally associated with opera. In an essay on Mann's *Dr. Faustus*, Erich Kahler has said that 'all the great novels of the twentieth century . . . are without exception terminal books' in which 'art has come to question its own existence'.[1] Kahler's statement applies not only to the novel. Like many twentieth-century works of art, one of the subjects of *Lulu* is the work itself; the opera is about writing an opera. In *Pandora's Box*, the second of Wedekind's two *Lulu* plays, Alwa, a writer, is revealed to be the author of *Earth Spirit*, the first of the *Lulu* plays; in Act II, sc. 2, of Berg's *Lulu*, Alwa is revealed as the composer of the first part of the opera.

Wedekind emphasized the grotesque nature of his *Lulu* plays by including in them parodies of other plays; similarly Berg's *Lulu*, while being an opera in the great nineteenth-century tradition of the lyric theatre, also questions the very tradition upon which it is based. The traditional love duet becomes Alwa's declaration of love for his father's murderess, the 'amour fou' of *Tristan* and *Pelléas* is shown as a monstrous and self-destructive madness. and the opera ends with the 'Liebestod' of the lesbian Countess Geschwitz, The traditional vocal forms, and numbers such as the Canon to which the Painter pursues Lulu in Act I, sc. 1 and the canonic letter duet of Act I, sc. 3, are not employed in any spirit of neo-classicism or intended as a parody of operatic conventions, as they are in, for example, Weill's *Threepenny Opera* or Hindemith's *Neues vom Tage*, but as a means of emphasizing the artificiality of the plot and the absurdity of the situations in which the characters

[1] Kahler, 'The Devil secularised' in Hatfield, *Thomas Mann*, New Jersey, 1964, p. 109.

find themselves. Indeed, so absurd is the plot that even the characters themselves find it unbelievable. In Act I, sc. 3, Alwa considers writing an opera about Lulu – 'One could write an interesting opera about her. Scene 1: The Medical Specialist – bad enough! Scene 2: The Painter – even more impossible! Scene 3 – can it really go on like this?' Although the opera is eventually composed, the composer is aware of, and has anticipated criticism of, the plot's absurdity.

In *Lulu* Berg is attempting something quite different from and far more difficult to achieve than that which he attempted in *Wozzeck*. In *Wozzeck* the listener is forced to identify with and involve himself in the fate of Wozzeck. In *Lulu* the overwhelming emotional impact of *Wozzeck* is replaced by something more complex and more deeply disturbing. Far from encouraging the spectator to identify with the characters involved, the structure of the work and the use of such Brechtian devices as the silent film between Act II, scenes 1 and 2, are designed to alienate the spectator and to encourage him to view the events and to consider their significance without emotional involvement. The involvement which the music encourages is deliberately undermined by a plot of such manifest absurdity that the listener is unable to suspend his disbelief and, as in *Così fan Tutte,* is forced to recognize the hypocrisy and the capacity for self-deception of both the characters on the stage and himself. The relevance which the series of sensational events on stage has to the listener in the opera house is made clear in Act I, sc. 3, when Alwa's soliloquy in Lulu's dressing room is interrupted by the shouts and cheers of those watching Lulu's act. 'It sounds like the menagerie at feeding time', comments Alwa, to the accompaniment of the opera's fateful Hauptrhythmus. The audience watching Berg's *Lulu* is thus equated with the off-stage theatre audience watching Lulu's stage performance. Having accepted the Animal Trainer's original invitation to step inside and see his menagerie the listener in the opera house is forced to realize that he is as much a part of that menagerie as the characters he has come to watch. Only in Act III is the listener obliged to abandon his objectivity and identify with the figure of Lulu herself, when she is forced to suffer the consequences of the hypocrisies and delusions which the other characters have projected upon her. George Perle has remarked on the 'incredible transformation that takes place' in Act III; 'not in Lulu but in our understanding of her character. In the concluding scene she has become clear to one in the way that Desdemona is in Act IV of *Otello,* a process that begins to take place as a result of Lulu's heroic struggle against the Marquis in Act III, sc. 1 . . . the following scene has a pathos beyond anything I know in opera.'[1]

Whereas *Wozzeck* is overtly concerned with the inhumanity and the in-

---

[1] Perle in a letter to Robert Craft, quoted in Offergeld, *Hi-fi Stereo Review,* Oct. 1964, p. 64.

justice of society, *Lulu* is primarily concerned with personal, and only incidentally with social, hypocrisy. The two operas do, however, share a common subject, although it is one that is not an obvious feature of the original Büchner or Wedekind plays. It is a subject that Berg imposes through his musical designs and through the way in which these designs relate to and emphasize certain elements in the verbal texts.

Karl Kraus, who produced the 1905 performance of *Pandora's Box* which Berg attended, called the final scene 'the revenge of a world of men which makes bold to avenge itself for its own guilt'.[1] By doubling the roles of Lulu's clients and husbands, Berg has found a striking way of symbolizing this revenge. There is, however, no real relationship between these and the other roles that are taken by the same performer in *Lulu* – between, for example, the roles of the Painter and the Negro, or of the Manservant and the Marquis. The choice of roles assigned to a performer is arbitrary, having the effect of equating certain characters in such a way that they seem interchangeable.

This feeling of interchangeability is basic to Berg's conception of the opera and applies not only to the characters played by a single performer but to all Lulu's admirers. Though each of the most important of Lulu's admirers is identified by a different series, these series have, as I have shown in Chapter III,[2] a number of features in common, the most important of which is the contrast, at certain transpositional levels, between a 'white-note' and a predominantly 'black-note' hexachord.

The constant exploitation of these musical similarities in Act II not only gives the act musical continuity but also has the effect of emphasizing the dramatic similarities between Lulu's admirers. These similarities are further emphasized by the fact that the note row associated with the minor figures of the Prince, the Manservant and the Marquis is itself derived from the basic set of the opera and from the note rows associated with the major figures of Dr. Schön and Alwa.

Lulu's admirers are also equated with one another through recurrent musical and dramatic events. In Act II, sc. 1, Lulu, now married to Dr. Schön, complains that they never see one another and that Schön does not treat her as his wife ('Couldn't you take the afternoon off? . . . I haven't seen you for months . . . you didn't marry me at all'). Her complaints are reminiscent of those about the Painter in Act I ('He sees nothing, neither me nor himself. He is blind! He knows nothing about me. What am I to him?') and the similarity is underlined by the music, the second half of Lulu's conversation with Schön in Act II being a restatement of one strophe of her Duettino with the Painter in Act I. Both the Act I Duettino and the conversation with Schön in Act II end with the ringing of the doorbell announcing the arrival

---

[1] Reich, *Alban Berg,* London, 1965, p. 158.
[2] See pp. 88–93 above.

of Schigolch. Later in Act II, sc. 1, Schön, returning home to find the house full of Lulu's lovers, notices the Athlete escaping up the stairs. 'What was that?' asks Schön. 'Nothing', replies Lulu, 'You're suffering from a persecution complex!' thereby imputing to Schön the mental unbalance that Schön himself had imputed to the Painter earlier in the opera to explain the Painter's suicide to the police.

Alwa, who becomes Lulu's lover after his father's death, is also equated with the Painter. The question and answer scene between Lulu and Alwa in Act II, sc. 1 ('Oh, this hand!' 'What do you find there?' 'An arm!' 'What do you find there?' 'A body!' 'What do you find there!' 'Mignon!') is reminiscent of the question and answer scene between Lulu and the Painter in Act I, sc. 1 ('Can you tell the truth?', 'I don't know', 'Do you believe in a creator?', 'I don't know', 'Can you swear on anything?', 'I don't know'). When, at the end of the question and answer scene in Act II, Alwa asks, 'Do you love me?' Lulu replies, 'I don't know', the answer she gave to the Painter's questions in the corresponding scene in Act I.

The music that leads up to the death of Alwa in Act III (he is murdered by the Negro, a role played by the same performer as played the role of the Painter in Act I) is a free recapitulation of the Monoritmica which led up to the death of the Painter. 'Ich werde doch nicht hier bleiben', – 'I shan't stay here' – says Lulu on realizing that Alwa is dead; 'Ich kann nicht hier bleiben' she says on discovering the corpse of the Painter in Act I.

Elsewhere in the opera Alwa is equated with Dr. Schön. Lulu's attempts to persuade Alwa to leave with her, at the end of Act II, are set to a reprise of the Musette of Dr. Schön's Sonata, the music which, in Act I, sc. 3, accompanied the writing of the letter that Schön described as his 'death warrant'. Knowing that Lulu has murdered his father and that he too is signing his 'death warrant', Alwa agrees to join her in fleeing across the frontier.

The sense of *déjà vu*[1] which these recurrent musical associations and dramatic situations give is further underlined by the curious repetitive nature of the libretto. Schön, having told the Painter of Lulu's past life in Act I, sc. 2, murmurs 'Das war ein Stück Arbeit' – 'That was a good piece of work'; in Act III, sc. 2, Jack, having murdered Lulu and the Countess, also murmurs, 'Das war ein Stück Arbeit'. When the doorbell rings at the beginning of Act I, sc. 2, the Painter says 'Vielleicht es ist aber der Kunsthändler' – 'But perhaps it is the art dealer'; when it rings again in the middle of the same scene Lulu says 'Vielleicht der Kunsthändler'. In Act I, sc. 2, Alwa bursts in upon Schön and Lulu with the news, 'In Paris ist Revolution ausgebrochen . . . In der Redaktion weiss keiner, was er schreiben soll' – 'A revolution has broken out in Paris . . . No one in the office knows what to write'; in Act II, sc. 1, Schön interrupts Alwa and Lulu with the same news.

---

[1] See Perle, *Music Review*, 25, 1964, p. 314.

Such textual, musical and dramatic repetitions lie at the heart of the work and give it its peculiar effect of always moving in circles. Lulu's admirers, whether husbands, lovers or clients, are not only equated with one another but *are* one another.

Each of Lulu's admirers calls her by a different name; none uses her real name even when told, as is the Painter in Act I, sc. 1, what it is. Only Schigolch, who shares her mythological origins, calls Lulu by her real name, recognizes her true nature, and survives at the end of the opera.[1] The other characters project upon her their own fantasies and self-delusions and, just as the single figure of Lulu represents different things to each of her admirers, so do these admirers represent the different forms which these self-delusions take. It is the refusal of these other characters to accept Lulu as she is that eventually leads to their destruction. As the same situation recurs time and time again the work becomes an absurd and dream-like dance of death. The continual circular progression of the work and the absurdities of the plot reduce the characters to puppets, unable to control their own fates, unable to communicate with one another and unable to break out of the grotesque circle of events within which they find themselves trapped. The circle is closed, but not broken, at the end of the opera with the death of Lulu. The survival of Schigolch suggests that we have seen only one episode in a continually repeating cycle of events.

Since palindromic or retrograde motion is, by its very nature, 'anti-time',[2] inevitably closing the circle by returning to the point at which it began and at which the whole process could begin again, the 'Film Music' interlude at the centre of the opera both marks the turning point of the drama and symbolizes the circular construction of the work as a whole. Through purely musical means Berg, thus, identifies as the central subject of the opera an idea that is only hinted at in the original Wedekind plays.

\*     \*     \*     \*

*Wozzeck* is also concerned with the idea of circular motion, an idea which again finds its musical equivalent in palindromic and retrograde motion and in complicated symmetries of the kind found in *Lulu*. The most important of these symmetries have been discussed in Chapter V,[3] although there also exist others which are quite imperceptible to the listener. The numerological correspondence between the Passacaglia Variations on a seven-bar theme in Act I, sc. 4, and the set of Variations, again on a seven-bar theme, which opens Act III, is one such.

Whereas in *Lulu* a fatalistic view of life is implied by the opera's musico-

[1] See Perle, *Music Review*, 26, 1965, p. 285.
[2] Adorno, *Alban Berg*, Vienna, 1968, p. 21.
[3] See pp. 190–91.

dramatic structure, in *Wozzeck* this fatalism is explicitly revealed in both the
text and the music of the opening scene of the work. Act I, sc. 1, of *Wozzeck*
is dominated by the idea of time moving in a circle to return to the point at
which it began, an idea expressed by the Captain's image of an endlessly
turning mill wheel. 'Consider, Wozzeck', says the Captain, 'that you have
at least 30 more years to live – that's 360 months and heaven knows how many
days, hours and minutes. What will you do with that vast expanse of time?
It frightens me to think of eternity – I'm terrified when I think that the
world revolves in one day and whenever I see a mill wheel turning I feel
depressed'.[1] The word 'eternity' is symbolized musically by the fragment of
the 'endless' circle of fifths which accompanies it[2] while the image of the
mill wheel is suggested by a retrograde, the music of the final part of the
scene being that of the opening backwards. The relevance which the Captain's obsession with time and the need to do everything slowly has to
the opera as a whole is indicated by the setting of the word 'Langsam',
when it appears at the end of the first sentence in the opera, and on its subsequent appearances, to the notes B and F which form the 'fate' dyad of the
work. The significance of this dyad has been discussed in Chapter II.[3] The
Captain's obsession has its counterpart in the Doctor's obsession with the
need for speed and his grandiose delusions of immortality. The appearance
of the Captain's and the Doctor's themes, when the two characters meet in
Act II, sc. 2, at a level at which both themes include the fateful B–F dyad
indicates the similarity of their obsessions.

The image of the endlessly turning mill wheel in Act I, sc. 1, mirrors the
circular construction of the work itself. In his lecture of *Wozzeck*, Berg himself mentions this circular construction, saying of the final scene that
'although the music steers again into the cadential haven of the final chord it
almost looks as if it was to go on. And it really does go on! As a matter of fact,
the initial bars of the opera could easily link up with these final bars and
thereby close the circle.'[4] I have shown in Chapter II how the two opening
chords, representing Marie and Wozzeck, are segments of the two cadential
chords which close the opera.

George Perle has called the D minor interlude, which precedes the final
scene of Act III, an 'overture',[5] and Misha Donat has pointed out that by
placing the 'overture' before this final scene Berg implies that the last scene
is the start of a fresh, inevitable tragedy.[6] The end of the opera thus 'closes
the circle' and the tragedy begins again with the child taking his father's

[1] The relationship between the musical structure of *Wozzeck* and the subject of time
and predestination is examined in Donat, *The Listener*, 2 April 1970.
[2] See Perle, *Music Review*, 32: 4, 1972, p. 304.
[3] See pp. 48–9 above.
[4] Redlich, *Alban Berg*, London, 1957, p. 265.
[5] See Perle, *Music Review*, 32: 4, 1971, p. 300.
[6] See Donat, *The Listener*, 2 April 1972.

place. The circular construction of the work, however, implies a tragic view of life that not only embraces Wozzeck and the social class to which he belongs but comments on the human condition itself.

At a number of points during the opera retrograde and palindromic figurations (which, in Act I, sc. 1, are associated with time and predestination) are specifically associated with Wozzeck's mental instability and with the terror of his existence. In Act I, sc. 3 (bars 459–60), an ascending arpeggio-like figuration and its retrograde accompany Marie's words, 'He'll lose his sense with these wild fancies'. In Act II, sc. 3, similar palindromic figurations accompany Wozzeck's words 'Man is a chasm, it makes one dizzy to look into his depths.' Two of the variations in the Passacaglia of Act I, sc. 4, are also based upon palindromic figurations. The first of these (Variation 7) is written in 7/4 time and accompanies Wozzeck's cry of pain following the words, 'The world is so dark that you have to feel around it with your hands searching and it seems to disappear like spider's webs – when it's there and isn't there'. The second palindromic variation (Variation 12), which is also written in 7/4, accompanies Wozzeck's description of the toadstool rings in the fields and the strange messages which he believes them to contain. The words 'Lines, circles and strange figures – would that one could read them' are set to a descending whole-tone scale and its retrograde in the voice part, and are accompanied by a diminution and an inverted diminution of the same scale and its retrograde on the strings and a further palindromic figure and its inversion on the celeste and harp. The mysterious-sounding musical patterns which result not only represent the 'lines, circles and strange figures' of the text but also, being palindromic, recall the retrograde motion which, in the first scene of the opera, symbolized the inescapable circle of time. On the written page the figurations which Berg uses to suggest the ominous message of the toadstool rings themselves describe circular patterns. Like the mill wheel of Act I, sc. 1, the toadstool rings stand as a symbol of the inevitability of the circular course of the opera. Although Wozzeck cannot read the strange figures which they present, he instinctively feels a terror of the predestined course which the musical palindromes reveal to be the message of the toadstool rings.[1]

\* \* \* \*

[1] The extent to which those procedures and ideas that dominate Berg's music – his love of palindromic structures, his interest in numerology, his use of isorhythmic techniques and his conception of time as cyclic – correspond to those of the composers of the late Middle Ages and early Renaissance is curious. The reader is referred to M. van Creel's essay *The Secret Structure*, which forms the preface to his complete edition of the work of Obrecht (Amsterdam 1964), for a detailed discussion of the role played by these and other, equally 'Bergian', techniques and concepts in Mediaeval and Renaissance music. The similarities between Berg's musical thought and that of the earlier composers is a striking example of the way in which composers of the pre- and post-tonal periods – composers separated by four centuries but facing similar structural problems – turned to similar devices as a way of solving these problems.

One need not take seriously Berg's claim, in his lecture on *Wozzeck*, that the link between the end of Act III and the beginning of the opera happened 'quite unintentionally'[1] for not only is this link implied by the whole design of the work itself but it is also the logical consequence of Berg's own outlook. Berg imposes such circular or symmetrical designs whenever the opportunity presents itself. Thus Berg decided to arrange movements II, III and IV of the *Lyric Suite* for string orchestra, placing the palindromic third movement in the centre of the set, even though Webern, whose advice Berg had specifically requested and who, unlike Berg, had vast experience as an orchestral conductor, advised against the inclusion of the third movement. Similarly, when arranging the orchestral version of the Seven Early Songs, Berg imposed a symmetrical shape upon the group by scoring the third song for strings and the fifth for wind alone, the second and sixth songs for reduced orchestra and the first and seventh songs for full orchestra so that the whole set pivots around the central fourth song.

So great a significance do such symmetrical designs seem to have assumed in Berg's private view of the world that his obsession with symmetry extended to many other aspects of his creative work. In a letter to Webern dated 18.8.1924, when Berg and Webern were preparing a book of appreciations in honour of Schoenberg's birthday, Berg writes:

> We should also try to get a kind of *symmetry* in the appreciation (such as Kraus often gives to the shape of 'Fackel' – Poems, commentaries, leading article, commentaries, poems . . . or: leading article 1, commentaries, notices, commentaries, leading article 2). Come to that, we could even put Schoenberg's article in the middle. But that's very tricky to deal with – one must be able to tell that that's the place of honour. Perhaps by putting it in another typeface or between two facsimiles . . . (one could get a kind of symmetry there – Kokoschka to start with and Schlosser to end).

In his article on Schumann's *Kinderszenen* Berg lays particular emphasis on the fact that *Träumerei*, as the seventh in a set of thirteen pieces, is distinguished by its central position 'and occupies, therefore, a very special position in the symmetrical structure of the whole opus and is a vital component – perhaps the most vital component – of the whole'.[2] Both the manuscript score of the Ostinato of the *Lulu* Suite[3] and a handwritten note concerning the publication of *Der Wein* ask the printer to place the central points of the palindromes in these two pieces (the point at which the music begins to move backwards) in the middle of the page and to arrange the bars on either side symmetrically around this point.[4] In the score of the Chamber

---

[1] Berg's 'Lecture on *Wozzeck*' in Redlich, *Alban Berg*, London, 1957, p. 265.
[2] Reich, *Alban Berg*, London, 1965, pp. 206–7.
[3] The score of the Ostinato is pasted into the manuscript score of the complete opera.
[4] This wish has been observed in the published orchestral score of *Der Wein* but not in the vocal score of the work or in the score of *Lulu*.

Concerto, which Berg himself prepared for publication, the turning point of the central movement of the work is laid out in this way.

So obsessional an interest in symmetry that it extends to his literary work and to the visual aspect of his music suggests that the circular, palindromic and other symmetrical designs which play so large a role in Berg's music are not simply technical conceits but, like his use of ciphers and number symbolism, are objective intellectual restraints which hide a deeply subjective significance.

Despite their obvious differences of setting, style and subject matter, both *Wozzeck* and *Lulu* have a similar preoccupation with the subject of time and with the idea of man trapped within a continually repeating cycle of events.[1] In both it is a subject that is peripheral to that of the original plays and that is revealed through the musical structures which Berg chooses to impose; in each opera the *structure* is the *subject*. Misha Donat's observation that, in Berg's music, retrograde and palindromic motion represent a 'view of life' is equally applicable to Berg's fascination with predetermined organizational schemes and his habitual use of arch-shaped symmetrical structures which, like palindromes, end at the point at which they began.

The similarity between the circular construction of the two operas and that of a work such as the *Lyric Suite*, in which the finale 'foreshadows' the thematic material of the opening movement and which, like *Wozzeck*, has no real ending but simply stops, is particularly striking. Such similarities demonstrate the consistency of Berg's view of man as a helpless creature unable to alter his preordained fate and unable to break out of the tragic and absurd dance of death within which he is trapped – a fatalistic and deeply pessimistic view of life that underlies all Berg's mature compositions.

[1] Peryne (*Studia Musicologica*, 9, 1967) has suggested that many of the numerological elements in Berg's music represent significant dates in the composer's life. Although, as I have pointed out (see footnote 3, p. 229 above), some of the information on which Peryne bases his study is incorrect, and although, by their very nature, such arguments can never be more than speculative, the possibility that Berg's use of number symbolism represents an attempt to embody past experiences in his music would accord with the preoccupation with the subject of time which one finds in his operas.

# Appendix I

### Catalogue of Berg's Works and Manuscripts

(i) *Early Songs*

Two volumes, entitled 'Jugendlieder' and including 73 unpublished songs, are contained in the collection deposited in the Musiksammlung of the Österreichische Nationalbibliothek by the late Helene Berg. A list of these songs can be found in Chadwick, *Music and Letters*, 52, No. 2, April 1971. Of those in Chadwick's list holographs of Nos. 3, 7, 12, 14, 17, 26, 31, 32, 33, 34(?), 36 and 38 are also in the possession of the Library of Congress, of Nos. 5, 9, 12, 19, 20 and 29 in the possession of Mrs. Susanne Szekely of New York and of No. 1 in the possession of the Houghton Library of Harvard University. Copies of those manuscripts in the possession of Mrs. Szekely have been deposited with the Library of the Performing Arts at Lincoln Center.

(ii) *Seven Early Songs*

Piano scores:

Nos. 1–7 Musiksammlung, Österreichische Nationalbibliothek, Vienna.
Nos. 5 and 6 Musiksammlung, Wiener Stadtbibliothek, Vienna
No. 7 Gesellschaft der Musikfreunde, Vienna.

Orchestral score:

Universal Edition, Vienna.

(iii) *Fugue with three subjects for String Quintet and Piano*

Whereabouts of manuscript unknown.

(iv) *Compositions for 6–8 part chorus*

Whereabouts of manuscript unknown.

(v) *Twelve Variations for Piano on an original theme*

Score: Alban Berg Stiftung, Vienna.

(vi) *Piano Sonata, op. 1*

Whereabouts of manuscript unknown.

(vii) *Four Songs, op. 2*

Score: F. H. Klein, Linz.

(viii) *String Quartet, op. 3*

Score: Musiksammlung, Österreichische Nationalbibliothek, Vienna.

(ix) *Altenberg Lieder, op. 4*
Orchestral Scores:
Nos. 1–5        Universal Edition, Vienna.
Nos. 4 and 5    Lincoln College (on deposit in the Bodleian Library), Oxford.
Piano scores:
Nos. 4 and 5    Wolfdietrich Hassfurther, Vienna.
No. 5           Gesellschaft der Musikfreunde, Vienna.
Note: Holograph copies of the first violin part of Nos. 2 and 3 are in the
    possession of the Musiksammlung, Wiener Stadtbibliothek.

(x) *Four Pieces for Clarinet and Piano, op. 5*
Score: Wolfdietrich Hassfurther, Vienna.
Sketches: Musiksammlung, Österreichische Nationalbibliothek, Vienna.

(xi) *Three Orchestral Pieces, op. 6*
Full score (revised version): Universal Edition, Vienna.
Short score: Musiksammlung, Österreichische Nationalbibliothek, Vienna.
Sketches: No. 3 Musiksammlung, Österreichische Nationalbibliothek,
    Vienna.

(xii) *Wozzeck, op. 7*
Full score: Library of Congress, Washington.
Short score: Musiksammlung, Österreichische Nationalbibliothek, Vienna.
Sketches: Musiksammlung, Österreichische Nationalbibliothek, Vienna.
        Staatsbibliothek, Berlin.
        Collection A. Meyer, Paris.

(xiii) *Chamber Concerto for Violin, Piano and thirteen Wind Instruments*
Full score: Alban Berg Stiftung, Vienna.
Score of wind parts: Rychenburg Stiftung, Winterthur.
Arrangement of second movement for Violin, Clarinet and Piano: Universal
Edition, Vienna.

(xiv) *Schliesse mir die Augen beide*
Song I (1907): whereabouts of manuscript score unknown.
Song II (1925): Universal Edition, Vienna.
Sketches for Song II: Musiksammlung, Österreichische Nationalbibliothek,
Vienna.

(xv) *Lyric Suite for String Quartet*
Score: Musiksammlung, Österreichische Nationalbibliothek, Vienna.
Sketches: Musiksammlung, Österreichische Nationalbibliothek, Vienna.
        Library of Congress, Washington.
Arrangement of movements two, three and four for string orchestra: Universal Edition, Vienna.

(xvi) *Der Wein*
Full score and short score: Musiksammlung, Österreichische Nationalbib-
    liothek, Vienna.
Sketches: Musiksammlung, Österreichische Nationalbibliothek, Vienna.
    Wiener Stadtbibliothek.
    Walter Jarry, Vienna.

(xvii) *Four-part canon*: Alban Berg an das Frankfurter Opernhaus
Score: Library of Congress, Washington.

(xviii) *Lulu*
Full scores:
Acts I and II: Universal Edition, Vienna (deposited in Musiksammlung,
    Österreichische Nationalbibliothek).
Act III: (scored portion): Universal Edition, Vienna.
Short scores:
Acts I and II: Musiksammlung, Österreichische Nationalbibliothek, Vienna.
Act III: Particell: Musiksammlung, Österreichische Nationalbibliothek,
    Vienna.
Vocal score (by Erwin Stein): Universal Edition, Vienna.
Sketches: Musiksammlung, Österreichische Nationalbibliothek, Vienna.

(xix) *Violin Concerto*
Full score: Louis Krasner, U.S.A.
Short score: Musiksammlung, Österreichische Nationalbibliothek, Vienna.
Sketches: Musiksammlung, Österreichische Nationalbibliothek, Vienna.

# Appendix II

Frank Wedekind: *Lautenlied* No. 10, 'Konfession'

1. With joy, by every oath, I swear before Almighty God, who is my judge, that I would far rather be a whore than richly possessed of fame and fortune.

2. In me, world, you have lost a woman, a woman self-possessed and free from inhibition. Was there ever anyone born for the business of love as I was born for it?

3. Is it not true that I have dedicated myself to love as others dedicate themselves to their work? Have I ever, once in my life, given my love to just one person?

4. To be in love? No, that brings no happiness in life. To love like that brings humiliation and jealousy. But to love passionately, vigorously again and again – that's ecstasy. That is real living.

5. But could it be, when the first flush of youth has faded, a sense of shame will prevent me from softening that exquisite pain – the child of mad fantasy?

6. A sense of shame? I have often experienced that: shame after many a noble act. Shame about abuse and pain. Shame when payment finally approaches.

7. But shame about my body – so rich a gift of pleasure and delight? I have not felt such ingratitude since that first kiss awakened me so long ago.

8. And a body, whose every part is desired as a fount of ecstasy. What more pure and exquisite goal is worth striving for in this life?

9. When the softest movement of the knee generates power like a burning flame, that power can no longer be contained out of passionate desire to overreach itself.

10. With every moment that power becomes more indestructible, more sweet; with every moment it is more fully realized in pleasure, so that he who indulges in it trembles, not with light-headedness, but in the face of its overwhelming force . . .

11. World, when I dream of such magic, the sins I have committed crumble to dust; then, I praise my being and reach to the stars, drunk with power's madness . . .

12. It would be unjust should I wish to conceal from the world what it is

that inflames my inner self; because, encouraged by many good souls,
I ask myself – in vain – where its source lies.

Translated by Susan Davies

Ex. 210

## KONFESSION

Freudig schwör'ich es mit jedem Schwure
Vor dem Allmacht, die mich züchtigen kann:
Wieviel lieber wär'ich eine Hure
Als an Ruhm und Glück der reichste Mann!

Welt, in mir ging dir ein Weib verloren,
Abgeklärt und jeder Hemmung bar.
Wer war für den Liebesmarkt geboren
So wie ich dafür geboren war?

Lebt ich nicht der Liebe treu ergeben
Wie es Andre ihrem Handwerk sind?
Liebt ich nur ein einzig Mal im Leben
Irgendein bestimmtes Menschenkind?

Lieben? – Nein, das bringt kein Glück auf Erden.
Lieben bringt Entwürdigung und Neid.
Heiss und oft und stark geliebt zu werden,
Das heisst Leben, das ist Seligkeit!

Oder sollte Schamgefühl mich hindern,
Wenn sich erste Jugendkraft verliert,
Jeden noch so seltnen Schmerz zu lindern,
Den verwegne Phantasie gebiert?

Schamgefühl? – Ich hab'es oft empfunden;
Schamgefühl nach mancher edlen Tat;
Schamgefühl vor Klagen und vor Wunden;
Scham, wenn endlich sich Belohnung naht.

Aber Schamgefühl des Körpers wegen,
Der mit Wonnen überreich begabt?
Solch ein Undank hat mir fern gelegen,
Seit mich einst der erste Kuss gelabt!

Und ein Leib, vom Scheitel bis zur Sohle
Allerwärts als Hochgenuss begehrt . . .
Welchem reinern, köstlichern Idole
Nachzustreben, ist dies Dasein wert?

Wenn der Knie leiseste Bewegung
Krafterzeugend wirkt wie Feuersglut,
Und die Kraft, aus wonniger Erregung
Sich zu überbieten, nicht mehr ruht;

Immer unverwüstlicher und süsser,
Immer klarer im Genuss geschaut,
Dass es statt vor Ohnmacht dem Geniesser
Nur vor seiner Riesenstärke graut . . .

Welt, wenn ich von solchem Zauber träume,
Dann zerstiebt zu nichts, was ich getan;
Dann preis'ich das Dasein und ich bäume
Zu den Sternen mich vor Grössenwahn! – – –

Unrecht wär's, wollt ich der Welt verhehlen,
Was mein Innerstes so wild entflammt,
Denn vom Beifall vieler braver Seelen
Frag'ich mich umsonst, woraus er stammt.

# Appendix III – Synopses

*WOZZECK*
*ACT I*
*Scene 1. The Captain's room. Early morning*
Wozzeck is shaving the Captain who begs him to take more time about it.
The Captain expresses his anxiety as to what he will do with the time which
Wozzeck is saving him, his fear of the idea of eternity and describes the feel-
ing of giddiness brought on by the sight of a revolving mill wheel. A worthy
man, says the Captain, takes his time.

Upset by Wozzeck's refusal to do more than simply agree with him, the
Captain attempts to draw Wozzeck into a conversation about the weather
and laughs derisively when he agrees that the wind is blowing from the
'South–North'.

Wozzeck, declares the Captain, has no moral sense, citing the fact that the
child of Wozzeck and Marie was born out of wedlock as evidence. Wozzeck
replies that the Lord, who said 'suffer little children to come unto me', will
not reject the child because of his illegitimacy and that it is easy to be
virtuous when one has money. The Captain, confused by Wozzeck's reply,
dismisses him, begging him, once more, to go more slowly.

*Scene 2. An open field outside the town. Late afternoon*
Wozzeck and Andres are cutting sticks. Wozzeck is disturbed by the place,
which he thinks evil, by the rising mist and by the toadstool rings which
seem to hide strange messages within them. Andres, unconcerned, sings a
folksong. Wozzeck hears noises beneath the ground; the rays of the setting
sun cause him to have a vision of the world in flames. The two of them leave
as darkness falls.

*Scene 3. Marie's room. Evening*
Marie is watching a military band passing by her window. Her neighbour,
Margaret, notices, and comments upon the way in which Marie is admiring
the Drum Major who leads the band. Marie closes her window and sings a
lullaby to her child.

Wozzeck comes in and attempts to describe the strange feelings and
hallucinations which he experienced while cutting sticks in the fields. He
leaves to report back to the barracks. Marie turns back to the child.

*Scene 4. The Doctor's study. A sunny afternoon*
Wozzeck is examined by the Doctor who is using him as guinea pig to test his bizarre dietary theories. The Doctor reprimands Wozzeck for not having the will power which would enable him to control his bodily responses and questions whether he has been following the prescribed diet. Wozzeck again attempts to describe his experiences while cutting sticks in the fields. The Doctor regards Wozzeck's description as the manifestation of some mental aberration and resolves to make this the basis of further scientific investigation. The Doctor reflects on the fame and immortality which his experiments will bring.

*Scene 5. The street outside Marie's house. Evening twilight*
The Drum Major is boasting to Marie and posturing in front of her. He attempts to embrace her and, after struggling, Marie gives in to him. They go into the house together.

*ACT II*
*Scene 1. Marie's room. Morning sunshine*
Marie is admiring the ear-rings, given to her by the Drum Major, in the mirror. The child is restless and twice she breaks off to sing him a song. Suddenly aware of Wozzeck's presence she attempts, unsuccessfully, to hide the ear-rings. When Wozzeck asks where they came from she tells him that she found them. Wozzeck comments that he has never had the luck to find two such together. He gives Marie his wages from the Captain and the Doctor and leaves.

*Scene 2. A street in the town. Day*
The Doctor and the Captain meet. The Captain tries to persuade the Doctor to take things more slowly. The Doctor, remarking on his poor physical condition, speculates on the likelihood of the Captain being struck down by a stroke in the immediate future. Wozzeck enters and the Captain and Doctor turn their attention to him, making pointed allusions to Marie's association with the Drum Major. Wozzeck rushes off.

*Scene 3. The street before Marie's house. A dull day*
Wozzeck confronts Marie with his suspicions of her infidelity and attempts to strike her. Marie warns him not to touch her: 'Rather a knife in my heart than lay a hand on me'. Wozzeck leaves, overcome by the image which Marie's remark opens up.

*Scene 4. A tavern garden. Late evening*
A group of soldiers, apprentices and girls are dancing to the music of the tavern band. A drunken apprentice breaks into song. Marie and the Drum Major join the dancers. Wozzeck sits on a bench watching them. The drunken

apprentice again breaks into song – a long monologue at the end of which he is carried out by his colleagues. The idiot, who has joined Wozzeck on the bench, tells him that the scene reeks with the smell of blood.

*Scene 5. Guard room in the barracks. Night*
Wozzeck is unable to sleep. He imagines that he can see a knife in front of him, hears voices from the wall and the music of the tavern band.

The Drum Major enters, drunk, boasting of his conquest of Marie. Wozzeck turns away from him, whistling. The Drum Major thrashes Wozzeck and goes out, leaving him on the floor.

## ACT III

*Scene 1. Marie's room. Night, candlelight*
Marie is sitting with the child, reading from the Bible on the table. She reads the story of the woman taken in adultery and of Mary Magdalene.

*Scene 2. A forest path by a pool. Dusk*
Marie and Wozzeck walk through the forest. The moon rises a blood red. Wozzeck plunges the knife into Marie's throat.

*Scene 3. A low tavern, badly lit. Night*
Wozzeck is drinking at one of the tables. He begins a song but stops himself and dances a few steps with Margaret. Margaret, sitting on Wozzeck's lap, notices the blood on his hand and, when he says that he has cut himself, remarks that he could not have wiped the blood from his right hand on his right elbow. Wozzeck rushes off.

*Scene 4. The forest path by the pool. Moonlit night as before*
Wozzeck returns to look for the knife with which he murdered Marie. He sees Marie's body and the line of blood, like a necklace, round her throat. He finds the knife and throws it into the pool. The red moon breaks through the clouds. Fearing that it will be found, Wozzeck wades into the pool to throw the knife in further. The moonlight makes both him and the water appear to be blood red and he wades in yet further, attempting to wash his hands white again. He drowns. The Captain and the Doctor pass and, hearing the sounds of someone drowning, hurry on so as not to be involved.

*Scene 5. In front of Marie's house. Bright morning sunshine*
A group of children are playing. The child of Marie and Wozzeck is riding a hobby horse. Another child runs on to announce the discovery of Marie's body. The children go off to look. Marie's child notices he is alone, hesitates for a moment and then follows the others.

*LULU*

*Prologue*

The Animal Trainer invites the audience to step inside the menagerie and see his animals – true wild animals, not conventional domesticated creatures like those in the orchestra. He lists the animals to be seen in his collection and calls for an assistant to bring the snake. A stagehand carries on Lulu, dressed in the Pierrot costume in which she appears in the first scene of the opera.

## ACT I

*Scene 1. The Painter's studio*

The Painter, watched and advised by Dr. Schön, is painting a portrait of Lulu. Schön's son, Alwa, a composer, arrives to invite his father to attend his dress rehearsal. As they leave Lulu asks that, although she doesn't know the lady, they convey her greetings to Schön's fiancée; Schön, in turn, asks Lulu to give her husband his regards.

The Painter, upset by Lulu's presence, is unable to work. Declaring that, although her name is Nelly (a misconception which Lulu corrects), he will call her Eva, he catches Lulu and attempts to kiss her.

Lulu's husband, the Medical Specialist, arrives, breaks down the door and, on seeing the couple, suffers a fatal heart attack. Shocked by the lack of emotion which Lulu shows at this event, the Painter questions whether she has any beliefs or is able to tell the truth. Lulu replies that she doesn't know and goes to change. The Painter is left alone with the corpse of Lulu's husband. With a sudden premonition of what lies before him, he prays that he will have the strength to achieve a little happiness.

*Scene 2. An elegant room in the Painter's house*

Lulu and the Painter are now married. The morning post brings news of Dr. Schön's engagement. The Painter answers the doorbell and leaves to get on with his work as Schigolch, whom the Painter assumes to be a beggar, arrives. Schigolch is an old acquaintance of Lulu's and the two reminisce about the past until another ring at the door announces the arrival of Dr. Schön. Schigolch leaves as Schön enters.

Schön has come to tell Lulu that their relationship must end and that she must stop visiting him; he has twice found her a husband, supports both her and her husband financially, and she must now leave him free to marry a respectable young lady. Lulu replies that the Painter has no interest in her as a person and that she owes everything to Schön.

The Painter returns, disturbed by the noise of their arguing, and Schön determines to tell him the truth about Lulu so that the Painter, as her husband, will exert greater control over her. Schön recounts how he adopted

Mignon (his own name for Lulu) as a child, saving her from Schigolch whom Schön assumes to be her father, and how, when, after the death of his wife, Lulu tried to come between Schön and his fiancée, he introduced her to her previous husband.

The Painter, shocked by Schön's revelations, leaves saying that he will speak to Lulu. As Alwa arrives Schön hears noises from the kitchen. Joined by Lulu the two men break down the door and discover the body of the Painter who, unable to face the truth about Lulu, has committed suicide. Schön calls the police who arrive a few moments later as Lulu, wiping the blood from Schön's hands, vows that he will yet marry her.

*Scene 3. A theatre dressing-room*
Alwa and Lulu are in her dressing room celebrating her triumphant stage appearance – an appearance arranged by Dr. Schön in the hope that Lulu will thereby meet someone who will marry her and finally take her off his hands. As Lulu goes back on stage, Alwa considers the possibility of using her story as the basis of an opera. His thoughts are interrupted by the noise of the audience cheering Lulu's performance and by the arrival of the Prince, one of Lulu's admirers.

Lulu rushes in, followed by an attendant and the theatre manager. She has caught sight of Dr. Schön and his fiancée in the audience and refuses to perform. Schön arrives and, left alone with him, Lulu makes it clear that she regards his bringing his fiancée to watch her as an insult. Having calmed her down Schön asks Lulu about the Prince. Lulu tells him that the Prince intends to take her to Africa with him. The threat of complete separation exposes Schön's inability to make a decisive break with Lulu and Lulu forces him to write a letter to his fiancée ending their engagement.

*ACT II*
*Scene 1. A magnificent room in Schön's house*
Lulu, now married to Schön, is visited by the lesbian Countess Geschwitz. The Countess leaves and Schön gives vent to his disgust at having to entertain such people in his home. Lulu complains that Schön doesn't pay her enough attention and begs him to take the afternoon off. Schön refuses and leaves for the stock exchange. Unseen by either Lulu or Dr. Schön, the Countess re-enters and hides behind the firescreen.

A trio of admirers – Schigolch, the Athlete and the Schoolboy – arrive, taking advantage of Schön's weekly visit to the stock exchange to pay their respects to Lulu. During the course of the following conversation it emerges that Schigolch is not Lulu's father and, indeed, at one time wanted to marry her; Schigolch doubts whether she had a father.

The Manservant, another of Lulu's admirers, announces the arrival of

Alwa. The three admirers rush to hide. The Athlete hides behind the window curtain, the Schoolboy beneath the table. The asthmatic Schigolch is still making his way upstairs as Alwa enters.

The Manservant serves a meal during the course of which Lulu declares her admiration for Alwa's 'strength of character'. Unseen by either, Dr. Schön returns and, standing in the gallery, overhears Alwa admit his love for Lulu. The Athlete, looking out from behind the curtain, sees Schön, who threatens him with a revolver. The Athlete starts back behind the curtain, the movement attracting the attention of Lulu who notices Schön in the gallery. Schön descends the staircase and escorts Alwa off stage. As Schön's back is turned the Athlete makes an unsuccessful attempt to escape and retires behind the door curtain. Dr. Schön returns and looks behind the now vacated window curtain; Lulu explains that, being an acrobat, the Athlete has escaped over the balcony.

Schön hands the revolver to Lulu, telling her that she must shoot herself. She fires a shot at the ceiling and the Athlete, in a panic, darts up the staircase and through the gallery. Schön, searching for other hidden guests, discovers Geschwitz behind the fire screen and pushes her into the next room. He tries to take the revolver from Lulu who breaks away from him, saying that he knew what she was when he married her; if he has sacrificed his old age to her she has sacrificed her youth in return.

Dr. Schön attempts to aim the revolver in Lulu's hand at her but is distracted by the Schoolboy who is still hidden under the table. As he turns, Lulu fires the revolver at Schön's back. As the Schoolboy and Alwa lead the dying Schön to the next room the Countess Geschwitz comes out.

Schön dies and the police arrive.

During the following orchestral interlude a silent film shows the events which take place between the end of Act II, sc. 1, and the beginning of Act II, sc. 2: Lulu's arrest and detention, her trial and imprisonment, her removal to the isolation ward (having deliberately contracted cholera from the Countess) and her disguising herself as Countess Geschwitz in preparation for her escape.

*Scene 2. As before but dusty, uninhabited and shuttered against the daylight*
Alwa, the Athlete and the Countess Geschwitz are awaiting the arrival of Schigolch. Once Lulu has escaped from prison, and he is sure that she is no longer contagious, the Athlete intends to marry her and make her an acrobat.

Schigolch arrives to take Geschwitz to the hospital where she will change places with Lulu. Alwa offers the Countess payment for the expenses which she has incurred. She refuses and leaves with Schigolch.

The Athlete suggests that he take the money offered to the Countess, and, when his offer is refused, denounces Alwa as a scoundrel whose only achievement has been to write an opera about Lulu which no respectable theatre will stage.

The Schoolboy arrives with a plan to free Lulu from prison but leaves when told that she has already died from the cholera.

Schigolch returns with Lulu. The Athlete, horrified at her physical deterioration and realizing that his plan to turn her into an acrobat is no longer practical, leaves to call the police.

Schigolch goes off to collect the train tickets. Alwa describes how the plan to effect Lulu's escape from prison was put into operation and how Geschwitz contracted cholera and infected Lulu so that they could change places in the isolation ward. They declare their love – sitting, as Lulu observes, on the divan on which Alwa's father died.

## ACT III
*Scene 1. A salon in a Parisian Casino. A door at the back leads to the gaming room*

The Athlete and the other members of the company drink a toast to Lulu. As they leave to go to the gaming room the Mother, the Banker, the Journalist and Alwa discuss the prices of the Jungfrau railway shares in which they have invested.

The Marquis stays behind with Lulu, whom he is blackmailing; he offers her the choice of either taking a job in a Cairo brothel or having her whereabouts revealed to the police. Lulu protests that she cannot descend to a life of prostitution and sell the only thing that she has ever owned. The Marquis gives her until eleven o'clock to decide.

The company return in jubilation from the gaming room; everyone has won. As they leave for the dining room the Athlete detains Lulu. He also is blackmailing her and threatens to denounce her to the police if she refuses to pay him 20,000 Marks.

The groom brings the Banker a telegram.

Schigolch comes to ask Lulu for some money with which to support his newly acquired mistress. Lulu tells him about the Athlete's threats. Schigolch promises to dispose of the Athlete by pushing him from the hotel window if Lulu undertakes to lure him to Schigolch's hotel room.

The Marquis meets the Athlete and accuses him of threatening to denounce Lulu; the Athlete denies it. The Marquis leaves to inform the police.

Lulu tells the Athlete that the Countess Geschwitz is waiting to go with him; believing that the Countess is willing to give him money the Athlete agrees to spend the night with her. Lulu persuades the Countess to take the Athlete to Schigolch's hotel room.

Everyone spills out of the gaming room in a commotion. The Banker has won everything. Since the telegram he received earlier brought news of the collapse of the Jungfrau shares he now refuses to accept payment in shares and insists on cash. Almost everyone present is bankrupt.

Lulu, having exchanged clothes with the groom, leaves with Alwa. The Marquis arrives with the police.

*Scene 2. A London attic*

Lulu, now reduced to prostitution, has gone on the streets to find clients. Alwa and Schigolch await her return. They hide at the sound of footsteps on the stairs. Lulu and her first client, the Professor, go across to Lulu's room.

Alwa and Schigolch emerge from hiding. Alwa listens outside Lulu's door: Schigolch searches the Professor's coat pockets. They return to their hiding place in the cupboard as the Professor leaves.

The sound of footsteps announces the arrival of Countess Geschwitz carrying Lulu's portrait. Alwa hangs it on the wall. Lulu, followed by the Countess, returns to the streets.

Schigolch hides as Lulu and her second client climb the stairs: Alwa stays where he is, covered by a rug.

Lulu and the Negro, her client, argue about payment. Alwa attempts to intervene. The Negro strikes Alwa on the head and leaves.

Lulu returns to the streets and Schigolch drags the corpse of Alwa away. Geschwitz enters and Schigolch leaves for the pub. The Countess contemplates suicide. Lulu enters with Jack the Ripper and they cross to her room. Alone again, the Countess resolves to return to Germany and fight for women's rights. Jack kills Lulu. Hearing Lulu scream the Countess rushes to her aid. She is confronted by Jack who stabs her before washing his hands and leaving. The Countess Geschwitz dies.

# Bibliography

*BOOKS*

Abraham, G., *A Hundred Years of Music*, Methuen, London, 1964 (first published 1938).

Adorno, T. W., *Alban Berg: Der Meister des Kleinsten Übergangs*, Verlag Elisabeth Lafite, Vienna, 1968.

Archibald, R. B., *Harmony in the early works of Alban Berg*, Harvard University, Ph.D. dissertation, 1965 (unpublished).

Barzun, J., *Berlioz and his century*, Meridian Books, New York, 1956.

Berg, A., *Écrits d'Alban Berg*. Choisis, traduits et commentés par Henri Pousseur, Éditions du Rocher, Monaco, 1957.

——, *Briefe an seine Frau*, Albert Langen and Georg Müller Verlag, Munich, 1965.

——, *Letters to his wife*, Faber and Faber, London, 1971.

Berg, E. A., *Alban Berg, Leben und Werken in Daten und Bildern*, Insel Verlag, Frankfurt, 1976.

Boulez, P., *Relevés d'apprenti*, Éditions du Seuil, Paris, 1966; John Calder, London, forthcoming.

Carner, M., *Alban Berg, the man and the work*, Duckworth, London, 1975.

DeVoto, M., *Alban Berg's Picture-postcard songs*, Princeton University, Ph.D. dissertation, 1967 (unpublished).

Forte, A., *The Structure of Atonal Music*, Yale University Press, New Haven and London, 1973.

Hauer, J. M., *Von Melos zur Pauke*, Universal Edition, Vienna, 1962.

——, *Zwölftontechnik*, Universal Edition, Vienna, 1962.

Hill, D. R., *Alban Berg. Leben und Wirken in Wies bis zur Uraufführung des Wozzeck*, University of Vienna, Phil. dissertation, 1974 (unpublished).

Hilmar, E., *Wozzeck von Alban Berg. Entstehung – erste Erfolge – Repression*, Universal Edition, Viennal, 1975.

Hoffman, W. (ed.), *Schoenberg–Webern–Berg: Bilder–Partituren–Dokumente*, Universal Edition, Vienna, 1969.

Jouve, P. J. and Fano, M., *Wozzeck d'Alban Berg*, Librairei Plon, Union Générale d'Éditions, Paris, 1953.

König, W., *Tonalitätstrukturen in Alban Bergs Oper 'Wozzeck'*, Hans Schneider, Tutzing, 1974.

Messiaen, O., *The Technique of my musical language*, Alphonse Leduc, Paris, 1950.

Mitchell, D., *Gustav Mahler: the Wunderhorn Years*, Faber and Faber, London, 1975.

——, *The Language of Modern Music*, Faber and Faber, London, 1953.

Perle, G., *Serial Composition and Atonality*, Second Edition: Faber and Faber, London, 1968; Third Edition: Univ. of California Press, Berkeley, 1972.

Ploebsch, G., *Alban Bergs Wozzeck*, P. H. Heitz Verlag, Strasbourg, 1968.

Rauchhaupt, U. von (ed.), *Schoenberg–Berg–Webern: The String Quartets. A documentary study*, Deutsche Gramaphon Gesellschaft, Hamburg, 1971.

Redlich H. F., *Alban Berg. The man and his music*, John Calder, London, 1957.

——, *Alban Berg. Versuch einer Würdigung*, Universal Edition, Vienna, 1957.

Reich, W., *Alban Berg, Bildnis im Wort*, Peter Schifferlei, Verlag 'Die Arche', Zurich, 1959.

——, *Alban Berg. Mit Bergs eigenen Schriften und Beitragen von T. W. Adorno und E. Krenek*, Herbert Reichner Verlag, Vienna, 1937.

——, *The Life and Work of Alban Berg* (trans. Cornelius Cardew), Thames and Hudson, London, 1965.

Reiter, M., *Die Zwölftontechnik in Alban Bergs Oper 'Lulu'*, Gustav Bosse Verlag, Regensburg, 1973.

Rosen, C., *Schoenberg*, Fontana Modern Masters, Collins Sons & Co., Glasgow, 1976.

Rufer, J., *Composition with Twelve Notes* (trans. Humphrey Searle), Rockliff, London, 1955.

Russell, J., *Erich Kleiber*, André Deutsch, London, 1957.

Scherliess, V., *Alban Berg in Selbstzeugnissen und Bilddokumenten*, Rowohlt Taschenbuch Verlag, Hamburg, 1975.

Schoenberg, A., *Style and Idea*, ed. Leonard Stein (trans. Leo Black), Faber and Faber, London, 1975.

Schweizer, K., *Die Sonatensatzform im Schaffen Alban Bergs*, Musikwissenschaftliche Verlags, Stuttgart, 1970.

Slonimsky, N., *Lexicon of Musical Invective*, Second Edition, Colman-Ross, New York, 1965.

Vogelsang, K., *Alban Berg, Leben und Werk*, Max Hesses Verlag, Berlin, 1959.

Waldberg, P., *Surrealism*, Thames and Hudson, London, 1965.

*ARTICLES*

Archibald, B., 'The Harmony of Berg's *Reigen*', *P.N.M.*, 6, Spring/Summer, 1964, pp. 73–91.

Blaukopf, K., 'Autobiographische Elemente in Alban Bergs *Wozzeck*,' *O.M.*, 9: 5, 1954, pp. 155–8.

——, 'New Light on *Wozzeck*', *S.R.*, Sept. 1953.

Bohm, J. D., 'Berg, Poet of the Atonal, tells of his new opera *Lulu*', *Musical America*, 51: 18, 25 Nov. 1931.

Carter, E., 'Shop Talk by an American composer', *M.Q.*, 46: 2, 1960, pp. 189–201.

Chadwick, N., 'Berg's unpublished songs in the Österreichische National-bibliothek', *M & L.*, 52: 2, April 1971, pp. 123–40.

Chittum, D., 'The triple fugue in Berg's *Wozzeck*', *M.R.*, 28, 1967, pp. 52–62.

Cone, E., 'Music: a view from Delft', in *Perspectives on Contemporary Music Theory*, W. W. Norton & Co., New York, 1972.

Crevel, M. van, preface to *Obrecht, Opera Omnia*, Vol. VII, Vereniging voor Nederlandse Musikgeschiedenis, Amsterdam, 1964.

DeVoto, M., 'Some notes on the unknown *Altenberg Lieder*', *P.N.M.*, 5, Fall/Winter, 1966, pp. 37–74.

Donat, M., 'Mathematical Mysticism', *The Listener*, 2 April 1970, p. 458.

Green, D. M., 'Berg's De Profundis: The Finale of the *Lyric Suite*', in *International Alban Berg Society Newsletter*, No. 5, April 1977.

Goldman, R. F., 'The Music of Elliott Carter', *M.Q.*, 43, 1957.

Gräbner, E., 'Some aspects of rhythm in Berlioz', *Soundings*, 2, University College, Cardiff, 1971–72, pp. 18–28.

Helm, H. G., 'Voraussetzungen eines neuen Musiktheaters', *Melos*, 34, 1967, pp. 122–3.

Jarman, D., 'Berg's Surrealist Opera', *M.R.*, 31:3, August 1970, pp. 232–40.

——, 'Dr. Schön's Five-Strophe Aria: some notes on tonality and pitch association in Berg's *Lulu*', *P.N.M.*, 8: 2, Spring/Summer 1970, pp. 23–48.

——, 'Some row techniques in Berg's *Der Wein*', *Soundings*, 2, University College, Cardiff, 1971–72, pp. 46–56.

——, 'Some Rhythmic and Metric Techniques in Alban Berg's *Lulu*', *M.Q.*, 56: 3, July 1970, pp. 349–66.

——, 'Two unpublished letters from Alban Berg to Růžena Herlinger', *M.T.*, 113: 1550, April 1972, pp. 350–2.

Kahler, E. 'The Devil Secularized: Thomas Mann's Faust', in Hatfield, H. (ed.) *Thomas Mann*, Prentice-Hall Inc., New Jersey, 1964.

Keller, H., '*Lulu*' (Holland Festival Review), *M.R.*, 14, 1953, pp. 302–33

Knaus, H., 'Berg's Carinthian Folk Tune', *M.T.*, 117: 1600, June 1976, p. 487.

Maegaard, J., 'Berg's 17 four-part canons', in *International Alban Berg Society Newsletter*, No. 3, June 1975.

Mitchell, D., 'The character of Lulu', *M.R.*, 15, Nov. 1954, pp. 268–74.

Neumann, K., 'Wedekind and Berg's *Lulu*', *M.R.*, 35, Feb. 1974, pp. 47-57.

Offergeld, R., 'Some questions about *Lulu*', *Hi-Fi Stereo Review*, Oct. 1964, pp. 58-76.

Perle, G., 'Berg's Master Array of the Interval Cycles', *M.Q.*, 63:1, Jan. 1977, pp. 1-30.

——, 'The character of Lulu: A sequel', *M.R.*, 25, Nov. 1964, pp. 311-9.

——, 'Current Chronicle: *Lulu*', *M.Q.*, 54, 1967, pp. 100-2.

——, 'Erwiderung auf Willi Reichs Aufsatz "Drei Notizblätter zu Alban Bergs *Lulu*" ', *S.M.*, May-June 1967, pp. 163-5.

——, '*Lulu*: The Formal Design', *J.A.M.S.*, 17: 2, 1964, pp. 179-92.

——, '*Lulu*: Thematic Material and Pitch Organization', *M.R.*, 26, 1965, pp. 269-302.

——, 'The Music of *Lulu*: A new analysis', *J.A.M.S.*, 12, 1959, pp. 182-200.

——, 'The Musical Language of *Wozzeck*', *Music Forum*, I, 1967, pp. 204-59.

——, 'A note on Act III of *Lulu*', *P.N.M.*, Spring/Summer 1964, pp. 8-13.

——, 'Die Personen in Bergs *Lulu*', *A.f.M.*, 24, 1967, pp. 283-90.

——, 'Representation and Symbol in the music of *Wozzeck*', *M.R.*, 32: 4, 1971, pp. 281-308.

——, 'The score of *Lulu*', *P.N.M.*, Spring/Summer, 1965, pp. 87-90.

——, 'The Secret Program of the *Lyric Suite*', *International Alban Berg Society Newsletter*, No. 5, April 1977.

——, 'Three Views of *Lulu*', *S.R.*, 25 May 1969, pp. 47-9.

——, 'Three Views of *Wozzeck*', *S.R.*, 2 Dec. 1967, pp. 54-5.

——, 'What they did to Berg's *Lulu*', *S.R.*, 30 Dec. 1967, pp. 43-5.

——, '*Wozzeck* and *Woyzeck*', *M.Q.*, 53: 2, April 1967.

Pernye, A., 'Alban Berg und die Zahlen', *Studia Musicologica*, 9, 1967, pp. 142-61.

Redlich, H. F., 'Bergs Konzertarie *Der Wein*', *O.M.*, 21, May-June 1966, pp. 284-91.

Reich, W., 'Alban Berg's "*Lulu*" ', *M.Q.*, 22, 1936, pp. 383-401.

——, 'An der seite von Alban Berg', *Melos*, 27, 1960, pp. 36-42.

——, 'Drei Notizblätter zu Alban Bergs "*Lulu*" ', *S.M.*, Nov.-Dec. 1967, pp. 336-9.

Scherliess, V., 'Briefe Alban Bergs aus der Entstehungszeit der "*Lulu*" ', *Melos*, 2, March-April 1976, pp. 108-14.

Stroh, W., 'Alban Berg's constructive Rhythm', *P.N.M.*, Fall/Winter 1968, pp. 18-31.

Weber, F., 'Der Literarische Gehalt von Bergs Musikdramatik', *Melos*, 35, 1968, pp. 144-9.

Westergaard, P., 'Toward a Twelve-Tone Polyphony' in *Perspectives on Contemporary Music Theory*, edited B. Boretz and E. Cone, W. W. Norton and Company Inc., New York, 1972.

Whittall, A., 'Tonality and the Whole Tone Scale in the music of Debussy', *M.R.*, 36: 4, Nov. 1975, pp. 261-8.

Abbreviations: *A.f.M.*: Archiv für Musikwissenschaft
     *J.A.M.S.*: Journal of the American Musicological Society, Boston
     *M. & L.*: Music and Letters, London
     *M.Q.*: Musical Quarterly, New York
     *M.R.*: Music Review, Cambridge
     *M.T.*: Musical Times, London
     *O.M.*: Österreichische Musikzeitschrift, Vienna
     *P.N.M.*: Perspectives of New Music, Yardley, Pennsylvania
     *S.M.*: Schweizerische Musikzeitschrift, Zürich
     *S.R.*: Saturday Review, New York

# Index

References to individual compositions or works are indexed under the name of their composer or author.

Page numbers in italic indicate more important references.

**NORMANDALE COMMUNITY
COLLEGE**
9700 FRANCE AVENUE S.
BLOOMINGTON, MN 55431

DEMCO